Spike Lee's *Bamboozled*
and Blackface
in American Culture

Spike Lee's *Bamboozled* and Blackface in American Culture

ELIZABETH L. SANDERSON

McFarland & Company, Inc., Publishers
Jefferson, North Carolina

LIBRARY OF CONGRESS CATALOGUING-IN-PUBLICATION DATA

Names: Sanderson, Elizabeth L., 1973– author.
Title: Spike Lee's Bamboozled and blackface in American culture / Elizabeth L. Sanderson.
Description: Jefferson, North Carolina : McFarland & Company, Inc., Publishers, 2019 | Includes bibliographical references and index.
Identifiers: LCCN 2019017085 | ISBN 9781476678634 (paperback : acid free paper) ♾
Subjects: LCSH: Bamboozled (Motion picture) | African Americans in the performing arts—History. | Race in motion pictures. | Racism in motion pictures. | Blackface entertainers—United States. | Minstrel shows—United States—History. | United States—Race relations—History. | Racism in popular culture—United States—History. | Popular culture—United States—History.
Classification: LCC PN1997.B2435 S26 2019 | DDC 791.43/72—dc23
LC record available at https://lccn.loc.gov/2019017085

BRITISH LIBRARY CATALOGUING DATA ARE AVAILABLE

ISBN (print) 978-1-4766-7863-4
ISBN (ebook) 978-1-4766-3695-5

© 2019 Elizabeth Sanderson. All rights reserved

No part of this book may be reproduced or transmitted in any form or by any means, electronic or mechanical, including photocopying or recording, or by any information storage and retrieval system, without permission in writing from the publisher.

Front cover: Savion Glover (center), Tyheesha Collins (right) and Cartier Williams (left) in the 2000 film *Bamboozled* (New Line Cinema/Photofest)

Printed in the United States of America

McFarland & Company, Inc., Publishers
 Box 611, Jefferson, North Carolina 28640
  www.mcfarlandpub.com

For my daughters, Emma and Rebecca,
and my husband Aaron.
This book wasn't possible without them

Table of Contents

Preface 1
Introduction 7
Historiography 9

1. Bert Williams: Minstrelsy, Vaudeville and Silent Film 23
2. Oscar Micheaux 32
3. Ralph Ellison 44
4. Michael Ray Charles 59
5. Spike Lee 79
6. The Problem of the Color Line 92
7. *Bamboozled*'s Reception 97
8. Symbolic Naming and Casting Practices 106
9. Signifyin' 124
10. Invoking History 140
11. Narrative Structures 153
12. Keeping It Real: A Conclusion 185

Chapter Notes 189
Bibliography 205
Index 211

All dreamers and sleepwalkers must pay the price, and even the invisible victim is responsible for the fate of all.
—Ralph Ellison, *Invisible Man*

Preface

As a student of art history, I learned that keeping your personal voice out of your writing was critical. As an academic, one's approach should be dispassionate and scholarly. However, when analyzing historical critical texts, context was always key. Every art historian—and every artist—approaches their subject matter from a unique viewpoint, mustering the impetus to tackle their subject through a journey which makes that context crucial to their practice. I am a white woman writing about the work of a black man, ultimately several black men. The journey that brought me to write this book is the same process that transformed me from an artist to an art historian. A process that changed me from a person mostly unaware about issues of race and gender to a hopefully aware and slightly less clueless scholar. In "Critical Interrogations" bell hooks writes about the importance of transparency for white academics whose thinking about race is transformed to include their own whiteness in developing the scholarship of the next generation. It's great to wake up, but to illuminate the why is just as crucial. "Understanding that process is important for the development of solidarity; it can enhance awareness of the epistemological shifts that enable all of us to move in oppositional directions."[1]

I wrote this text because the film *Bamboozled* challenged me. I found myself thirsty to understand it. Although I had first viewed the film in its theater release, I didn't write about it until about half a decade later when—studying as an undergraduate—I encountered the film again in two art history courses, *Black Art* and *Race Films*. I had been working as an art teacher at a summer camp where none of the youth were white. Upon taking the kids to the museum of the Art Institute of Chicago where I was a student, the trip had fallen flat. The kids were not engaged with the content as I had presented it. One of my older students told me that she didn't see herself represented there. My own mask shattered. I felt embarrassed over their lack of interest resulting from my lack of foresight and insight into how to bridge my cultural knowledge gap to make the trip more fruitful for all of us. It was exactly the opposite of every white savior education movie. The kids treated me with acceptance and kindness despite my inadequacies and inexperience as a teacher. Through my quest to become less embarrassingly inadequate, I enrolled in classes that could broaden my worldview. I encountered rich, complex art that challenged my limited understanding of the world and forced me to grow. Rael Salley's *Black Art* and Romi Crawford's *Race Films* provided me more enjoyment than my own art making did. The more I learned, the more connections I made between the work I encountered and the themes within Lee's unsettling movie.

When I had watched *Bamboozled* in the theater the first time, I had felt the film's biting satire, been shocked by its images but remained unsure of its messages. *Do the Right Thing* had felt partially accessible to me, so *Bamboozled's* inaccessibility felt deliberately disquieting. I also would see *Summer of Sam*, which I strongly identified with because I had been a punk before Nirvana broke, and as a teenager I had felt my own form of Difference. That film made me love the song *Baba O'Riley*. But sitting watching *Bamboozled* at the 400 Theater in the racially diverse Chicago neighborhood of Rogers Park, I had been very aware of my whiteness. My embarrassment was hot and flushing as a child who had done something wrong and Mr. Lee was going to deal with me in a moment but for right now, he was *not talking to me*. Something significant happened within that film, but I didn't understand what because so much was outside of my knowledge base. *Bamboozled* problematized me as an audience member. The film dared me to do something about it.

Progressing on the journey to unpack the film that wasn't made for me, I have discovered so much work that I love. I am grateful for the textual richness of the film. The discomfiture I experienced through *Bamboozled* became more understandable to me, and gradually, my worldview changed, as it does whenever you encounter information that doesn't match your experiences. You either change or you double down. I chose to adapt, because I could see I had only been partially informed about the world. I know sometimes that the moments where I encounter new information or experience moments of insight might not be as revelatory to people not so white, and not so clueless; but, this book is my encounter. This book is the best representation of *Bamboozled's* influence on my development as a scholar. Louis Chude-Sokei has written that it is a troubled film,[2] and it is not a perfect film, but it is the film that changed my mind. The argument of this text is that this is the goal of the film. *Bamboozled* wants me to be uncomfortable in my whiteness to the point where I can no longer pretend to sympathize as a neutral outsider for people of color suffering under oppressive, systemic racism but must instead actively work to help dismantle the system that keeps blackness—and therefore whiteness—in place. This work involves talking about whiteness in order to make it visible. This work means moving beyond a superficial encounter with a romanticized past into having radical conversations about difficult topics. It involves no back patting. If we "get woke", we are not awakening into becoming "good white people" like Miss Daisy. We are acknowledging that the existence of whiteness is what prevents equity in America. We cannot be "good" or "reconciled" and also continue to be white. This truth is why racial reconciliation is a harmful myth, and why we must stop making and watching movies like *Driving Miss Daisy*.

Or *Green Book*.

On February 25, 2019, Spike Lee won his first competitive Oscar for Best Adapted Screenplay for his masterpiece *The BlacKkKlansman*. In his acceptance speech, he told his personal history and an American shared story, highlighting injustices of the past, and hopefulness for the future. Later that evening, *Green Book* won the Oscar for Best Picture and Spike Lee walked out. *Green Book* echoed the themes of *Miss Daisy* which had won in 1989 when Lee was denied even a nomination for the film that by many believe—as Kim Basinger said that night—should have won best picture that year, *Do the Right Thing*. But Spike Lee's watershed masterwork had not even been nominated.

Like *Driving Miss Daisy, Green Book* is a film that creates a racial reconciliation story by highlighting a white person's journey in which the white person becomes less racist after being exposed to a black person who does not have their own journey and whose life remains unseen except in relation to the white protagonist. It reduces the agency of the black character by showing them only as an agent for white change. As the man says, "it's the same thing, just done over." Lee said that he had a second speech in his pocket that was a thank you speech, but he wasn't sure he would return to the podium and he wanted to get the first speech said. Spike Lee is always vigilant and he has a plan. He is aware of the limitations of the system he operates inside and always makes maximum use of his opportunities. If the Academy shared his values, perhaps a different picture would have won Best Picture, but *Green Book* stole that honor.

Monique Judge wrote the *Green Book* review for The Root. The title for her review was straightforward, "*Green Book* Has Great Acting, a Misleading Title and Palatable Racism for White People." In the review, Judge described her experience watching the film and the audible gasps of the audience as they witnessed scenes of explicit racism portrayed in the film. She wrote, "We have a sitting president who declared to the world he is a [white] nationalist and who enacts policies that are harmful to blacks and people of color in general—but somehow white people were surprised to see a scene in which a white man who hired Don Shirley to entertain his party guests insists that his black entertainment go outside to use an outhouse rather than the restroom inside his home."³ This surprise is one reason why *The BlacKkKlansman* could not win the Best Picture Oscar. White people as a group do not know the history of racism in the United States and have maintained its invisibility by delegating black history to a separate conversation. By doing so, when white people—like the author of this book—discover the depth of its entrenchment in our culture, a re-education is required and a film like *Green Book* pretends to do that work in a way that allows those same white people a way to remain comfortable, and to view themselves as aligned with the right side of history.

White people want to believe that when they see injustice, they recognize it and will be appropriately appalled. They want to maintain the idea that they do not benefit from racism because if they are benefitting, they will then be forced to make a choice between their own comfortability and justice. They want comfort and justice. So they choose *Green Book* over *BlacKkKlansman* or *Black Panther* or *Sorry to Bother You* or *Roma*. They leave the struggle with race in a past that is ripe with nostalgia. Never dealing with the marriage they create in the mythic language of these films. Never moving beyond the Civil Rights Era and imagining a more recent racism. *Green Book*—and other stories like it—never require the white viewer to move beyond that journey. *Green Book* will never require its characters to encounter race in circumstances as the continually inadequate learner. The white viewer emphasizes with the racist white who is redeemed. They believe and feel that watching these films has engaged them with race, but unlike the characters in this film trope, the white audiences of films like *Green Book* aren't even witnessing or believing in the current acts of racism that occur in front of them, or in the daily news. *Green Book* allows for an acknowledgement of racism that nevertheless maintains and naturalizes whiteness. *Bamboozled* works differently. It points to whiteness, but intends to smash it to pieces, because if we destroy blackness, we also destroy whiteness. That is meant to make us all very uncomfortable.

You can't talk about blackface or blackness without encountering whiteness. Whiteness in America formed itself by drawing a boundary around blackness. For white viewers and scholars, it is difficult not to be the hero in a story you think might include you. But when your eyes adjust to see forms in the darkness, you must acknowledge that the artistry in the shadows is not absence. And this is the doubly signified intention of Darby English's book title *How to See a Work of Art in Total Darkness*. It's both about finding the beauty when you have been in the dark, and seeing the beauty in the darkness.

However, whiteness is not the ending, it is a point of noticing on a journey. James Baldwin said "As long as you think you're white, there's no hope for you."⁴ David Roediger—whose *Wages of Whiteness* highly influenced this book—wrote in his autobiographical introduction' "The main body of writing by white Marxists in the United States has both 'naturalized' whiteness and oversimplified race."[5] It is the intention of this book to make visible the methods and intentions of whiteness. So it will begin with a history of whiteness by talking about the history of blackface in America.

Introduction

Spike Lee released the film *Bamboozled* at the dawn of a new millennium. The close of the 1900s invited Lee to revisit W. E. B. Du Bois' claim that "the problem of the twentieth century is the problem of the color line."[1] *Bamboozled* is the result of Lee's interrogation into the state of the color line in the year 2000. The film unveils a nuanced vision of the history of a hundred years of black performance through a re-presentation of the past. This practice is rooted in the fiction writing of Du Bois. In the postscript to *The Ordeal of Mansart*, Du Bois makes plain the relationship between history, fiction, and truth. In the face of the inadequacy of memory and documentation, Du Bois recognized the role of fiction in conveying an essence of history, "To me it seems wiser and fairer to interpret historical truth by the use of creative imagination, provided the method is acknowledged and clear."[2] In other words, as long as a writer acknowledges the fictional nature of their account, rather than presenting it as history, fiction can often illuminate truths that elude us in the recitation of facts.

This book is not a recitation of facts but a cultural analysis of a turbulent and difficult movie. I will be examining the film as a piece of literature and as a visual document, exploring its cultural and historical context. In order to do that, I must cast my nets widely, to paraphrase Cornel West,[3] for *Bamboozled* satirizes a wide array of sources. Lee draws narratively on Ralph Ellison's *Invisible Man* as well as *Network*, with a nod to *The Producers*. Visually and thematically, Lee riffs on television, vaudeville and minstrelsy, and theoretically on Post black art.[4] As is characteristic of Post black art, Lee uses historically based icons and signs to illuminate, confront, and critique culture. As is also characteristic of Post black art, Lee draws upon sometimes shocking and racially loaded imagery. Although Lee references many black performers and artists over the course of the film, four heavily influence the form the film takes: Bert Williams, Oscar Micheaux, Ralph Ellison, and Michael Ray Charles.

The first half of this book outlines the significance of these four men, and Lee, in relation to Du Bois' project of using fiction to convey the truth of history. These chapters are part biography, and part cultural analysis of each artist's overall body of work, to familiarize the reader with the work and its meaning.

The second half offers an analysis of *Bamboozled*, documenting the intersections between the film and Williams, Micheaux, Ellison, and Charles. These chapters document repeating themes and forms employed by Lee to create referents: double articulation as Du Bois' double-consciousness, naming and casting practices, objects as signs, and the content of narrative structures, including satire.

The third section "keepin' it real" is the conclusion, in which it is determined where the didactics are pointing. Having proven in the previous sections that Lee is trying to illuminate the past, this section explores Lee's purpose, the *why* of the undertaking, and whether or not he is successful in enlightening the intended audience.

Historiography

In 1997, the sculptor Charles Ray salvaged a wrecked 1991 Pontiac Grand Am and took it apart recasting the pieces in fiberglass. A team of assistants assembled the fiberglass pieces to recreate the wreck. The casts, though literal duplicates, did not fit together easily. The shape and scale of the pieces all measured fractions off. This Ray work is a treatise on wonky perception, the failure of best efforts, and the inadequacy of painstaking intimacy and precision to create a likeness of a thing that exists. It is a critique of the copy of a copy. It is a critique of images. It is the sum of Gilles Deleuze's difference in repetition. This book undertakes the same painstaking process of disassembling parts in an attempt to understand the whole, to fully know the purpose of Spike Lee's film *Bamboozled*. The end result may feel wonky despite the care and precision with which it was executed. Hopefully any present wonkiness will engage the reader into a conversation that inspires an even broader dialogue about the film.

Not that *Bamboozled* needs help starting conversations. Audiences have been arguing about its purpose and meaning for years. The film caused controversy with popular critics following its release. In 2001, "Race, Media, and Money: A Critical Symposium on Spike Lee's Bamboozled" was held in response to the film, with Armond White leading the charge of dissidence against Lee's project. Jason Vest outlines the film's reception in his chapter on *Bamboozled*—"Facing Back, Facing Black"—within his 2014 book *Spike Lee: Finding the Story and Forcing the Issue*. Vest notes the misunderstanding that has clouded the film's reception and does a solid job unpacking why the film has been wrongly received, noting "Lee's film, in perhaps its greatest affront to easy viewing, strikes unsympathetic audience members as a text that destroys its own artistic foundation, with its director emerging as little more than a cinematic killjoy."[1] Just in the last several years, scholarship on *Bamboozled* has produced several serious texts, which though quite different from this project, have made their own contribution to the discourse. Ashley

Clark's *Facing Blackness: Media and Minstrelsy in Spike Lee's Bamboozled* does a good job analyzing its technical aspects and noting the film's importance. Clark sharply recognizes the centrality of *Bamboozled* to the thesis of Lee's career. Alessandro Raengo's *Critical Race Theory and Bamboozled* offers up a case study of *Bamboozled* as an argument for using critical race theory to unpack images and representations within film. Raengo's convincing argument provides a practical method for use in analysis. These methods can apply to many difficult films. Both of these texts are more solidly grounded in film studies' approaches than the book in your hands. If this book has a true home, it is likely in cultural studies. However, the methodology comes from the work of Darby English in the art historical text *How to See a Work of Art in Total Darkness*.

In his book, English identifies a loose ideological connection between a group of five black artists—Glenn Ligon, Fred Wilson, Isaac Julien, William Pope L., and Kara Walker—who problematize the idea of a black art and vigorously interrogate race and racial representations. These artists all question the yoke of the past and do not flinch from dredging up uncomfortable histories to force the question of what work race does and for whom. While English's text stands in agreement with critical race theory in some respects—viewing race as socially constructed—it also asserts that attempts to curtail the image making of black cultural producers to images of positivity are by necessity limiting and that, "There is no Black representational space outside of politics." The artwork of these five artists refuse prescribed limitations and assert the importance of remembering history.

English's book opens with a reference to David Hammons' installation *Concerto in Black and Blue*, which is itself a reference to the opening of Ralph Ellison's *Invisible Man*. English begins with the art, insisting that we do not assume that the subject is race, but rather examine how the work of art operates. Then, English unpacks the history of the conversation about blackness and art and its political connections. Turning to Frantz Fanon for inspiration, he infers that black artists are not trapped by history, but through his exposition of the same within the introduction, English mirrors the work he analyzes in asserting its importance.

Although not included within English's work, Michael Ray Charles—Lee's artistic consultant on *Bamboozled*—rose to prominence around the same time as Kara Walker and was attacked in similar ways over his use of negative imagery by black artists. The conversation that surrounds Walker's and Charles' work echoes inside *Bamboozled*'s reception. Persistently, in popular reviews and in the public conversation surrounding the film, Lee's choice to use blackface is criticized and condemned on the grounds that blackface is only able to say one thing.

Because of the clear connection between Lee's project and the artists

English addresses—and because of English's influence on the author of this text—the first half of this book follows English's outline. Beginning with an exposition of necessary historical background for its thesis and exploring the work of the five artists whose influence feels clear and present in *Bamboozled*: Bert Williams, Oscar Micheaux, Ralph Ellison, Michael Ray Charles and, of course, Spike Lee. There are direct and indirect references to these individuals within the film. This fact is undeniable. Bert Williams' costumes and catchphrases appear in the film and he is mentioned by name. Within Lee's company name "40 Acres and a Mule," he references not only the case for slavery reparations and the promise of restitution for freed black men following the Civil War, but also Oscar Micheaux's vision of homesteading as an alternative to northern migration. The portraits in Dunwitty's office reflect the portraits of Booker T. Washington that hung in Micheaux's race heroes' homes. The Jolly Nigger Bank scene within *Invisible Man* is almost precisely repeated by Delacroix within the film. And the artwork of Michael Ray Charles appears on the walls and interrupts the action of the film. Like blackface itself, these histories are a current running through the film. Learning the stories exposes the intent of the film.

Like English, this text looks to the art's work to tell us what it means. How does it operate and what are its ends? When approaching analysis of an artwork, a helpful approach is to unpack the referents in the search for meaning and to place those referents within the context of the works making. In applying this method to *Bamboozled*, we must understand the broad history that Lee draws from in this film and then posit an educated thesis about the why.

Several times over the course of the film, Lee asserts that this is the new millennium. Even the minstrel show in the film contains the phrasing "new millennium." The thesis of this book is that Lee uses this phrase to refer to W. E. B. Du Bois' assertion that the problem of the twentieth century is the problem of the color line. Lee revisits this conclusion at the century's close and questions what if anything has changed. So, *Bamboozled* contends with the rich history of black performance within that past century. Therefore, to contend with *Bamboozled*, any analysis must recognize the importance of historical narratives to the film.

A thoughtful analysis of this film must also acknowledge W.J.T. Mitchell's important assertion in *What Do Pictures Want?* that *Bamboozled* is a metapicture about images. Mitchell's argument rightly identifies the film's interests, but examines the implications of this assertion only in respect to the film's struggle as an image bearer (a picture being the image married to its support.) He writes that "[Lee] talks sometimes as if he had achieved a standpoint outside the 'madness' of images, the 'distorted' images of film and television. And yet if there is one thing Bamboozled makes clear, it is just how difficult it is to find this critical standpoint, to achieve a 'just estimation' of images that transcends distortion and madness."[2] Mitchell leaves room in this statement for the possibility that one might achieve a purely critical standpoint, but he remains skeptical that Lee has managed these ends. Mitchell asserts that *Bamboozled* operates as an image. And his definition of an image is broad enough to include *Bamboozled*. According to Mitchell, "By 'image' I mean any likeness, figure, motif, or form that appears in some medium or other."[3] However, the term is more historically fraught than this straightforward definition suggests.

Is there a critical foundation for the idea that *Bamboozled* in fact did manage these ends and what are the strategies employed in the film that accomplish them? Looking at the history of the term's use in critical theory, there are other ontological possibilities identified for film's function other than as an image. Mitchell's image functions representationally, therefore the strategies of *Bamboozled* must be representational in order for the struggle as an image bearer to be a correct understanding of the ultimate failure or success of the film. Gilles Deleuze also uses the term image to point to a fixed state of representation, the "snapshot" moment, which is the ontological essence of photography. Deleuze, however, views film as potentially antithetical to the image when the viewer is replaced by the visionary. He seeks within "aberrant" and "abnormal" films a moment of nooshock—defined by French dramatist Antonin Artaud as a state of neuro-physiological overload, brought about by the rapid presentation of on-screen images. Cinema makes it impossible to think, because before we can interpret one image, it is already replaced by another. Before we can grasp an image it is already passed, the process of association is constantly interrupted, deconstructed, dislocated.

That awakens the viewer to their subjectivity and smashes that subjectivity to pieces. Art—which stands in opposition to images for Deleuze—has only one form of politics, which is to dismantle the strategies of representational thought. In this sublime moment, according to Deleuze, the problematic Idea creates it's "vital-intuition."[4] I argue that this moment of nooshock, which is rare within film, is present within *Bamboozled*. Even the language from the film points to subjectivity and stirs within the viewer a call to awaken. We are left in intentional discomfort.

I am aware of the irony exemplified in utilizing some of the techniques within this text that Deleuze condemns as ontologically photographic—particularly the application of linguistics—but Lee hits all of these images to make them resound and therefore I use every tool that exposes the strategies he employs. Strikingly, in analyzing this meta-picture, the real question is: does it transcend its form and spark a nooshock, or has it failed in that large sense? Mitchell's interest in the desires of images provides a crucial form of entry that envisions a different criteria for seeing. This criteria asks larger questions that helps to position the film in a critical world.

In addition to the influence of English and Mitchell, the collective works of W. E. B. Du Bois are an essential influence on the theory of this text. Also, a large debt is owed to Stuart Hall and his seminal text *Representation: Cultural Representations and Signifying Practices*. Hall's Cultural Theory provides a means for making connections across academic disciplines through the common sense application of semiotics to all forms of cultural production as a tool for unpacking context.[5]

Clearly influential on my own ideas about liberating identity and history is Deleuze's *Difference and Repetition*. Deleuze's conception of difference ascribed value to what Western philosophy—through the influence of Plato—devalued as debased copies or simulacra. Deleuze marks a Platonic conception of simulacra as what is excluded from participating, "Subordinating difference to the powers of the Same and the Similar, in declaring difference unthinkable in itself, and sending difference and simulacrum back to the bottomless ocean."[6] The simulacrum is rendered Invisible, discarded. The redemption of simulacra is rooted in an assertion of difference, in the individual over the communal, acknowledging similarity but finding the difference to be the value. Concepts that seem to be duplicates are actually events unto themselves and don't require a return to an original.[7] In relation to identity and the ideas of writers and thinkers like Lee, Ellison and Du Bois there is an undercurrent of an assertion of difference to the work of all three. This critical viewpoint is theoretically significant within Postmodernism and encountered within Post black art.

I interpret the work of Post black art of the 1990s as a push back against the pressure of Identity politics, a concept derived from my reading of Studio of Harlem Director and Chief Curator Thelma Golden's essays within *Freestyle*, *Black Male*, and the *1993 Whitney Biennial* catalogs. Along with English, Golden's work introduced me to the concept of the political basis for assigning ideologies to systems of representations and visual conventions and sent me running down the rabbit hole that became this book. The lectures of Rael Salley and Romi Crawford demonstrated the connections between Oscar Micheaux and Spike Lee. Through the teaching of Corey Capers, I came to understand the importance of the black/white binary in fashioning "American-ness."[8]

Also important are the work of several scholars whose own writing pointed towards connections that have contributed to my understanding of the film. Michael Germana's *Standards and Values* examines the connections between Ralph Ellison, Michael Ray Charles, and Lee in relation to the use of the coin and the Jolly Nigger Bank. And while their inclusion is primarily a minor point in a greater project, Germana connects all three works to Herman Melville's *The Confidence Man*.[9]

Louis Chude-Sokei's work on Bert Williams in *The Last Darky: Bert*

Williams, Black-on-Black Minstrelsy, and the African Diaspora locates an origin for the discourses about systems of black representation within the communities of the black diaspora, focusing particularly on Harlem and the clashing views of the thinkers arising during the period, particularly W. E. B. Du Bois, Marcus Garvey, Booker T. Washington and Claude McKay. Chude-Sokei de-centers the discourse surrounding Williams' minstrelsy from a conversation about the limitations and misrepresentations inherent within minstrelsy to a complex dialogue about the building of blackness and modern black community. Chude-Sokei cites Williams' performances as a critique of both these conversations. Bert Williams is perhaps the origin for the trajectory that my book seeks to establish, and Chude-Sokei's theories on his performances anchor the continuity of the project, establishing an understanding of the contextual richness of the history of the performance of blackness within the arts. Subversion and critique, two main themes of his work, are prevalent within this specific trajectory.[10]

Also, Chude-Sokei has written specifically on Spike Lee's *Bamboozled* and its use of blackface in the anthology *Burnt Cork*. Although, I disagree with Chude-Sokei's assessment of Lee's use of Williams within *Bamboozled*, I find his work insightful and invaluable overall. As a proof that *Bamboozled* synthesizes the thread of performance history and contains echoes of each of the other men's work, Chude-Sokei's work demonstrates connections between Williams and the Harlem Renaissance. This point allows correlations to be drawn between Williams and Micheaux and secondarily, Ellison, which broadens the discourse.[11]

Jacqueline Stewart's *Migrating to the Movies: Cinema and Black Urban Modernity* uniquely pulls together theory, history and technological understanding to write comprehensively about the role of film in the early twentieth century. Stewart's project brings a technical understanding to the greater sociological issues surrounding the role of film in helping to achieve a transition to urban modernity during this time period. Stewart ends her volume by focusing on the work of Micheaux, particularly his silent films. Stewart's grounding of this project within Chicago's story highlights its significance in black film history and sets the scene for Micheaux's work. Stewart's writing illuminates a specific historical understanding of black audiences and provides a context for some of the pushback that occurred in reaction to Micheaux's films.[12]

Pearl Bowser and Louise Spence's *Writing Himself into History: Oscar Micheaux, His Silent Films and His Audiences* situates Micheaux outside of the mainstream discourse surrounding the Race Films of the Silent Era, noting the dissension many critics had with some of the negative characterizations contained within Micheaux's films, like *The Brute* and *The Symbol of the Unconquered*. Bowser and Spence identify Micheaux as a trickster and able businessman who calculatedly created a persona designed to sell his films. *Writing Himself into History* primarily concerns itself with the first ten years of Micheaux's directing career, prior to the advent of the "talkie." Bowser and Spence have comprehensively documented this time period, contextualizing Micheaux's work within it and very successfully sift through the self-generated myth that Micheaux made of himself through his fictional work. Bowser and Spence's project to locate Micheaux's films historically and within community serves as a beginning point for this examination, which locates Micheaux within a pattern of intellectual history that seeks to subvert the dominant narrative of not only the history but also of community.

In greater history, many volumes have been written on the broad subject of black film and blacks working in film in general, examining their cultural impact and providing a methodology through which to do so. The three volumes of greatest significance for this writing are *Forgeries of Memory and Meaning* by Cedric Robinson, *Toms, Coons, Mulattoes, Mammies and Bucks* by Donald Bogle, and Thomas Cripp's *Slow Fade to Black*. The methodologies of these three men do specific work related to the goals of the book. Robinson uses the transition period from theater to film to analyze how and why tropes of race permeated the early narrative of film using a Marxist lens, ascribing the employment of these tropes to economic and cultural forces with a political significance.[13] Bogle has a similar project, only he is interested in unpacking the cultural conditions of the black actors who undertook many of the roles also described by Robinson. Bogle assigns agency to these figures and asserts the need for their stories to be documented and located within the limitations of the time, while still acknowledging the part they had to play in opening doors for those who came after them. Bogle asserts that there has been, historically, an interest in dismissing the work of these figures because of the racial content of the projects they were involved with, but that this is somewhat dishonoring. Lee's treatment of performers like Bert Williams within the film, as well as some of his public statements, echo Bogle's assertions.[14] *Slow Fade to Black* chronicles the period of black film history from 1900–1942, looking at blacks in front of and behind the camera. Cripps documents a slow change in the representations of blacks during this time and cites the work of the NAACP against racist stereotypes as crucial to this process.[15]

This book has been years in the making. When I first began research on *Bamboozled* in 2007, there were no full-length books that I could find on the film and locating and accessing articles was a more painstaking project than it is today. One monograph I was able to locate was a small but textually dense volume by Gerald Powell devoted to *Bamboozled* and *X*. It was invaluable for raising my own level of thinking about the film. Gerald, if you're reading this. Thanks for giving me a place to begin.

History as Didactics through Fiction: The Legacy of W. E. B. Du Bois

In 1915, the year Booker T. Washington passed away, D. W. Griffith released the film *Birth of a Nation*, which would indelibly mark film history with the legacy of minstrelsy's racist stereotypes: the mammy, the Uncle Tom, the black buck, the tragic mulatto, the pick-a-ninny, and the coon. Griffith's film broke new ground visually, establishing a cinematic language that is still drawn from today. However, these same elements also furthered an agenda of white supremacy, using epic grandeur and visual power to frighten white audiences about a set of imagined consequences arising from the abolition of slavery. The strides black Americans made during the initial stages of Reconstruction were lampooned as chaotic savagery. The film's tragic plot and melodrama worked to incite opposition to the advancement of civil rights for black Americans. Through its renewed visual investment in minstrelsy—the first truly American form of entertainment—its narrative sought to reaffirm the ways in which the United States historically had defined American identity, in opposition to blackness. Famously, Woodrow Wilson would call the film "like writing history with lightning."[16] *Birth of a Nation* framed the blackface performances of its white actors as straightforward representations, making-believe a space in which white bodies could define authentic blackness. However, in actuality, the characteristics ascribed to blackness within the film's characterizations served as a cautionary tale that was really about regulating the behavior of disenfranchised impoverished white people.

Like many accounts of history in film that would follow this epic, the story conveyed within *Birth of a Nation* tells us less about the Civil War and Reconstruction than it does about the time period the film was produced in. The Progressive Era—from 1900 to 1915—witnessed the arrival of over 15 million immigrants to the United States. According to the Library of Congress, by 1910 three quarters of New York City's population were either new immigrants, or the daughters and sons of immigrants. The face of America was changing rapidly.[17] What it meant to be American was changing as well. The country whose founders had argued for their separation from the British Empire based on a broken contract between a British King and his equally British subjects had written into the fabric of its constitution a definition of American that worked to uphold the hierarchies of the preexisting social structures that operated within the colonies.[18]

Prior to the American Revolution, English citizens of the British colonies in America constructed social divisions between themselves and others rooted in nationality. These colonists justified the indentured servitude and enslavement of people groups like the Irish and Africans of varying ethnicity based on their status as non-citizens, as opposed to their ethnicity. In the same way, these colonists in their list of grievances within the Declaration of Independence invoked their right to fair treatment as British royal subjects and citizens, citing the Enlightenment logic of Rousseau's *Social Contract*.

Upon winning the Revolution, the newly founded country needed to find different criteria for citizenship. According to David Waldstreicher's *Slavery's Constitution*, the framers of the U.S. Constitution knowingly employed language that would institutionalize slavery in order to appease the slavery dependent South, preventing an immediate secession. As Waldstreicher points out, "Because the Constitution had economic implications and set the stage for a National economy, it could not avoid slavery and creating a constitutional politics of slavery."[19] Waldstreicher defines the Constitution as a document that outlines the governance of the people within the nation, establishing rule and a hierarchy over them. The U.S. Constitution outlines who is included in U.S. citizenship and who is not and whose rights are protected under the law, marking through its wording a very clear and distinctive line between the idea of people and property. Rather than situating citizenship geographically—if you were here, you were a citizen—this American identity was formed through adherence to behaviors that Rousseau defined as civilized and therefore human. For the most part, these behaviors conformed to Judeo-Christian values, which the constitution's formers used to justify a hierarchy that maintained the divisions of class upheld in colonial times.[20]

The behaviors identifying *civilized* people included lawfulness, discipline, good manners, education, cultural awareness and participation in government. Through law—and through image making in print and illustration—groups were included or excluded within this definition. In subsequent attempts to justify the practice of slavery, and to define what it meant to be American, these citizens of a new nation drew boundaries based on "race," inscribing meaning onto black bodies, creating justification for and through their continued enslavement.[21]

Through law, enslaved blacks were kept undereducated and unable to participate in government. Through grotesque characterizations in tracts and newspapers, and then, in minstrel shows, and eventually films like *Birth*, writers and artists repeatedly imbued blackness with unruliness, disorder, shiftlessness, and lawlessness.[22] Through this practice—this enacting of race—a working definition of whiteness or Americanness was established. Americanization became a process through which immigrants and excluded peoples could earn inclusion by enacting their separateness from blackness. Through ritual behaviors like racial violence against blacks—as described by David Roediger within *The Wages of Whiteness*—and performing in blackface, ethnic groups like the Irish proved their whiteness and so their Americanness. Roediger argues that the use of language was essential in establishing this new white identity.[23] As Stuart Hall notes in *Representations*, "Language is central to meaning and culture and has always been regarded as the key repository of cultural values and meanings."[24] Writing intentional meaning into blackness and linking these written words with illustrations that supported the text gave these representations weight. These enacted constructed representations turned black bodies into signifiers of uncivilized behaviors.[25] People striving for citizenship adhered to the standards of civility in order to argue their case for inclusion.[26] However, as black bodies stood in for savagery, there was no possibility for blacks to access the privileges of whiteness or Americanness. As a result, the historical defining of American identity continued to be positioned as opposed to blackness. Therefore, when the wave of immigration at the turn of the twentieth century occurred, performing blackface minstrelsy served as a shortcut to assimilation. For white performers, the removal of the mask underscored their whiteness. If you could put the mask on, you could take it off. Blackface operated as a didactic pointing to the whiteness of its performers. The necessity of the application of burnt cork functioned as a proof.[27]

Blackface's mechanics belied a complicated system of representations, the least of which were straightforward negative characterizations. Minstrelsy's stereotypes helped establish a definition of blackness repetitiously building agreed meanings. Over time, these meanings became naturalized, an invisible part of the hegemony of the American fabric. These representations and the oppositional framework they maintained manufactured a rift in identity for black Americans who, in actuality, operated inside the fabric of American society, not outside of it. Nevertheless, they were viewed by white Americans as separate. W. E. B. Du Bois would call this rift double-consciousness, when your own understanding and perception of yourself doesn't match how you are perceived by others and you are made aware of the difference.[28] Frantz Fanon describes this realization as the shattering of the mask.[29]

Under slavery, this separation enabled white Americans to ignore the inherent inequity of the plantation model. After slavery's end, the promise of whiteness prevented black and white workers in a newly industrialized society from organizing together. By representationally affixing blackness to uncivilized behavior, both disenfranchised black and white Americans were curtailed from accessing the tools that allowed British colonists to separate from the British crown to begin with: active forms of resistance.[30]

Blackness was fashioned as a threat of reprisal. Hosea Easton—a black American Chaplain and staunch abolitionist—wrote about these practices in *A Treatise on the Intellectual Character, and Civil and Political Condition of the Colored People of the United States and the Prejudice Exercised Toward Them*.

[I]n some families it is almost the only method of correcting their children.
   To inspire their half grown misses and masters to improvement, they are told that if they do this or that, or if they do thus or so, they will be poor or ignorant as a nigger; or that they will be black as a nigger; or they will have no more credit than a nigger; that they will have hair, lips, feet, or something of the kind, like a nigger.... This display of American civility is under the daily observation of every class of society, even New England. But this kind of education is not only systemized but legalized.[31]

This form of warning and admonition was a cousin to the literary form the cautionary tale, in which the protagonist of the story illuminates the folly of specific behaviors by exhibiting the dire consequences of engaging in those same behaviors. The trope of the cautionary tale has been used for centuries as a didactic tool for regulating the moral behavior of children. Charles Perrault published *Little Red Riding-hood* in France, in 1697. Heinrich Hoffmann's *Struwelpeter* appears in Germany in 1845. *Struwelpeter* was remarkable in its morbidity, with its characters often meeting terrible violent ends.[32] The McLoughlin Brothers Publishing Company of New York was a primary purveyor of the genre in America from the mid–1800s to the early 1900s.[33] In 1859, McLoughlin published a collection of tales that included "The Little Girl Who Inked Herself." In this story, Miss Mopsa, when learning to write with ink, frequently spills on herself and her work, sucking ink out of the pen. Her skin grows blacker and blacker until she is no longer considered a suitable daughter and is given up by her family for a rag doll.[34] In many cases, the cautionary tale results in the punishment of the child in question for uncivilized behavior by the loss of his/her ethnic purity. This trope often alluded to the broader theme of miscegenation. In literature, and later films, miscegenation was discouraged through imagery that invoked animalistic character traits as inherent in black characters, referring to cautionary tales like *Little Red Riding-hood*. In *Birth,* the animalistic Gus' proposal of marriage was enough to send Flora Cameron hurling to her death. Gus would serve as a mirror for the character Silas Lynch who would attempt to rape Elsie Stoneman because—within the logic of the film—even after clothed in a position of respectability within society, Lynch couldn't control himself. Charlene Regester writes that in Griffith's world, "Blacks, despite their sophistication, cannot disconnect themselves from beastliness; being black renders them beastly attackers, desirous of White women."[35] Griffith positions Lynch as a sophisticated statesman *and* attacker in order to demonstrate that race not class is the marker for exclusion from full participation in American identity. This illustration reinforces the work of blackface minstrelsy, closing doors to social improvement for blacks and dangling a carrot of inclusion and mobility in front of working class whites in exchange for their complicity in black disenfranchisement.

   Eric Lott argued within his book *Love and Theft* that the story of blackface minstrelsy is more complex than racist caricature. "The minstrel show was less the incarnation of an age old racism than an emergent social semantic figure highly responsive to the emotional demands and troubled fantasies of its audiences."[36] The elasticity of blackface performance allowed for critiques of class and recognition of the malleable slippage of race to play out in an arena where these same ideas could be easily disavowed. Blackface minstrelsy allowed white performers an opportunity to enact the characteristics made unavailable to them and marked those behaviors—and the desire to enact them—as separate from themselves. Blackface minstrelsy functioned as parody or burlesque. Parody—as opposed to the concise and biting critique of satire—is ambivalent. A host of meanings can be discerned within its loose spaces.[37]

What work the parody within blackface minstrelsy did and how it is received depended on who performed it and who its audience was. For black Americans performing blackface minstrelsy, the work done through the performance was no less dense than that of white performers. The black Americans who performed these roles frequently used them as a means of pushing back against these representations. Because of the limits imposed upon the criteria for citizenship, during the Reconstruction and the Progressive Era, many forms of resistance by black Americans to these characterizations necessarily came from within the structure of the stereotypes themselves, as a means to challenge and deconstruct their authority. According to theater historian David Krasner, "Since parody, and not direct satire or social confrontation, was all that was available, it was the ability to parody class, race, gender, and social conditions that provided black performers an opportunity to call minstrelsy's racism into question."[38]

As Louis Chude-Sokei points out, the flattening of black performed blackface minstrelsy into pure racist caricature is something that occurred in retrospect in an attempt to distance other black modernisms from the genre, despite their connections and debt to its legacy. Writes Chude-Sokei,

> Their transformations of the form of minstrelsy would be repressed or evoked as a sign of racial trauma by subsequent generations of black cultural producers in the United States; from the Harlem Renaissance up to the contemporary moment, as, for example, in Spike Lee's deeply troubled film *Bamboozled*, which features multiple images of Bert Williams as well as some of his most well-known costumes.[39]

Chude-Sokei's thoughtful analysis of the work of Bert Williams inside his book *The Last Darky* historicizes Williams' performances within the context of his identity as a West Indian immigrant and in conversation with the approval of both Booker T. Washington and W. E. B. Du Bois. Chude-Sokei notes that Washington conflates the person Bert Williams with the identity statement of Williams' performances.[40] The quotation from Chude-Sokei in the previous paragraph demarcates a belief that Lee also misunderstood or flattened the performances of Bert Williams perhaps because of their inclusion and reference within a film, which works very hard to condemn contemporary ways in which Black performers function, even now, within the constraints of minstrelsy. Chude-Sokei locates the pulse of conflict within the film, but also subjects *Bamboozled* to a similar flattening. Chude-Sokei continues:

> For these generations the very mask was too shameful to even quibble about its various and intricate semantic or signifying possibilities or to even dare connect to Du Boisian double-consciousness or assimilation. It was too traumatic a sign to even mention in the context of both of these latter concepts; after all, to do so would be to suggest that these notions were mere performances.[41]

Lee made this connection within *Bamboozled*. He employed the cork mask for the purpose of critique and commentary, using it in the way that Williams did, as a complex sign and a referent for talking about blackness and how it operates. Lee also strives to draw comparisons between black image making that acknowledges and challenges historical and contemporary representations with those that do not. The troubled nature of the film—which Chude-Sokei rightly picks up on—builds from the seething wrath Lee rains upon what he marks as buffoonery. The subtext is strong and present, "Bert Williams, he was brilliant."[42] and about Mantan Mooreland, "That's not funny."[43] That Lee chooses Savion Glover—whose choreography for *Bring Da Noise, Bring Da Funk*, the 1996 Broadway musical that chronicled black history through tap and reclaimed and reinvigorated this art form long associated with racist stereotypes in Hollywood—to portray the character Manray who stands in for Williams in the film, didactically establishes Lee's framing intent.[44] Furthermore, the characterization of Manray and his partner Womack as "lazy, ignorant, and unlucky"[45] is an artifice of character ascribed to them by Pierre Delacroix. Their early rising in the initial scene "We snooze, we lose,"[46] and the rehearsal scene in which Manray goes over and over the choreography with the dancers demonstrate these characterizations as false. Lee's film agrees with Du Bois' concept of the work of art. When Du Bois maintains that, "Again artists have used Goodness—goodness in all its aspects of justice, honor and right—not for the sake of ethical sanction but as the one true method of gaining sympathy and human interest."[47]

Lee responds, pulls threads of history, making connections from one generation of image making in black performance, art, and literature to the next to engage in the conversation black Art inevitably returns to over and again. Images and words always carry meaning. To not regulate the content of images and words contained within a work of art with precision and awareness is tantamount to surrendering agency. The performance history that Lee invokes to critique contemporary black performances draws a line between art that compels a recognition of black humanity through its portrayals and those performances that operate as a reduction. Various historians and cultural producers and artists have argued that images of black Americans must necessarily be images of positivity and uplift, or that there is a certain aesthetic character to black art that should be maintained. This is not what Du Bois argues for in "Criteria of Negro Art." Rather he wrote,

> On the other hand, the young and slowly growing black public still wants its prophets almost equally unfree. We are bound by all sorts of customs that have come down as second-hand soul clothes of White patrons.... Our worst side has been so shamelessly emphasized that we are denying we have or have ever had a worst side. In all sorts of ways we are hemmed in and our new young artists have got to fight their way to freedom.[48]

Du Bois argues for speaking truth through art. "The apostle of Beauty thus becomes the apostle of Truth and Right not by choice but by inner and outer compulsion. Free he is but his freedom is ever bounded by Truth and Justice; and slavery only dogs him when he is denied the right to tell the Truth or recognize an ideal of Justice."[49] Like Du Bois, Lee does not care for art that is not propaganda, because like Du Bois he recognizes that all art functions as propaganda for some idea. *Bamboozled* is Lee's historically based argument for that concept. Lee demonstrates within *Bamboozled* a willingness to make a failed or flawed film in service to a greater idea. Roger Ebert noted this tendency in his review of *She Hate Me*: "By getting mad at the movie, we arrive at the conclusions he intends. In a sense, he is sacrificing himself to get his message across."[50] Lee's efforts to spark conversations about black representation and racial politics in America are successful and they are the point. *Bamboozled* stands as a testament to Lee's career project. In Spike Lee's films, consistently, some character calls for the audience to "wake up." If we examined the body of Lee's work and imagined that one film could mark the "wake up" moment of the arc of his filmography, *Bamboozled* would be it. The five chapters that follow highlight the work of men who fall on the Du Boisian side of Lee's line in the sand.

1
Bert Williams: Minstrelsy, Vaudeville and Silent Film

> *Williams and Walker lifted minstrelsy by sheer force of genius into the beginning of a new drama.*—W. E. B. Du Bois

One of the dominant contrasts within *Bamboozled* is the difference between the cinematography of the narrative sections of the film—shot in video with the Sony DCR-VX1000 and later converted—and the minstrel sequences, which were shot on Super 16 film. The result is a hyperrealism in the minstrel sequences, which are lush and rich in feel compared with the flat affect of the video sequences.

Lee constructed the minstrel show very carefully attempting accurate authenticity to history. To this end, Lee drew heavily upon Bert Williams' performances using his tagline, costumes, and formula—a duo with George Walker. Lee even references Williams within the film, calling him brilliant. Clearly, by outfitting Manray in Williams' costumes—including his infamous chicken suit legs—Lee draws parallels between Williams and Manray.

Lee wants the audience to view Manray as an artist and sympathetic character. Lee emphasizes that Manray's options are limited in similar ways to how Williams' options were limited and through those associations that Manray's talents are as genuine as Williams' were. Simultaneously, Lee thus frames Manray's abilities and legacy as disregarded; his talents ignored by many of his contemporaries—the Mau Maus, Dunwitty, even Delacroix—as a result of the burnt cork. All of these connections are made clear through viewing the film in light of the critical histories of Williams' life by historians like Louis Chude-Sokei and Eric Lott. Williams' story broadens the discourse that surrounds blackface and gives credence to an argument of agency for those who wore the mask.

Born in the Bahamas, Bert Williams grew up in the British West Indies. In 1885, he moved with his family to the United States, living first in Florida

Savion Glover as Manray (center)—with Tyheesha Collins (front right), Cartier Williams (front left), Baakari Wilder (back left), Dormeshia Sumbry (back left center), Jason Bernard (back right center), and Sekou Torbet (back right)—appearing in *Mantan: The New Millennium Minstrel Show* from Spike Lee's *Bamboozled* (2000).

before finally settling in Riverside in Southern California; where he graduated from high school. After spending a brief time studying engineering at Stanford, Williams left the school after being unable to afford the tuition. In part to raise funds for his education, Williams began to fall back on a set of talents he had been developing while cutting up in class; telling jokes and singing. At first, Williams set out to be a serious actor and musician, but it became clear quite quickly that this was impossible due to the limited opportunities for blacks within the field. White audiences wanted a coon show. Williams performed with Martin and Seig's Mastodon Minstrels before finally meeting George Walker who would be his onstage partner for almost 20 years. Walker and Williams found some work performing as a duo in California, but eventually left with the hope of securing a spot in the Octoroons show in Chicago. As they moved across the Southwest and performed their way towards the Midwest, Williams and Walker encountered difficulty because white audience members disliked the fact that they dressed well and refused to wear blackface.[1] One incident in Colorado scared the duo particularly. Following their performance, audience members approached Williams and Walker forcing them to disrobe and don burlap sacks.[2] The vitriol grew so intense as they

Bert Williams in a chicken suit for the performance of "White Folks Call It Chantecler," performed at the Ziegfeld Follies in New York (1910).

crossed the country that the pair decided to stop performing in the South altogether. Upon reaching Chicago, both gentlemen were accepted into Octoroons, and both were fired soon after. The necessity to quickly secure work finally forced the duo to wear the cork mask. While performing in Detroit, Williams applied blackface for the first time while performing his own composition, "Oh, I Don't Know, You're Not So Warm." The audience response was manic. Ann Charters wrote in her biography *Nobody: The Story of Bert Williams* that Williams despised having to wear blackface, but simultaneously discovered that it allowed him to perform comedy in a way that he previously had been unable to do.[3] This decision to perform in blackface would become both the source of the duo's initial successes and the source of Williams' lifelong regret. However, the brilliance of their performances did not lie within the mask but rather within Williams' and Walkers' ability to surpass it. As Walker wrote in 1906:

> Bert and I watched the White "coons," and were often much amused at seeing White men with black cork on their faces trying to imitate black folks. Nothing about these White men's actions was natural, and therefore nothing was as interesting as if black performers had been dancing or singing in their own way.[4]

In recent years, historians and theorists have reexamined Williams' filmed performances and the documents surrounding Williams' and Walkers' stage shows, finding a complexity and nuance overlooked in the past because of the overtly racist nature of blackface itself.[5] Cedric Robinson wrote in *Forgeries of Memory and Meaning*:

> In the process of spawning Black musical theater from Black Minstrelsy,[6] a remarkable cluster of Black performers, choreographers, and writers—Bob Cole, Bert Williams, George Walker, Aida Overton Walker, James Weldon Johnson and his brother J. Rosamund Johnson, Will Marion Cook, and Paul Laurence Dunbar—perfected a host of Black resistance gestures for display before largely White audiences. Acutely race-conscious, this group recovered and invented much of the moral and conceptual vocabulary and the sly oppositional stratagems which would sluice Black resistance into public entertainment.[7]

Finding the subversions inherent within Williams' performances due in part to his complicated personal identity, Louis Chude-Sokei documents painstakingly the duality of the performance of blackface within Williams' work, inside *The Last Darky*. He views Williams' performances as functioning in separate ways in the presence of racially different audiences, citing Williams' West Indies ancestry as an area of conflict that prevented his true integration into black Harlem during this time just prior to the Harlem Renaissance.[8] Williams, Chude-Sokei argues, drew upon the negotiations and mimicry essential to operating as an immigrant inside black culture in Harlem to feed the characterizations within his blackface performances. Therefore, Williams performed a complicated presentation of the black dual identities built into American culture, while truly viewing himself as an outsider to the dichotomy of the black/white binary.[9] Chude-Sokei writes, "The minstrel mask mediates and silently complicates the institutional dynamics of black and White through an intra-racial and cross-cultural signifying."[10] For Chude-Sokei, Harlem Renaissance participants and the critical thinkers and activists of the time invested in a black identity that was as constructed as the one within minstrelsy and also as singularly American.[11] Williams, as an immigrant, was in the unique position to view the constructed-ness of both of these manifestations of American blackness and play upon that irony within his performances. Unfortunately, as generations have passed, the context of Williams' work as both a black blackface performer and an immigrant has been largely forgotten and—as is noted by Chude-Sokei in the text—eventually, Williams' use of blackface leads largely to the erasure of his entry from black history for some time, despite his strong influence on the founders of the Harlem Renaissance.

In part, this erasure is the effect of *Birth of a Nation*. The racist stigma of blackface—as transferred to the film epic narrative through Griffith's vision—led to a massive dispossession of the legacy of black performers within the early history of both film and American theater. As Donald Bogle expressed within his seminal work *Toms, Coons, Mulattoes, Mammies & Bucks*, black Americans in early film history had been largely "dismissed, ignored or even vilified because no one knew anything about the nature of their work and the conditions under which they performed."[12] Bogle believed that the history of black film must be "contended with ... defined, recorded, reasoned with, and interpreted."[13,14] Unpacking this contentious legacy of the past and locating its connections to the present provides a fuller understanding of current context, allowing us to locate places of difference within history significant in their Deleuzian returns. Difference—the small slippage between an original and its copy—is the site of parody and satire.[15] Difference marks the birth of change, and as Darby English wrote, "Art is a function of change."[16] Striving for change within a performance by a person struggling under a veil of oppression of limited forms is an act of resistance. Change the joke, slip the yoke. This is precisely the kind of performance Williams strived for,

> I shuffle onstage, not as myself, but as a lazy, slow going negro ... the real Bert Williams is crouched deep down inside the coon who sings and tells stories.... I'd like a piece that would give me an opportunity to express the whole of the negro's character. The laughter I have caused is only on the surface. Now I'd like to go much deeper and show our depths that few understand yet.[17]

Chude-Sokei argued that the work of Bert Williams is difficult to dismiss as a mere "coon show" and is rather specifically complex.[18,19] Spike Lee directly quotes Williams' act with George Walker in the context of *Mantan: The New Millennium Minstrel Show*. Manray and Womack—performing as Mantan and Sleep'n'Eat—open a starting segment of the show with an introduction that calls up Williams and Walker stating "we are two *real coons*."[20] Williams and Walker used this phrase to introduce their act, calling attention to the white audience's characterization of them and problematizing it in the process. Coons were characters drawn from within the context of minstrelsy.

In the early days, there existed two stereotypes related to what would become the coon type, the zip coon, and the Sambo. George Dixon first portrayed the zip coon in 1834. This type was differentiated from the Sambo character by his fancy dress. His fancy dress signified his position as a freed black man. The Sambo was the superstitious, lazier version of the docile Uncle Tom. Jim Crow became the face of this character, eventually becoming the face of racism against blacks in the United States. The two eventually merged into one type, the coon.

The use of the moniker "two real coons" highlights the issue of constructed-ness inherent within a performance of blackness. The phrase does work on two levels. First, "Two real coons" maintains that there can be an authentic coon. It does not, however, unpack what a coon is, the ambivalence of parody. To a white audience from this time period, a coon was a lazy, amiable mischievous black person, a trickster. For white audiences then, the authenticity of the performance rested within an understanding of Williams and Walker as black men. Their blackness was equivalent to coon-ness. And unlike white minstrel performers, Williams and Walker were defined by white audiences as authentically black.

However, performing in front of black audiences, the emphasis on how one can be an authentic coon shifts. The phrase takes on a different connotation, in front of black audiences who did not necessarily believe blackness to be equivalent to coon-ness[21]; Williams and Walker are asserting that they—as individuals—are indeed coons, irrespective of their blackness. In the same way, Delacroix and Sloan identify Manray and Womack as representative of Dunwitty's understanding of blackness and therefore separate this vision from themselves. This displacement enables the recognition of a space in which coon-ness is de-centered from black Americans as a whole and situated upon the behavior of individuals. Thus, this assertion recognized the misnomer of the equivalency of blackness and disorder maintained by greater American culture. The double meaning inherent within the phrase undermines the audience's ability to locate a stable definition of *coon*. Second, the term *real* emphasizes the humanity of Williams' and Walker's performances. Despite the adherence to the racist stereotypes, they managed to convey a poignancy inside their portrayals that reached beyond this adherence to type towards an authentic feeling. This poignancy is present inside Williams' poker game pantomime at the end of 1916's *Natural Born Gambler*.

In this routine—a staple within Williams' vaudeville act—Williams mimes a hand of poker. Within this scene, a shift occurs; the former slapstick cadence of the film slows. Williams conveys a sadness, trapped alone within his jail cell, performing this behavior of gambling. It's an odd moment within the arc of the narrative because it breaks form. Prior to this concierto, all of Williams' exaggerated gestures, comic facial expressions, and slapstick antics

1. Bert Williams: Minstrelsy, Vaudeville and Silent Film 29

Bert Williams (front left) in *Natural Born Gambler* (1916).

are put in service to the plot: Bert is a gambling man. Gambling is illegal and frowned upon by the more upstanding members of the community.[22]

Bert is arrested, perhaps as a comeuppance for both his decision to gamble and his willingness to cheat. The farcical method of cheating he undertakes—using his toes to pass cards under the table—is an example of how these actions manifest. When he enters the cell, however, we see that instead, the plot has been contrived to put on display the brilliance of the performer Bert Williams. This film documents Williams' abilities and marks the man himself as significant.[23]

That Williams is the only character appearing in blackface in both *Natural Born Gambler* and *Lime Kiln Field Day* (1913) also bears significance. The blackface marks his performance of comic blackness as masked and serves as a marker of his celebrity. Also, because of Williams' mask, the other performers need not wear the same. In the didactics to *Lime Kiln Field Day*, the Metropolitan Museum of Modern Art, or MoMA, contends that Williams was forced to wear blackface within the film because of his light skin, but without any evidence in support of this assertion—other than the accurate but general understanding that black performers given a choice would choose to not wear blackface—a stronger argument could be made that Bert Williams wore blackface because his masked visage was recognizable to audiences while his bare countenance was markedly less so.[24] Williams' minstrel persona had been long established by the time *Lime Kiln Field Day* was filmed. Biograph—who produced the film—doubtless understood the significance blackface held for Williams' public persona. As was underscored earlier in this chapter, the external force of the historic racial schema did indeed compel Williams to wear blackface, it just happened long before the date of this film.

The MoMA presents a reduction here that belittles Williams' agency and his success. Williams was a celebrity, a man considered irreplaceable by the *Ziegfeld Follies*. King Edward VII requested a command performance by Williams at Buckingham Palace. Part and parcel with the success of first Williams and Walker and later Williams alone was an association by their audiences of the performer with his identity statement. Years earlier, Walker noted in an interview with the *Indianapolis Freeman* that the public "expects to see me as a flashy sort of a darky and I do not disappoint them as far as that goes."[25] Walker's witticism expresses three aspects of his resistance. First, he acknowledges a public expectation of his appearance that corresponds directly to his fame. In the incident that persuaded Williams and Walker to stop performing in the South, the audiences were angered by the fancy dress of the duo and humiliated and inflicted bodily harm on them as a result. The only thing that had changed between the earlier incident and the time of the *Indianapolis Freeman* interview was the increase in visibility and public knowledge of Williams and Walker as performers. David Krasner asserts that "few if any, black males at the time were allowed to display as much dash, wit, and style as George Walker."[26] Walker's fame then gave him license to dress in a way unavailable to many black men. However, Walker's agency was not untethered. This limitation defines the second aspect of the resistance. Clearly, Walker's stage persona developed out of the zip coon type, an urban dandy that put on airs.[27]

Walker's words, "A flashy sort of darky" mark his understanding—his double-consciousness—of his public perception, indicating a reflexive self-awareness. The third aspect is Walker's use of the stage persona to carve out an area of public life that was previously unavailable. In relation to this, *Lime Kiln Field Day* is the first known feature-length production with a black male lead actor. The film features what was the first recorded screen kiss of a black couple. The MoMA didactics note the significance of this, yet reduce the importance of Williams as a figure for getting this film made at all. More judiciously, the MoMA asserts that it is not known why the film was never brought to post-production.[28] According to UCLA Film & Television Archive director Jan-Christopher Horak, MoMA curator Ron Magliozzi theorized that the release of *Birth of a Nation* may have contributed to the abandonment of the film, a point Horak finds unlikely.[29] More likely, the riots that followed the 1914 New York opening of Williams' first cinematic appearance in the Biograph short *Darktown Follies* caused the notion of continuing work on the film to seem ill-advised.[30] The film not only starred a largely black cast but cast these members in a decidedly more positive light than was usual. Doubtless, as a result, Biograph would have had sufficient motivation to withdraw.

Lime Kiln Field Day is notable for its depiction of black Americans at leisure, and also for the inclusion of the phenomenon the cakewalk. Although they did not invent the form, Williams' and Walker's stage productions helped to popularize the practice. Aida Overton Walker, George Walker's wife, had introduced the dance to their productions years earlier. Aida Walker would identify her introduction of the cakewalk as barrier-breaking, noting, "It has been my good fortune to entertain and instruct, privately, many members of the most select circles—both in this country and abroad—and I can truthfully state that my profession has given me entree to residences which members of my race in other professions would have a hard task gaining if they ever did."[31] Within these negotiations of agency, the frank awareness of both the limitations set before them and the greater access allowed them as a result, black performers like the Walkers and Williams strived to break open the spaces in which they were hemmed. The disavowal of that aspect of their work reads as an erasure. The inclusion of dress and strategies and images of Williams and Walker within *Bamboozled* (2000) is not a reduction but a reclamation. The casting of Savion Glover—the dancer and choreographer who strove to reclaim tap through the exposition of its history in *Bring in Da Noise, Bring in Da Funk*—symbolizes this reclamation. To read Manray as a coon without concluding the context is intentional is problematic.

In *Bamboozled,* Manray dies as Williams did—performing. Lee respects the character of Manray and showcases his talent within the final dance. Lee uses the vehicle of Bert Williams' history to complicate a straightforward reading of Manray as coon. To acknowledge the complexity of blackface's place in black performative history is not to deny the racist intentions of its invention but to broaden the empathy for the experiences of the performers who operated within its constraints. *Bamboozled* desires us to have empathy for Manray and Womack but not to desire to participate in our own blackening as an affectation of style.

2
Oscar Micheaux

The man, who sets the ideals of the community where he lives, directs its thoughts and heads its social movements."—W. E. B. Du Bois

Lee's first attempt at addressing the legacy of *Birth of a Nation* was a 20 minute short called *The Answer*. A film that—according to Ashley Clark—almost got him kicked out of NYU.[1] *Bamboozled* was the next attempt. *Birth* takes its place among the racist montage Delacroix watches as his final moments unfold. Lee was not the first black director to respond to the blatant racism of Griffith's film. Race film giant Oscar Micheaux wrote and directed *Within Our Gates* (1920) as a direct response to *Birth*.[2] Micheaux's picture served as a counterpoint to the lynching and rape portrayed within *Birth of a Nation*, framing these incidents with greater historical accuracy.

Micheaux's pioneering work as a filmmaker inspired Lee to make movies. Perhaps Micheaux's greatest achievement was simply telling black stories that grew from his own experiences. In doing so, he challenged commonly understood ideas about black experience and possibility. Micheaux gave Lee a different road map for filmmaking than the cannon that included Griffith. Challenging that cannon became Lee's mission. The methodologies employed by Micheaux—his tropes and symbols appear in not only *Bamboozled* but the greater body of Lee's work. *Bamboozled* is at its heart a race film. Micheaux's experiences are foundational to Lee's work.

Feminist labor historian Joan Scott wrote, "Experience can both confirm what is already known (we see what we have learned to see) and upset what has been taken for granted (when different meanings are in conflict we adjust our vision to take account of the conflict or to resolve it-that is what is meant by 'learning from experience'). Experience is a subject's history. Language is the site of history's enactment. Historical explanation, therefore, cannot separate the two."[3] Oscar Micheaux's experience of life in the first half of the twentieth century was perhaps unusual. Born in 1884, the fifth child of former slaves, Micheaux began life in Metropolis, IL. His family would move to Kansas after his father inherited land. Several of his older siblings chose to stay in Illinois, migrating to Chicago to find work. Eventually, Micheaux followed them, living and working first in Carbondale, IL before finally arriving in Chicago in 1901. While in Chicago, Micheaux worked as a Pullman porter. Micheaux was impatient with routine and had ambition and wanderlust, which his travels as a porter reinforced and encouraged. Becoming dissatisfied with the rote nature of the job, and ex-

Grant Gorman as Armand Griddlestone and Evelyn Preer as Sylvia Landry in Oscar Micheaux's *Within Our Gates* (1920).

periencing firsthand the beauty of the western expanse, Micheaux longed for a different sort of life from the one he had built in Chicago. He saved his money and dreamt of owning his own land. Eventually, Micheaux left the city to homestead in the Dakotas, living and working there for eight years, until he lost his land to drought and the dissolution of his marriage. In part, Micheaux brought the latter upon himself, after claiming an additional plot of land in his young wife Jessie's name and she was obligated to occupy the land or lose it. As a result, husband and wife spent most of their married life living separately. When his wife left him, his father-in-law seized control of the property.[4]

Despite this, Micheaux enjoyed his experiences of homesteading, ultimately becoming an advocate for that lifestyle over migration to the large northern cities. The richness of his time there would inspire him to write about his experiences. Micheaux sent an open letter to the *Chicago Defender* in 1910, encouraging others to follow his example. "Any energetic young man with as little as $1000 and up and willing to give all of his time and attention can go to Wyoming, Montana or Idaho and get himself a homestead."[5] Micheaux envisioned a different sort of future for young black men than the one that would be formed in context of the Great Migration. For Micheaux, the prospect of homesteading offered a scenario in which black men willing to work hard could own property and stake a claim for themselves within a society that was newly forming and which offered them a chance to impact that formation. Year after year, Micheaux watched poor white men migrate west and build better lives for themselves. A believer in the hard work philosophy of Booker T. Washington, Micheaux grew frustrated at a rift he saw developing within the black community at this time. John Howard, Micheaux's biographer, identifies Micheaux's categorization of these groups as progressives and reactionaries. Writes Howard:

> [Progressives] believed that blacks should acquire the necessary skills that would allow them a place for themselves in the economy. The reactionaries were, in his [Micheaux's] view, people overly concerned with civil rights and who were given to complaining about disabilities whites placed on blacks without having a clear strategy for overcoming those disabilities. In simple terms, [Micheaux] divided the race into those who "do" and those who complain.[6]

This viewpoint reflected Micheaux's personality as a man of action and demonstrated his belief in the basic correctness of American moral values represented within civilized behavior. Micheaux in this sense did not have awareness of the exceptional nature of his position, and he, therefore, expected that what he attained was within reach of most. Micheaux viewed himself as abiding by the principles of Washington's philosophy, despite the fact that he more accurately presented as a member of Du Bois' Talented Tenth. In the words of Du Bois, "The Negro race, like all races, is going to be saved by its exceptional men. The problem of education, then among Negroes must first of all deal with the Talented Tenth; it is the problem of developing the best of this race that they may guide the mass away from the contamination and the death of the worst, in their own and other races."[7] In this sense, Micheaux embodied a cultural rift within the black community of the early 20th century that was exemplified within the debate of letters between Booker T. Washington and W. E. B. Du Bois. Within his treatise *The Souls of Black Folk*, Du Bois writes of Washington, "The question then comes: Is it possible, and probable, that nine millions of men can make effective progress in economic lines if they are deprived of political rights, made a servile caste, and allowed only the most meager chance for developing their exceptional men? If history and reason give any distinct answer to these questions, it is an emphatic No."[8]

For Micheaux, however, an existence outside of the racial strictures of the Jim Crow South, and the heightened racial teension of the Midwestern cities seemed tenable. His experiences homesteading in the Dakotas backed by the force of his hard work and charismatic personality had resulted in Micheaux being liked and respected amongst his white neighbors, many of whom would invest in his publishing company after he began writing. It was in part this integration that would influence his way of thinking. These experiences in the Dakotas would become the basis for his first novel: *The Conquest: The Story of a Negro Pioneer* which would eventually become *The*

Homesteader, his most famous novel, and the plot source of his first film in 1919. Micheaux's tireless optimism colored his perspective of future possibilities and his perception of the past.

As noted by Pearl Bowser and Louise Spence in *Writing Himself into History*, while the novel, and the subsequent film, contain some factual biography, they also are heavily fictionalized. Micheaux manipulated circumstances to build a myth that better expressed his hopes. It is likely that the picture as Micheaux painted it inside his open letter to the *Defender* was partially fiction as well. Micheaux's ability to tell stories that blended historical events with romanticized themes of the furthering of the race and striking characters with complicated motives resulted in tales of heightened drama that moved audiences. It is fortunate

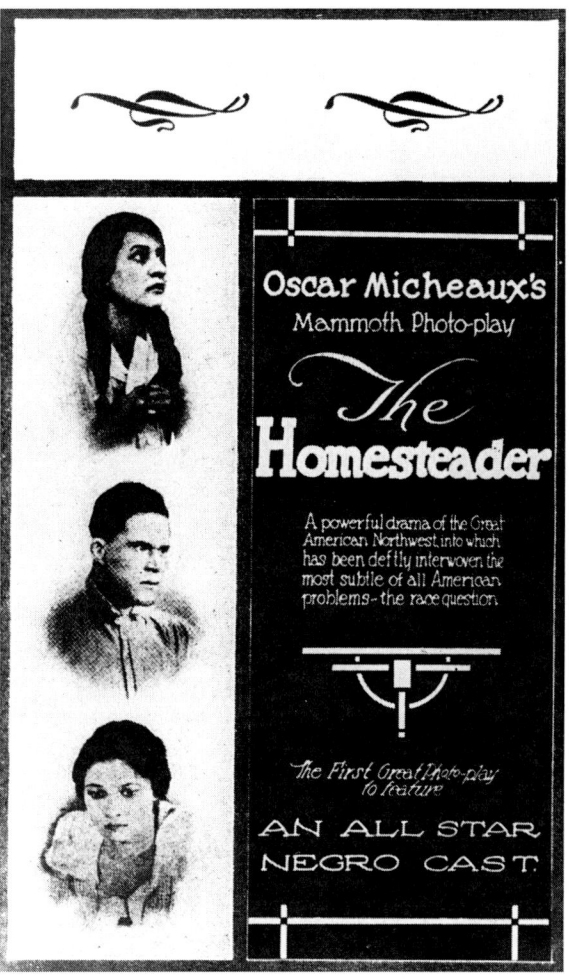

Lobby card for Oscar Micheaux's *The Homesteader* (1919), featuring Evelyn Preer (top), Charles D. Lucas and Iris Hall.

for the audiences of then and today that Micheaux was both approached by the Lincoln Motion Picture Co.—which inserted within Micheaux's mind the idea of making movies in the first place—and that the venture never took off under its auspices, as Micheaux's vision in his silent race films is quite strong, taking on many topics and situations that intimidated other companies, a quality he shares with Lee. George P. Johnson had approached Micheaux about producing the film after reading *The Homesteader* (1917) Jacqueline Stewart notes in her book *Migrating to the Movies* that Johnson and Micheaux "shared a conviction that the West was the ideal space for Negro self-improvement and self-definition. In this way, the West serves a mythic function for these Black filmmakers much as it does in white-produced western films."[9] Micheaux learned a great deal about the film business from his correspondences with Johnson about the possible production of the film and after the deal fell through their letters continued.

The Homesteader flirted with themes of miscegenation. Jean Baptiste, the hero of the story, migrates from Chicago to South Dakota and meets a beautiful light-skinned woman, Agnes Stewart. Convinced she is white, Baptiste returns to Chicago where he marries Orlean, the daughter of an influential black minister. In the end, it is proved beyond a doubt that Agnes has black ancestry, and the romance is saved.[10] Orlean is abandoned for his more suitable race heroine partner, as assuredly as Chicago is abandoned for the promise of the West. That Orlean is fashioned after Jessie Micheaux is clear. That the critique leveled against the minister within the film was directed towards his father-in-law was also clear. As a result of these biographic elements, his father-in-law protested the film, appealing to the censor board that the film was anti-religious in feeling. In addition, the theme of a possible interracial romance gave Micheaux problems with the censor boards as well. White theater owners in the South would refuse the film altogether, while theaters and censor boards in other areas of the country would require serious cuts. Over time, it would become common practice for Micheaux to show very different versions of his films in different cities. One result of this censor process is that it is very difficult to know how Micheaux's original vision for his films might have looked as most that remain are not intact, and many of his films are considered lost. However, Micheaux's depictions of black uplift as results of migration and his critique of negative stereotypes of black characters are evident in his films. Micheaux's didacticism attempts to negotiate a vision of Truth in a truly Du Boisian sense of the word. While Micheaux is highly critical of what Jacqueline Stewart calls white-lies—meaning falsehoods perpetuated by white Americans that distort historical fact for the purpose of black disenfranchisement—he is not afraid to level critique to the shortcomings of the black community either, a trait he shares with Lee. This vision is evident particularly in Micheaux's films: *Within Our Gates* and *Body and Soul*.

Within Our Gates was Micheaux's Book and Film Company's second film, released in 1920. The plot loosely follows selected events outlined in *Birth of a Nation,* although it is not set during the Reconstruction, but in contemporary times, in the time of the New Negro, after the Great Migration. A rape attempt and a lynching undertaken by a powerful Southern family are depicted in *Within Our Gates* that mirror the attacks in *Birth*. Micheaux reframed the context of racial violence during this time, demonstrating that the white landowners of the South were not victims, but rather perpetrators of these acts, historically. Although the film lacks the epic mastery of Griffith's work technically—Micheaux is a far greater storyteller than he is a cinematic director—Micheaux powerfully communicates the difficulty of negotiating modern black identity in a country boiling with racial tensions.

In the film, Sylvia Landry—our heroine, played by Evelyn Preer—is in love with a young man named Conrad, and visits Conrad and her cousin Alma in the urban North. Alma also loves Conrad. In an attempt to discredit Sylvia, Alma arranges for her brother—the drunken gambler Larry—to put Sylvia in a compromising position and for Conrad to find them together, all the while hinting at sordid aspects of Sylvia's past. Returning to the South, Sylvia learns of the great need of the Piney Woods School, and therefore Sylvia again heads to the North to attempt to raise funds for the school. In the course of her travels, Sylvia gets hit by a car and the wealthy white woman who hits her turns out to be benevolent and helps Sylvia save Piney Woods from closing down. During the treatment of her injuries, Sylvia develops a friendship with Dr. Vivian—a black doctor who is interested in questions of race and uplift. When horrific events of Sylvia's past are revealed to Dr. Vivian, his enlightened reactions of sympathy for her racial trauma stand as proofs that he—not Conrad—is a progressive match for her. The truth of Sylvia's past is disclosed by Alma who reveals her former falsehoods in a quest for redemption.

Jack Chenault as Larry Prichard and Evelyn Preer as Sylvia Landry in Oscar Micheaux's *Within Our Gates* (1920).

Micheaux frames these scenes in the form of a flashback, graphically depicting for the audience what exactly unfolded. Sylvia's adoptive parents were lynched when falsely accused of their landlord Griddlestone's murder, and as this grisly scene unfolds, the landlord's brother attempts to have his way with Sylvia—despite her resistance—only stopping when he realizes that Sylvia is his daughter. White and black characters are portrayed as complicated people within the film for the most part, and though melodramatically situated; its events were inside the spectrum of the reality of the day to day lives of blacks. This follow-up to the successful *Homesteader,* of 1919, would be plagued with controversy due to its portrayal of lynching and the attempted rape of the black main character, Sylvia Landry by the white Southern character, Mr. Griddlestone.[11] The Chicago censor boards—where the film premiered—took exception to the highlighting of violence perpetrated by white characters against black characters within the film. black critics found the negative characters within the film like Efrem, who betrays the Landry's to Griddlestone's brother, and Larry—who drinks, gambles and kills a man over a poker game—an affront to a wanted program of uplift. The critics of Micheaux's characterizations seemed to have difficulty with the parallels drawn between these characters and ones within the mainstream of the film industry. Wrote Bowser and Spence:

> Micheaux's silent films deflated the pretensions of an expanding middle-class culture.... Many of his critics were successful professionals of "respectable" taste and manners who wanted their own self-image to be heard, seen, and understood. They wished to distance themselves not only from the drunken dice throwing lore that black skin (as some would have it) signaled to the world, but also from the newly arrived migrants and the working poor (although many of them were not more than a generation or two removed from the same conditions and aspirations).[12]

To many within the black community, the negative portrayals did not do the work to establish the program of race pride reformers strove for.[13] These characterizations read to them as the tropes of minstrelsy; of films like *Birth of a Nation*. In *Within Our Gates*, the poorly behaved characters' inter-titles presented ways of speaking that are contained inside supposedly anthropological works of collected folktales like Joel Chandler Harris' *Uncle Remus*, which—in reality—bore little relationship to the speech patterns of any real people.

Undoubtedly, there are some underlying issues of class that arise within these films, as well as in other race films of the era and these critiques directly speak to Micheaux's employment of didactic notions of blackness as visual indicators of misguided attempts at reforming behaviors occurring as tropes in Hollywood films of the era. Ironically, the practice within the race films of the silent era of highlighting representations of what later would become Alain Locke's *New Negro* and bore a resemblance to Du Bois' talented tenth demonstrated an agreement with the standard being set by Hollywood. The insistence of the elimination of negative character types still reduced representations of blackness to a monolith, which worked against a building of a diverse identity for black Americans, and affirmed the moral justness of the white standard of behavior just as Du Bois notes within "Criteria of Negro Art."

To complicate matters further, other critics noted that Micheaux seemed to perpetuate this standard within his casting practices. Later critiques of *Within Our Gates* would note the probable favoritism Micheaux exhibited through casting light-skinned black people to play the heroes or heroines within his films. Such is the case with the casting of Evelyn Preer as Sylvia Landry. This characterization of nobility within light-skinned blacks contrasted with the casting of the dark-skinned actors as the villains of the stories—who behaved within the film in ways perceived as detrimental to the elevation of the race—was problematic for many who would note that the correlations perpetuated existing stereotypes. However, there are additional reasons that Micheaux may have used light-skinned actors for lead roles. Micheaux's focused interest with passing and miscegenation themes began within *The Conquest*. In the novel, the lead character falls in love with a young Scottish woman but refuses to give into his overwhelming desires so as not to be a traitor to the race. Both Bowser and Howard mention this aspect of the story and speculate about the possibility of its biographical accuracy. Given the almost obsessive exploration of variations on this theme, Micheaux possibly did experience feelings of attraction towards a young white woman, although there is no evidence outside of *The Conquest* to substantiate this claim. It is, at least, one possible explanation that seems consistent with Micheaux's character. Another possibility was that Micheaux used this trope as a way to break down racial barriers in culture. The great fear which served as the center for ideologies of films like *Birth of a Nation* was the fear of miscegenation. He was not the only black writer during this time to explore pushing the boundaries of the taboo of miscegenation for subversive purposes.

In the short story *The Comet,* also of 1920, Du Bois writes about a black man and a white woman who almost become romantically entwined when they believe that they may be the last two people on the face of the earth after a comet hits New York. Before they kiss, their loved ones find them and they realize that it is only the island of Manhattan that has been destroyed. Novelist Nella Larsen would take up this same topic in a complex way within 1929's *Passing*, the story of a bi-racial woman who marries a white man. There exists a third possibility, however, that Micheaux used light-skinned blacks within his films with multiple purposes: to highlight the existence of a wide variety of skin types for those who are identified and identify as black, to underscore the constructed or manufactured nature of race, and to visually represent what was being strived for in these representations of positivity, an achievement of citizenship, which historically involved a disavowal of blackness. The content of the films is complex enough to allow for a combination of these factors. Film—with its grand weight, visual authority and moldable narrative—offered a unique space within which to battle over the control of self-representation. The intensity of the debate over Micheaux's films provides evidence for the seriousness of the power of the medium. This chasm between how black citizenry viewed themselves and how Hollywood films had depicted blackness was the site of struggle for many reformers in regard to Micheaux's images.

For the mass audiences, *Within Our Gates* seemed to have fallen from the headlines of papers like the *Chicago Defender*, a realistic rendering of the injustices black people had endured and were enduring. After seeing *Within Our Gates*, a local school teacher, Willis Huggins was moved to write this to the *Chicago Defender*:

> The startling revelation now slowly coming to light that White men committed the murders in Arkansas for which men of our race are condemned to die are indeed fittingly coincident with the present run of the Micheaux picture which aims to expose just that sort of double-dealing all over the South.... *Within Our Gates* is written by the oppressed and shows in a mild way the degree and kind of his oppression.[14]

Public reception of *Within Our Gates* might have been related to the palpable increasing racial tension over the summer of 1919. Relations between the black and white citizens on Chicago's Southside came to a head on July 27, 1919, when a young black male swam into "white" territory at a public beach. White youth would stone the young man as he swam. The police on the scene would refuse to help or arrest the perpetrators. A riot ensued with both black and white folks hurling stones at each other. As Carl Sandberg would later write in *The Chicago Race Riots*, "The score at the end of three days was recorded as 20 negroes dead, 14 white dead and a number of negro houses burned."[15] In light of these events, the subject matter inside *Within Our Gates* came across as almost inflammatory.

When Micheaux released *Body and Soul* in 1924, his controversial themes were well known to audiences, but the uncompromising critique of corruption within the black church forged new ground for Micheaux critically. Paul Robeson played twin brothers in the film, powerfully. Robeson would become a major figure in black film and later a Hollywood star until his personal political activism would inspire the U.S. Government to dismantle his career under McCarthyism in the 1950s. The film is Robeson's debut. One brother, Sylvester, was a model citizen, meek and comely in his affections toward Isabella the film's heroine.

The other is an escaped convict and a brutal killer who poses as Revered Isaiah Jenkins and dupes the congregation of the black church in Tatesville,

Paul Robeson as Sylvester Jenkins and Julia Theresa Russell as Isabelle in Oscar Micheaux's *Body and Soul* **(1925).**

GA, into giving him their hard earned money by whipping them into a frenzy during sermons that he delivers while intoxicated. The Reverend Jenkins spends his time outside of church gambling, and pursuing the affections of Isabella as well, under the encouragement of Isabella's mother, Martha Jane. Martha Jane is pleased with the Reverend and excited by the social prestige of a match between her daughter and such an important vocal community figure. Isabella is aware, in a personal way of the bankruptcy of the Reverend Jenkins character as he attempts and finally succeeds in raping Isabella. The original film was nine reels long and the version that has survived is the one ultimately approved by the New York censor board, only five reels long. Although the unedited version appeared in other places, no known surviving version of the whole nine reels exists. The rape scene, which occurs within a cabin Isabella and the Reverend Jenkins are forced to take shelter in during a storm, is a masterful piece of editing and direction, which carries heavy emotional impact. Following this incident, Isabella becomes despondent of her life and leaves for Atlanta, where she struggles to stay alive. Martha Jane searches for her, finally finding her as she is dying. A manhunt for the

Reverend Jenkins ensues and in the process, Jenkins kills a man. Ultimately, the whole unfolding of events is proved to be Martha Jane's dream, and when she wakes to find Isabella still alive and seeking her approval for marriage to Sylvester, she offers it to them freely, trusting in her daughters judgment and gives them money she has saved to start a new life in the North; where Sylvester has received a monetary grant to pursue study.

Despite the masterful performances of Robeson in the film, or maybe because of them, there was a strong outcry against the themes of the film that went beyond mere negative portrayals of blacks to critiques of its institutions. In a letter to the editor of the *Chicago Defender,* William Henry asks:

> What screen production [*Birth of a Nation* or *Body and Soul*] does our people more harm? One would expect a White screenwriter to "fan the flame of hatred," but what can we say when a Black man portrays our people in the same way?[16]

The subtleties between what behaviors constitute advancement for the race in this film versus those in *Within Our Gates* refine Micheaux's vision of advancement as character driven, and not ascribed to a fixed class. Micheaux's race woman is nearly brought down by a corrupt community leader and the social climbing and ignorance of her mother.[17] Martha Jane's transformation is the vehicle of revealing within the film. The realities of everyday life and the consequences of Martha Jane's decisions ultimately belong within the realm of her influence. Her actions have an impact not only on herself but on others. Her initial ignorance leads to not only the rape and death of her daughter but her financial destitution, as well when the Reverend Jenkins steals the money she has been saving.

In *Body and Soul*, Micheaux provides a roadmap for the realization of race aspirations and roots them firmly within character and the bootstrap building promoted by Booker T. Washington, whose portrait hangs prominently on Martha Jane's walls.[18] First, Micheaux calls for a critical evaluation of the institutions and community leaders. Then he condemns Martha Jane's social climbing and associates this behavior with that of Efram by use of the same types of inter-titles when Martha Jane first speaks in the film. Martha Jane also characterizes a character as a "niggah"[19] and is admonished by Isabella, who calls her mother's speech vulgar.

The ability to advance the race is not location dependent. Even though Isabella and Sylvester head North at the end of the film, it is the hard work of Martha Jane that sends them there prepared and financially blessed. And Martha Jane, whose transformation is ultimately the central narrative of the film, does not need to leave either the rural neighborhood or the South in order to achieve its aims. Micheaux's emphasis on the connections, or lack thereof, between black modern identity and urbanity underscores interesting parallels to the performances of Bert Williams. He also called into question the efforts of black leaders to ascribe authenticity to a black urbanity as superior to other types of black identity. Williams performed a complicated presentation of black identities as he perceived them built into American culture, limited to a talented tenth. Micheaux mimics this way of operating presenting the tropes found within minstrelsy and ultimately complicating them in order to extend beyond a program of uplift to a necessary critique of that program.

Micheaux's personal tropes: manipulation of biography into persona, employing history to speak out on current events, and as a means of highlighting greater theoretical ideas, his critical engagement of multiple aspects of culture and community and his refusal of purely positive imagery mirror the time period of the turn of the millennium, in 2000, the time period in which a resurgence of interest began to occur in regard to his work. Bowser and Spence's book was released at this time, it had been three years since the MacArthur Foundation had awarded Kara Walker a genius grant and the arrival of 2000 marked an interest in revisiting Du Bois' assertion that the problem of the 20th century is "the color line." September 2000 would mark the release of Spike Lee's *Bamboozled,* which would mirror the format of Micheaux's race films, ultimately aligning the purposes of his film with that of Micheaux: to educate and elevate the audience to a greater understanding of history in context with current events, and the power of representations. To get woke.

3
Ralph Ellison

He began to have a dim feeling that, to attain his place in the world, he must be himself, and not another.—W. E. B. Du Bois

Undeniably, Ralph Ellison's *Invisible Man* remains one of the most important American literary works of the 20th century. It was the first novel authored by a black writer to receive the National Book Award for Fiction. However, critics have been divided over the prudence of its perspective and representations. At a 50th anniversary symposium, Ellison biographer and scholar Arnold Rampersad said that some black critics like Marguerite Cartwright were "livid about the extent to which the novel, like Richard Wright's *Native Son* and others, wallowed in what she saw as, quote, 'self-hate and disesteem among black males.'"[1] For many other critics, the response was positive. In 1952, *New York Times'* reviewer Orville Prescott wrote that "*Invisible Man* has many flaws. It is a sensational and feverishly emotional book. It will shock and sicken some of its readers.... It is uneven in quality. But it blazes with authentic talent."[2]

This uneven reception and caution-filled praise mirrors *Bamboozled*'s critical response. The similarity is not surprising given the many references to *Invisible Man* in the film. The central character is a narrator. Junebug's fatherly advice mimics the grandfather's. And there appears within *Bamboozled* both a dancing Sambo doll and a Jolly Nigger Bank. There exists as well a connection between Ellison's critical writings and the work of Post black artists, whose connection to Lee and *Bamboozled* are the subject of the upcoming chapter on Michael Ray Charles. A large hunk of the theoretical basis for Post black art's ideas about the intersection of art and blackness arises from Ellison's critical writing.

Both Ellison's novel and his other writings on jazz and art stood opposed to the agenda of many activists—like Amiri Baraka—who wanted to employ the arts as a cohesive black public voice and platform. For Ellison, delineating the possibilities for black art aesthetically was an unnecessary limitation for artists who were already hemmed in. The only way to exercise agency was to be oneself. "Life is to be lived, not controlled; and humanity is won by continuing to play in the face of certain defeat."[3] In the essay "Change the Joke and Slip the Yoke," Ellison confronts his friend Stanley Edgar Hyman's critical arguments about *Invisible Man* that reduced his novel's characterizations to mythic archetypes. Ellison believed that pigeon-holing characters into preexisting types usurped the specificity of individual literary works. Ellison asserts that literary works must be viewed as created by "the living human being in a specific texture of time, place and circumstance; who must respond, make choices, achieve eloquence and create specific works of art."[4] Flattening Ellison's characters to try to force them to adhere to myth is problematic. As Ellison says, "If the symbols appearing in a novel link up with those of universal myth they do so by virtue of their emergence from the specific texture of a specific form of social reality."[5]

Therefore, the characterizations within his novel—or within Lee's film—require historical grounding in their analysis even if they appear to conform to myth. For example, Ellison writes that the narrator's descent into the cave is "not into a 'sewer,' but into a coal cellar, a source of heat, light, power and, through association with the character's motivation, self-perception is a process of rising to an understanding of his human condition."[6,7] For Ellison, the inability of the white public to see the narrator's humanity is the means through which that humanity can be exercised. "Invisibility is not simply affliction; instead it becomes a strategy and a praxis."[8] This use of invisibility mirrors the strategy employed by Bert Williams working from within the veil rather than seeking a way to overcome it. This same argument will be employed by Post black artists a generation later and serves as a counterargument to Armond White's critique of *Bamboozled* itself. In the same way that Lee uses blackface to eviscerate unwitting use of its types, Ellison uses Tod Clifton's Sambo dolls to unpack a correct relationship to representations. At first the narrator is angered and dismayed by Clifton's sale of the dolls. When the narrator attempts to reconcile Clifton's actions to the man he knows, he arrives at the realization that Clifton controls the paper puppet through an invisible string. Manray is Lee's Tod Clifton. As with Williams' and Micheaux's lives, we see in the experiences of Ralph Ellison a narrative that is not the commonly understood narrative of black life in the early twentieth century. His experiences formed the ideologies present in his writings, which influenced black representational expressions for generations.

Ralph Waldo Ellison was born in Oklahoma in 1913. Lewis and Ida Ellison named their second born son after the famed writer Ralph Waldo Emerson. Lewis, who loved to read, fostered ambitions for his son to become a poet. He would never see these ambitions fulfilled. Ralph Ellison's father worked as a construction foreman and was killed in 1916 after an ice block dropped and shattered sending shards into Lewis' abdomen. Attempts to save him in surgery proved unsuccessful. This loss marked the end of a solidly middle class existence for the Ellison family. Ida would strive to hold things together for her two surviving sons, Ralph and Herbert, but their social status slipped steadily over the course of Ralph's boyhood. She would find work taking care of other people's homes and children. Ida's closest friend Edna Slaughter came alongside the Ellisons following Lewis' death and her extended family would include the Ellison boys in trips to the family farm and holiday celebrations. J.D. Randolph, Edna's father, instilled within young Ralph his own great love of books. According to Rampersad, Randolph's use of language inspired Ellison,

> Here facts melded with myth and legend, truth morphed into the inspired lie, and the comic vied with the solemn and tragic to assert the vitality of life. Ralph would remain a lover of this dynamic American approach to language. In it, the black and white rhetorical traditions of the South blended with Southwestern humor to create an expressive style that was both unique and uniquely American.[9]

Thus, Randolph picked up where Lewis had left off, instilling within young Ellison the love of a good book. However, this love took time to blossom into Ellison's acceptance of his looming name, and an idea about himself as a writer.

His youth was preoccupied by an affinity and an obsession with gadgets and electronics. This would translate into an embracing of instruments and cameras and—according to Ellison scholar John Wright—also influence his writing. Ellison graduated from high school in 1931, although his graduation was slightly delayed. That he managed to graduate relatively on time was an accomplishment. From a very young age, Ralph took on responsibilities for the upkeep of the household, working jobs and assisting his mother with the care of his younger brother. Ida Ellison for her part invested her hopes for the future heavily within young Ralph, always striving to improve their situation by whatever limited means available. At one point, Ida Ellison attempted to relocate her family to Gary, Indiana in hope of a new start and with an idea that better job prospects might be waiting in the Northern city where Ida's brother worked in the steel industry. Shortly after their arrival, her brother lost his job. Ida, in turn, was unsuccessful finding work. Thankfully, their burden was short lived. A chance arrival of unexpected visitors from back home in Oklahoma City enabled a return trip for the Ellisons who were enduring a poverty beyond anything they had experienced back home. The cost of the venture left the family worse off than they had been before they left. This experience may have contributed to Ellison's critique of the Great Migration as an uplift strategy within *Invisible Man*.

Mrs. Ellison was by all accounts a beautiful woman, and she remarried three times after Lewis' death. However, Ida's marriages did little to increase stability for the family instead fostering young Ellison's resentment. During his teenage years, Ellison immersed himself in music. He spent a year after high school working to save money for a trumpet. After acquiring one, he left Oklahoma for the Tuskegee Institute where he attended on scholarship. Despite studying for several years at Tuskegee, Ellison would leave the school without attaining his degree and head north to New York to pursue a career in the arts.

In New York, he would meet two key figures to his formation as an artist and author; Richard Wright and Romare Bearden. Although Ellison nursed a desire to study sculpture and photography, it was as a writer that Ellison garnered the most financial success. He began getting steady work writing reviews for magazines. His initial offerings were written for *New Challenge,* a magazine Richard Wright edited. Wright asked Ellison to submit a piece on Water E. Turpin's "These Low Grounds." This review would prompt Wright to encourage Ellison to begin writing fiction. Around this same time, Ellison also began work for the Works Progress Administration as a writer, again because of Wright's connections. He wandered through New York, through Harlem, knocking on doors and interviewing people many of whom had come to New York during the Great Migration. Like many other authors who pounded the streets for the WPA, Ellison would draw upon these narratives for inspiration within his own personal writing. Wright, Zora Neale Hurston, Saul Bellow and many others used their experiences as fodder for their own work, building a new American vernacular just as FDR had envisioned. Albert Murray—a writer and a great friend of Ellison—believed that without his time at the Project, Ellison would never have written *Invisible Man.* According to Murray:

> It was because of the Writer's Project that I first got to read the pieces Ralph was writing on his own. It pulled him away from the music and focused him on writing. It put writers and artists in touch as they had never been before. It was even more intense than the Harlem Renaissance. Throughout "Invisible Man" there are sketches and caricatures of people he met during the Federal Writers' Project.[10]

One such sketch shows up within *Invisible Man* through a direct quote from a New York transplant from Jacksonville, Florida who told Ellison, "I'm in New York, but New York ain't in me."[11] Within the novel, Mary would deliver this line as a warning against the corrupting influence of the city, revealing herself as a woman from the South; awakening a reminder of home within the narrator and instilling within him a sense of pride of his heritage.

Eventually, as World War II ended, the WPA was disbanded because of its perceived Communist leanings. Rampersad writes, "The Communist dominance of the Project in New York made it a target of the conservative congressman Martin Dies of Texas and his new House Committee on Un-American Activities."[12] Indeed, many artists and writers employed by the Project were affiliated with the Communist party prior to 1945, an affiliation which in many cases withered to a whisper upon the emergence of the blacklist and the increasing scrutiny of the HUAC. This affiliation was certainly true of Wright—who wrote for publications like the *Daily Worker*—and Ellison himself found his viewpoint influenced by its principles, which were mixed up in his relationship with his mentor. In letters written to Wright during the 1940s Ellison described this influence, asserting that Wright's *12 Million Black Voices* had made him a better Communist. Ellison told Wright the text unleashed from him "tears of impatience and anger. When experience such as ours is organized as you have done it here, there is nothing left for a man to do but fight!"[13] The attraction was understandable. The Communist Party in its American incarnation—prior to Soviet involvement with World War II—focused on a platform of Civil Rights for black Americans and stood against the war. The meetings and social gatherings provided an interracial sociality and intellectual exchange. When the official views of the Party shifted to a pro-war stance because of the Soviets' alliance with the United States against Germany, the American Party members abandoned Civil Rights. Ellison and Wright would both become disillusioned with the Communists as a result. Wright would eloquently express this sense of betrayal within his essay in the collection "The God that Failed." Within it Wright unveils the story of his friend Ross, who is put on trial by the Party as a traitor. Wright describes the unfolding of Ross' censor and witnesses the man he knew well break down in the face of the pressure of his peers. Communist party members Ross counted as friends cite him as an enemy under crimes of disagreement with Party leadership. This trial leads to a moment of decision for Wright, their condemnation of Ross mirroring what would inevitably be his own trial if he did not expel himself. Wright wrote:

> The communists had talked to him until they had given him new eyes with which to see his own crime.... This, to me, was a spectacle of glory; and yet, because it had condemned me, because it was blind and ignorant, I felt it was a spectacle of horror. The blindness of their limited lives—lives truncated and impoverished by the oppression they had suffered long before they had ever heard of Communism—made them think that I was with their enemies. American life had so corrupted their consciousness that they were unable to recognize their friends when they saw them.[14]

A similar disillusionment would also surface within *Invisible Man*. The Brotherhood was commonly thought to represent the kind of mistreatment Ellison believed the Communists subjected upon its black members, if not actually standing in for the Party itself. Their leader, Brother Jack, with his red hair and glass eye appears in the novel at first to be kind and fair, but turns out to be racist and dogmatic; inflexible when the narrator won't follow orders. Communism is not the only ideological platform to be critiqued within the novel. This particular illustration of ideological platforms as inadequate tools for change is one among many.

Although Ellison categorically denied many connections readers made between characters within the novel and specific political leaders within the black community during the Great Migration and Harlem Renaissance, there are correlations that can be drawn. Through his allusions and markers, Ellison built a historiography that problematized the platforms of critical thinkers like Booker T. Washington and Marcus Garvey. Importantly, Ellison places the allusions to these men's works, black folklore and the works of contemporaries like Wright within the context of allusions to Mark Twain, Herman Melville and Joel Chandler Harris creating a layered work that speaks with a singularly American voice. As Du Bois noted, "Once in a while through all of us there flashes some clairvoyance, some clear idea, of what America really is. We who are dark can see America in a way that White Americans cannot. And seeing our country thus, are we satisfied with its present goals and ideals?"[15] *Invisible Man* demonstrates the individual recounting of history as a necessary precursor to action. Here, the fruits of the novel are found. Understanding one's own historical context is essential to form an individual identity and to gain a consciousness about what America is, but understanding the historical context of one's own identity should not be conflated with the acceptance of cultural designators as truth. Ellison marked this search for identity as the central theme for the American novel. In a 1954 interview with the Paris Review, Ellison said:

> Each section [of the novel] begins with a sheet of paper; each piece of paper is exchanged for another and contains a definition of his identity, or the social role he is to play as defined for him by others. But they all say essentially the same thing: "Keep this nigger boy running." Before he could have some voice in his own destiny, he had to discard these old identities and illusions; his enlightenment couldn't come until then.[16]

Enlightenment is a key concept for the novel. In it, Ellison explores how enlightenment is achieved and defined through the narrator's experiences. Many scholars have noted the parallels between *Invisible Man* and the Wright novella "The Man Who Lived Underground." There are many correlations in events and motifs between these two works. Most significant—particularly to the theme of enlightenment—are their underground descents and naming in relationship to identity. Both protagonists end up underground after police suspect them of a crime that they did not commit. In *Invisible Man*, the narrator falls into the sewers as he flees police after the riots in Harlem near the end of the novel. The police are under the misapprehension that his briefcase—which contains the smashed pieces of the Jolly Nigger Bank wrapped in paper—is filled with goods from the looting that is taking place during the riots. The policemen close the manhole cover over him, encasing the narrator in darkness, laughing as they do so. After the narrator enters the sewer, he decides to remain underground, believing that his participation in the world above is folly.

In "The Man Who Lived Underground," Fred Daniels is falsely accused of murder. He had been tortured by police into confessing and finds himself on the run; under chase. Looking for a place to escape, he sees the manhole and approaches it apprehensively, observing the flooding torrent beneath him. Although he is afraid to descend into the sewers, he fears the police more and so he plunges into the water below, struggling at first, nearly drowning. The story focuses on Daniels' navigations of the world beneath the surface and his burgeoning enlightenment as he struggles with questions about innocence and guilt and what his role is within society. He encounters several rooms, each of which unveil aspects of his becoming and some of which provide him tools for survival, as he grows to understand that even in his freedom to act as he wants, his actions affect the lives of others. Daniels believes he sees differently within the cave.

Two of the rooms represent aspects of daily life that Wright finds illusory, church and movies. Daniels reaction to the church-going black people dressed in white robes and pleading with God for mercy is a desire to tell them that they are as innocent as he is. His encounter with the crowd in the movie theater strikes a chord of absurdity in him. Approaching life from behind, from underneath the world that is hidden and ignored gives Daniels a vantage point that up ends his worldview. "Sprawling before him was a stretch of human faces, tilted upward, chanting, whistling, screaming, laughing. Dangling before the faces, high upon a screen of silver, were jerking shadows. A movie, he said with slow laughter breaking from his lips."[17] He concludes from observing people distracting themselves with illusions that man must feel guilty because why otherwise deceive himself with manipulations?

His behavior transforms from that of a hunted animal to a god, who exerts an amoral control over this underground tomb. Daniels begins to think that perhaps anything he does is okay. He steals tools and a workman's lunch and then food from a market, a radio from a shop. Daniels finds his way into a jeweler's store, where he had previously spied a white hand turning the combination of the safe. As the store's guard sleeps, Daniels opens the safe emptying it of its contents, money and jewels. Seeing a typewriter, he walks over and types his own name. Up until this point, Daniels' name had not been revealed, and even now, Daniels' use of it feels tentative, almost as if he is trying it on. Wright's use of namelessness in the first half of the novella enables Daniels to stand in for Everyman, it also demonstrates his existence as a precursor to his assertion of essence. When Daniels types his name, it is a revealing of the individual, of the individual responsibility of this man, as opposed to the condition of every man. It reaffirms that he has an identity. However, the significance has shifted. Daniels actions are building the kind of man he is.

Daniels' lights and radio enliven his quarters below. He lines the walls with money like wallpaper, and spreads diamonds under his feet. Daniels tells himself that this isn't morally like stealing because he doesn't care about the value of the objects. In the underground world, the things from above lose their meaning, their assumed value is displaced. When Daniels sits in front of the typewriter to try to type his name again, he can't remember what it is. His identity has also become valueless below ground.

His voyages above the surface, his encounters with the usher in the theater and the white couple in the market, all reinforce the difference between the prescriptions of the world above with Daniels' untethered subterranean existence. The couple assumes he is a shopkeeper's assistant when his likely waterlogged and disheveled physical appearance works against this assumption. The usher directs him towards the men's room. In both cases, expectations subsume truth. This pattern escalates as the novella progresses. Daniels observes behind the scenes as the consequences of his actions are taken out on the bodies of others. First, a young boy is beaten for stealing the radio Daniels himself stole. Then Daniels observes the guard from the jewelry store being tortured by the same police who tortured his false confession from him. He then witnesses the suicide of the night watchman, which the police take as a confirmation of his guilt. As he watches these events unfold, Daniels exchanges the personal feelings of guilt for an existential release, justifying his behavior. He thinks that, "Perhaps it was a good thing that they were beating the boy; perhaps the beating would bring to the boy's attention, for the first time in his life, the secret of his existence, the guilt he could never get rid of."[18]

This guilt while manifested in Daniels as a racial conscription is decentered to a human condition in the context of the cave. Removing Daniels from the context of the world above and erasing his identity does not change the fact of his guilt, just his understanding of what it stems from. In the end, as Daniels makes the decision to turn himself into the police, he chooses to do so not because of his belief in his personal guilt of the crime but because of his belief in his fundamental guilt. When he arrives, however, Daniels discovers that the police are no longer interested in him. They have located the actual murderer and they refuse to listen to Daniels' words. To the officers, his ideas are lunacy. Officer Lawson—whose name represents the law—shoots Daniels in the back, as he attempts to bring the police into the sewer, to make them see the world and people as he does, through the lens of the underground, from behind a veil. Ultimately, the policemen's apathy and blindness result in this end: the structures and functions of civilized society stand in the way of enlightenment. These brutal infrastructures cannot become enlightened; to undertake this process would undermine their power, to surrender their will to the individual man would be tantamount to their undoing.

It is significant that Wright wrote this during his involvement with the Communist Party. Although some historians argue that the novella reflects the beginning of Wright's separation with the party, Daniels' relationship with the established order, his treatment of money and items of value as insignificant, and his belief he is not stealing because he doesn't believe in the economic value of the items he acquires all align with this ideology. This is perhaps a meaningful motivation for Daniels to evaluate the beating of the boy as a possible good; the ultimate goal being the changing of the order, not Daniel's enlightenment itself. He desires change and action; a conversion of a cultural mind. The established order within the above-ground world in the novella is complacent and can be overthrown when enough of the disenfranchised find enlightenment. For Daniels—and presumably for Wright—enlightenment requires the assertion of freedom for all.

This valuation reveals the very different and distinct philosophies engaged within "The Man Who Lived Underground" and *Invisible Man*. Daniels acts upon his epiphany in an outward way, seeking to convert the world to the viewpoint he believes will save it. In contrast, when Ellison's narrator describes the encounter with the white man whom he begins to beat, he recognizes that the man cannot see him because he is invisible and therefore stops. The newspaper story that describes the beating as a mugging makes the narrator rueful and amused rather than afraid as Daniels was when he saw the newspaper story about himself. Ellison locates the narrator's impetus within himself and for himself and assigns him agency. The narrator's own choices drive the action of the novel. He cannot alter the minds of others, but he can act upon his own beliefs and refuse the ascriptions of others, acting as he would within the world as an ultimate good. In his reevaluation of the advice of his grandfather, the narrator opens a space wherein the implementation of a new agreed philosophy is demonstrated to be futile and unnecessary. "My problem is that I always tried to go in everyone's way but my own. I have also been called one thing and then another while no one really wished to hear what I called myself. So after years of trying to adopt the opinions of others I finally rebelled. I am an invisible man."[19]

The identity of invisibility is how the narrator views himself. It is not how others believe that they see him. The names ascribed to the narrator at various times: the socially responsible Negro by the audience of the battle royal, "nigger" by Dr. Bledsoe, the unidentified name assigned to him at the hospital, the unknown name given him by the Brotherhood, his misidentification as Rhinehart, Sybil's fantasy of a black rapist, the police's identification of the narrator as a looter, the unshakable Sambo imagery through the Jolly Nigger Bank and Tod Clifton's puppet all fail to locate an authentic identity for the narrator. The location of his identity is found within the difference that he only begins to explore as the novel closes. His identity is rooted in the undeniable presencing of his life as an individuated event. Gilles Deleuze's notion of difference and repetition applies here. A return to an original ideal is not necessary in the bringing forth of the Essence which declares its being within a man. Therefore, locating one's identity within a conscription to someone's exterior notion of blackness, or Americanness, or in opposition to whiteness is not necessary. What is necessary is an understanding of the context of history so that one can be aware of how and where these conscriptions operate within culture and recognize when they are exerting pressure. As Sartre writes, "Authenticity, it is almost needless to say, consists in having a true and lucid consciousness of the situation, in assuming the responsibilities and risks it involves, in accepting it ... sometimes in horror and hate." Ellison is clearly exploring Existentialist themes, the search for an authentic way of Being within the World, and the tension of the individual versus the public.

In the Wright novella, there are also connections to Existentialism as well as nihilism. Jean Paul Sartre writes, "Man first of all exists, encounters himself, surges up in the world, and defines himself afterwards."[20] Before he entered the sewers, Daniels only existed. The process of the unconcealing of his historical context happens after the novella reveals the fact of his being. Then his essence is brought forth. In his time living beneath the ground, during his time in the cave, he confronts himself, a process at the end of which his name is revealed. Existentialism argues that man can choose to do right or to do wrong, so man is essentially neither good nor bad. The moment of enlightenment for Daniels manifests as an understanding that he is not only responsible for himself but also responsible for the way events play out in the lives of others; what Sartre describes as anguish. Wright was heavily influenced by Fyodor Dostoyevsky whose *Notes from the Underground* is considered by many to be the first Existential novel. Despite the strong connections to the Christ story—three days buried—there is no redemption. Daniels emerges from the tomb to be returned back into nothingness, to be forgotten.

Ellison's prologue, on the other hand, begins with the narrator beneath the surface, there for the purpose of enlightenment, removing himself first from the ideas of others by burning his papers that represent the will others imposed upon his life. Unlike Fred Daniels, Ellison's narrator remains removed from society and unseen. Daniels interactions with others do not cease, he just views them differently. Daniels moment of double-consciousness— or enlightenment—occurs outside of the underground, it is contained within the moment when the police beat him for what he did not do, that leads him to his understanding about guilt, one he hopes to have triggered within the young boy accused of stealing the radio.

Through the staging of a relationship between enlightenment and the underground, both Wright's novella and Ellison's novel upset the trope of Plato's cave allegory. In doing so, they each take on the point of origin in Western thought for the humanist Ideal. Robin McNallie writes that Wright's cave is "the opposite of Plato's—that it is, in fact, connected oddly to both truth and renewal of life."[21] McNallie views Wright's cave as a womb that brings about a rebirth for Daniels. However, it is a stillbirth. Daniels—like Plato's philosopher—returns to enlighten those he left behind on the surface, to wake them up. And his efforts are resisted with a mighty hand. While this doesn't necessarily negate the importance or the meaning of Daniels' enlightenment, it does paint a bleak picture of the hope in overcoming the blindness and point to a dark future for the enlightened as they maneuver within the world. The narrator's cave is also opposite. Rather than beginning the process of enlightenment beneath the cave and realizing that all that he had observed within it are but flickering reflections of the original things that exist outside the cave, the narrator removes himself from the world completely and illuminates his cave, brightly with 1369 bulbs, eliminating the possibility of any of images from above the surface to reflect upon his place of contemplation. The narrator in identifying himself as the invisible man confronts his own existence away from its association with any representations. Ellison's narrator eschews the authority of representations to exercise a relationship to him. The place of resistance is not within a dismantling of the status quo through conversion but rather through the exercise of self-determination as a right that is inherent within Being.

Ellison's great project within *Invisible Man* and within his critical essays—particularly his review of LeRoi Jones' (Amiri Baraka) *Blues People* and the excellent "The Art of Romare Bearden"—is resistance to the limitations imposed upon black people by ascribing authentic ways of being or imposing aesthetic or behavioral standards, conventions or associations. Ellison wrote:

> ... For although Bearden is by self-affirmation no less than by public identification a Negro American, the quality of his artistic culture can by no means be conveyed by that term. Nor does it help to apply the designation "black" (even more amorphous for conveying a sense of cultural complexity) and since such terms tell us little about the unique individuality of the artist or anyone else, it is well to have them out in the open.... I refer to that imbalance in American society which leads to a distorted perception of social reality, to a stubborn blindness to the creative possibilities of cultural diversity, to the prevalence of negative myths, racial stereotypes and dangerous allusions about art, humanity and society.[22]

For Ellison, Bearden's work stood as an example of art that neither denied ancestry or cultural identification as black nor relied upon the same to dictate the forms that his art took. This refusal of ascriptions that were considered by either nonblack people or black people to be visions of an authentically black culture asserted the agency of self-determination that Ellison strived for within his own work. Written in 1977, this essay stood in contrast to the views of identity based art in conventions like those ascribed to by the Black Arts Movement, of which Amiri Baraka was a founding member and whose views aligned with that of the Black Panthers and Black Nationalism. Ellison asserted a Du Boisian consciousness into a conversation dominated by more radical voices. He reaffirmed Du Bois' words,

> On the other hand, the young and slowly growing black public still wants its prophets almost equally unfree. We are bound by all sorts of customs that have come down as second-hand soul clothes of White patrons.... Our worst side has been so shamelessly emphasized that we are denying we have or have ever had a worst side. In all sorts of ways we are hemmed in and our new young artists have got to fight their way to freedom.[23]

This same fight is the one that Ellison undertakes. He is concerned with the determination that blackness ascribes to people that aids cultural blindness towards the individual's ability to break forth into Being through Difference as opposed to commonality. So, *Invisible Man* is written as a memoir of a tale of invisibility, which the narrator recounts from his underground hideaway. He is draining power from the Monopolated Power & Light Company. He is listening to "(What Did I Do to Be So) Black and Blue?" as performed by Louis Armstrong. The song was written for *Hot Chocolates* (1929)—a musical revue about nightlife in Harlem in which Armstrong performed the solo on "Ain't Misbehavin'" and appeared in the orchestra. Edith Wilson performed *Black and Blue* on Broadway as a woman done wrong by love. Armstrong lifted the song out of its context performing it with lyrics that made it read as a plaintive on the plight of the Negro race.

> I'm white inside but that don't help my case.
> Cause I can't hide what is on my face
> I says, How will it end, ain't got a friend
> My only sin is in my skin
> What did I do to be so black and blue?[24]

In Armstrong's version, the lyrics:

> No joys for me. No company[25]

are removed from the second verse. The third verse:

> I'm so forlorn, life's just a thorn.
> My heart is torn, why was I born?[26]

is eliminated altogether and alternate versions of the lyrics for the final verse exist that read:

> I'm sad inside, but it don't help my case.
> Cause I can't hide all the sorrow that's on my face.[27]

These changes to the lyrics make a very clear statement about race, displacing the intent of the song from a lovelorn lament to a question about the status of blackness as an identity during the twentieth century. They also subtly delineate the motivations of the narrator and the novel. In choosing this version of this song for the prologue Ellison marks the project of the novel an interrogation of the color line, and links the narrator's invisibility to the color of his skin.

The narrator attends the graduation ceremony of his high school, where he has been invited to speak. Before the speech commences, however, he and other black youth are required to participate in a "battle royal" in which the participants are blindfolded and given boxing gloves and compelled to fight one another for the amusement of the white audience.[28] At the end of the battle, the youth scramble for money on the carpeted floor, which they learn is electrified, as they attempt to scoop up as many coins as they can. This hullaballoo is all later shown to be a farce as the coins are made of brass, and are worthless. At the end of these gruesome festivities, the men award the narrator with a scholarship to a college that is reminiscent of the Tuskegee Institute. Despite the abhorrent behavior of the benefactors, the narrator is grateful for the honor and respectful to the group. Through the narrator's speech, Ellison connects the rhetoric of submission to Booker T. Washington; the narrator argues that a platform of acceptance of status quo and hard work is what will prove the value of the Negro to white society, quoting from large hunks of Washington's Atlanta Exposition Address. This section of the narrative demonstrates the first in a series of ideologies that set expectations of behavior upon black people and that are associated with specific character types. Ellison identifies a dichotomy in thinking about race and identity that has set the tone for the twentieth century, and which divided the sensibilities of the time. He outlined for us that *Invisible Man* is about identity, and that the novel lays bare the claims of black critical thought and platforms for action. Immediately, through the reactions of the audience to the speech, Ellison undermines Washington, and following the expulsion of the narrator from the black college, will dismiss Washington's efforts completely as unrealistic optimism based on false hopes for white generosity and strength of character at best, and cynical self-serving behavior of black leadership at worst. The Founder is omnipresent but never seen in person. He is used as a figure head, a myth meant to prove the truth of the school's mission. Keeping your head down and working hard will result in a better place within society for the Negro. To quote Du Bois within *The Souls of Black Folk*:

> In answer to this, it has been claimed that the Negro can survive only through submission. Mr. Washington distinctly asks that black people give up, at least for the present, three things: first, political power; second, insistence on civil rights; third, higher education of Negro youth—and concentrate all their energies on industrial education, the

accumulation of wealth, and the conciliation of the South. This policy has been courageously and insistently advocated for over fifteen years, and has been triumphant for perhaps ten years. As a result of this tender of the palm-branch, what has been the return? In these years there have occurred:
1. The disfranchisement of the Negro.
2. The legal creation of a distinct status of civil inferiority for the Negro.
3. The steady withdrawal of aid from institutions for the higher training of the Negro.[29]

Dr. Bledsoe maintains a face of submission to white benefactors like Mr. Norton, while hiding behaviors of actual community members that live in the land surrounding the school. Bledsoe seeks to maintain an illusion that primarily benefits him solely, maintaining his power and position despite the fact that his school and his philosophy do not provide the results that they claim. When the narrator acts as chauffeur for Mr. Norton and takes him first on a journey where they encounter Trueblood and his tales of incest and then to the operating brothel where they encounter the veteran, the result is the narrator's expulsion from the school. Mr. Norton attempts to reassure the narrator that he will exert his influence over Dr. Bledsoe, and it appears at first that this will be the case. However when the narrator has his interview with Bledsoe, he learns that Bledsoe wants him punished. Bledsoe says,

> You're nobody, son. You don't exist—can't you see that? The white folk tell everybody what to think—except men like me. I tell *them*, that's my life, telling white folk how to think about things I know about.... I'll have every Negro in the country swinging on tree limbs by morning if it means staying where I am.[30]

Purportedly, Bledsoe gives the narrator letters of recommendation to help him secure work in the city, but as is discovered later, the letters contain instructions to refuse help to the young man. This is revealed when the son of one of the men takes pity on the narrator and finally offers him a job. The narrator goes to work mixing optic white, a paint whose whiteness is made white by the drops of black added into its mix. In this we see a mirror opposite to the Zora Neale Hurston quote, "I feel most colored when I am thrown against a sharp white background."[31] Like the inky darkness of blackface, the white thrown against it appears purer and brighter by comparison. This incident exposes the connection between whiteness and blackness, and lays bare for the reader—and the narrator—the necessity of maintaining blackness in order to maintain whiteness.

Thus far we have discussed several ideologies unpacked and examined within the novel: that of the Brotherhood, that of the white benefactors, that of Mary, and that of Bledsoe. The final ideology represented within the book is that of black Nationalism through the character of Ras the Exhorter/Destroyer. Ras stands in for Marcus Garvey. Garvey was an advocate for Pan Africanism, believing that equality was not possible for blacks outside of

Africa. Garvey wanted to pursue a life in which black people and white people lived separately. He had been known to compliment the Ku Klux Klan for its separatist policies. In the novel, Ras' accent is Jamaican, referencing Garvey's Caribbean ancestry. He is described as wearing theatrical African dress, a practice Garvey was known to partake in. As the novel progresses, Ras the Exhorter becomes Ras the Destroyer. He believes that black people should not integrate with white people but rather begin their own nation. Ras is described in the novel as kingly, a leader who is dismissed because of his blackness. Ellison frames him as an exceptional orator. Ras persuades Tod Clifton to leave the Brotherhood and join the Nationalists, a decision which ultimately leads to his death. Ras is the one who starts the riots in Harlem, although he is acting under Brother Jack's impetus. His radical ideology leads to destruction and tragedy. Ras' anger and rebellion cause him to set aside other black people who disagree as the enemy. He ends up working against the narrator and Clifton and helping the cause of those who are further away from him as a result.

Ultimately, none of the ideologies espoused by the leaders that the narrator encounters are save-all solutions. They are as fallen as the human characters who espouse them. The narrator through his own journey, which is necessary as an experience towards unconcealing his becoming, realizes the futility of striving after the ideals of others and the futility of convincing others of the Truth of his own understanding. "Life's but a walking shadow, a poor player that struts and frets his hour upon the stage and then is heard no more: it is the tale told by an idiot, full of sound and fury, signifying nothing."[32] The narrator stands poised to return to the world he left; ready to live out his existence as the Invisible Man he has determined himself to be. The world is not changed, it may not change. But life lived underground is temporary. It is the life beyond the walls of the cave that will determine what is to come. The hope of *Invisible Man* is the hope of Ellison, an affirmation of the irrelevance of race as a limiting force in life; or in the arts. It is when we operate within the world in reaction only to the ideas of others that we lose sight of truth. These are the works of a man possessing a rare lucidity of vision."[33]

4
Michael Ray Charles

A black artist is first of all a black artist.
—W. E. B. Du Bois[1]

In 2007 Darby English published a book called *How to See a Work of Art in Total Darkness*. The book highlighted the work of five black artists whose art contested the limited confines of the ideologies of a black art. In the introduction, English examined the critical conversations surrounding the work *Concerto in Black and Blue* by the artist David Hammons. Hammons began making work in the late 1960s, creating politically charged images like the body print *Injustice Case*. Hammons had himself bound to a chair—in imitation of the court drawings of Bobby Seale during the Chicago 8 trial—his body covered with margarine. Then he was pressed down upon the surface of the work, leaving an indexical impression that read like a photo negative. The final step was to dust pigment over the surface of the impression. Through this work, Hammons critiqued the control exercised on vocal black bodies by the U. S. government, and offered a narrative of difference to the objectifying nature of the work of artists like Yves Klein who painted the bodies of others and then had them perform the painting as a spectacle; rolling around on the surface of the canvas to create the work. Hammons clearly made work investigating race. English chose to begin this contemplation on black artists' resistance to the politics of blackness with Hammons' *Concerto in Black and Blue*. The piece operated this way: a gallery space was made light tight. Those who entered the gallery to view the work were given flashlights that provided a blue light through which they were able to view and navigate the rooms. Thus, the only substance of the work was the light which burst forth with the presence of a public inside the space.

So the work was socially constructed, built by the participation of its observers. As English points out, the work was impossible to view objectively for the viewer couldn't remove themselves from the context. Conceptually, *Concerto in Black and Blue* referenced the opening scene of *Invisible Man*.

The title referred to the Louis Armstrong song that the narrator listens to as the story begins and ends, the "concerto" of the title connecting the work to music and "black and blue" pointing to the song Ellison referenced. Like the narrator, the audience enters the cave, and the flashlights become the lights of the narrator that assist in the enlightenment; a symbol for 1369 points of light. Like Ellison's novel, the work then functioned as an investigation into the prescriptive way black art is considered and talked about; always first in relationship to race. The reviews of the work bear this concept out with general references to music and to race. A *Gathering of the Tribes'* review indeed sees a connection in the title of *Concerto* to "(What Did I Do to Be So) Black and Blue." However, it is one among many songs referenced which contain "black and blue" in their titles and the significance of Louis Armstrong and Ralph Ellison are not noted. This same article reads, "There is a sense, then, in which the entire history of Africans in North America can be told through reference to these two colors."[2] English identifies here a "tendency to limit the significance of works assignable to artists by referencing their purportedly racial character."[3] English argued that the critiques leveled upon the work done by black artists subsume the art within ideologies about black political strategies for images rather than unpacking the way individual art objects operate. By opening his essay with an examination of this piece, English conceptually links *his* book—and the work of the five artists analyzed within the text—to Ellison's project of resistance to the limitations of prescriptive conceptions of black representational space.

The remainder of the introduction unpacks the history of a system of black representations which English connects to the work of the artists highlighted within the bulk of the text: Kara Walker, Fred Wilson, Isaac Julien, William Pope L. and Glenn Ligon. He frames this conversation by unpacking how black representational space was constructed, focusing particularly on the historical positions of Alain Locke (artists should make art, not propaganda) and W. E. B. Du Bois (I do not care for any art that is not propaganda) and building chronologically from there. He states that there is no black representational space outside of politics. English's project is effective in demonstrating why such a representational space was established and is sympathetic to the historical necessity of its political function. English also establishes a strong argument that the same political functions for these prescriptions can be, in fact, limiting. English structures his argument as *Invisible Man* is structured, ideological narratives are explored and removed from a briefcase in order to burn them, releasing the artist of today from the past. English sounds this call in part so that his work inside the text functions like the work he analyzes: with an awareness of the past for the purpose of first, getting the history heard; second, engaging its ideas and third, critiquing its concepts. Like the artwork English analyzes, his text is complexly structured with multiple layers and referents. As English unravels the work done with uplift as a conscription; a limitation, he simultaneously honors what has gone before. For though English critiques Du Bois, by doing this, he also engages him, and critically unpacks his ideas about art; setting them within their historical context and thus echoes Du Bois' project and his forms. Doubtless, English has made the connection, as Ellison did before him, that he is paying homage to Du Bois by opening with a song, just as is done within *The Souls of Black Folk*.

English engages historical context for the purpose of illumination and enlightenment. In the same way, English wrote these words in a specific historical moment for a specific reason. Understanding that context, will help us to unpack the work of Michael Ray Charles—an artist whose work functions in a similar way to the work described in English's text and was made during a similar time period—and also helps us pin down the point of crisis within Lee's film *Bamboozled*. Within the conflict between Ralph Ellison's project of shedding conscripted identities in favor of the assertion of the individual and Du Bois' "Criteria of Negro Art" *Bamboozled* sets its teeth to chew. The influence of Michael Ray Charles and Post black art is Lee's motivation for undertaking the project. The context of events occurring within the art community of the late 1980s and early 1990s shed light upon the work of both men.

In 1989 the artist Robert Mapplethorpe passed away from complications arising from HIV/AIDS. Just prior to his death, at the end of 1988, Janet Kardon organized a retrospective of his work called "The Perfect Moment" at the Institute of Contemporary Arts in Philadelphia. Detractors considered Mapplethorpe's photography controversial because of its graphic depictions of queer sexuality in work like the "X Portfolio" series. To complicate matters, during this time, a conservative Congress wanted to eliminate funding to the National Endowment of the Arts. The NEA had given financial awards to the Mapplethorpe exhibition and individual controversial artists like André Serrano, whose photograph *Piss Christ* portrayed an image of a crucifix suspended in the artist's urine. The NEA came under fire for their endorsements of art considered by members of congress like Sen. Jesse Helms and Sen. Dick Armey to be obscene, offensive and/or sacrilegious. The Mapplethorpe retrospective was scheduled to tour five cities. "The Perfect Moment" opened to positive reviews and without incident in Philadelphia and the Museum of Contemporary Art in Chicago, Illinois. Pressure on institutions to refuse the show increased. Christina Orr-Cayhall at the Corcoran Gallery in Washington, D.C., canceled the exhibition's stop at her institution over her growing concern about the fall out that might result. When the exhibition came to the Contemporary Arts Center in Cincinnati, Ohio, the local authorities arrested museum director Dennis Barrie for pandering obscenity. On April

7, 1990, Cincinnati police handed Barrie an indictment and kept several hundred museum patrons waiting in the museum atrium while they took photographs and videos of the exhibition for court. A jury eventually found Barrie and the museum not guilty of the obscenity charges determining that the Mapplethorpe images didn't meet the Supreme Court test for obscenity, which requires work to both be offensive and lacking in artistic value. However, the indictment lessened many museums willingness to host controversial exhibitions out of a fear of losing federal funding.

Adding to this atmosphere of fear, in June of 1990, Congress passed the decency clause. This legislative action empowered the NEA to refuse grants to individual artists based on content. As a result, NEA chairman John Frohnmayer vetoed the funding to artists Karen Finley, Holly Hughes, John Fleck and Tim Miller, who became known as the NEA Four. The artists—whose work had already passed a vetting process by a peer review for quality—sued the NEA, eventually settling out of court for money that equaled their grant awards. The NEA Four would continue to pursue the case against the decency clause, taking the litigation all the way to the Supreme Court. They argued that their work was denied on the basis of their political views rather than the merit of their art. They had a point. This Congress was a conservative body and the artists' work highlighted either LGBT or feminist political viewpoints. This controversy unfolded as the HIV/AIDS crisis was at its peak in the United States with nearly 300,000 people dying from complications of the disease between 1987 and 1997.[4] The Supreme Court would ultimately choose to uphold the decency clause in 1998, but call the language advisory.

The controversy highlighted the plight of artists and others who had been politically marginalized. Around this time, Thelma Golden's star was rising as a curator for the Whitney Museum. Golden helped Elizabeth Sussman curate—and also wrote an essay for—the famous 1993 Whitney Biennial, which would become known as the multicultural biennial. The exhibition followed in the wake of the acquittal of the Los Angeles Police Department for the beating of Rodney King and the riots that ensued as a direct result. King led the LAPD on a high-speed chase on March 3, 1991. At the chase's end, the police officers pulled King from his car and beat him brutally. These incidents gained a national audience because George Holliday caught the beating on his video camera. Spike Lee's biopic X (1992), on the life of Malcolm X, opened with the Holliday video and an American flag burning. This statement echoed within the biennial which played the video on screens within the exhibition. As Roberta Smith, art critic for the *New York Times* noted,

> With its persistent references to race, class, gender, sexuality, the AIDS crisis, imperialism and poverty, the work on view touches on many of the most pressing problems facing the country at the dawn of the Clinton Administration and tries to show how artists are grappling with them. The wall labels and text are rife with fashionable buzz-

words: identity, difference, otherness.... The presence of Mr. Holliday's tape signals one of the shows basic flaws, which is that it is less about the art of our times than it is about the times themselves.[5]

Smith's critique of the show is that controversy and /or political statements don't necessarily translate to effective pieces of art. Smith held up for example works within the show that read as one-liners, pieces that never seemed to get to the point and artworks that should be effective pieces in one medium clumsily and ineffectively rendered within another. She admired the few moments of visual pleasure, like Charles Ray's sculpture of a fire truck, and moments where all of the elements seemed to work in tandem to communicate effectively with skill, and a strong voice.

One such piece was Glenn Ligon's *Notes from the Margin of a Black Book*. This work is Ligon's encounter with the series of Robert Mapplethorpe's photographs entitled *The Black Book* which eroticized and objectified the black male body through a queer white male gaze. Ligon—a queer black male—found himself simultaneously drawn to and disturbed by the images because although he understood the eye of desire that gazed upon these bodies, he was also bothered by the fetishizing that Mapplethorpe had done to the black men, Many of the photographs cropped out the faces of the men and focused on highly sexualized body parts. Mapplethorpe's title for the series referenced the notion of a black book that contained numbers for sexual trysts and conquests, and carried the connotation of promiscuity. Ligon had taken the images cut from his own copy of *The Black Book* and framed them hanging the photographs in juxtaposition with quotes from the media, critics and politicians about Mapplethorpe's work during "The Perfect Moment" controversy. Ligon's piece was a nuanced conceptual artwork that complicated the dynamics of race and sexuality, and interrogated presumed intersections and overlap between spheres of difference. Despite the inclusion of controversial images, it read as thought-provoking instead of merely provocative, in contrast to much of the work on display within the biennial, as Smith notes in her assessment of the overall exhibition:

> Committed, provocative and informative, it should not be missed, as its flaws and achievements will be debated for some time. But it too often loses sight of the fact that art is a form of visual communication that must exist for its own sake before it can further a cause. In the end, this ambitious show illuminates the pitfalls of politically inclined art more than its triumphs.[6]

Smith's analysis of the trappings of much of the work hanging within the exhibition was that the propaganda had lost its artistry. This argument related to art critic and historian David Hickey's defense of Mapplethorpe's work several years earlier. Hickey argued that all art eventually loses its contextual vibrancy as the time in which it was made recedes into the past. Beauty is what remains when context is gone. If it is never beautiful to begin with, it will not last beyond the immediacy of its message. Hickey asserted that the reason conservatives were so concerned by Mapplethorpe's images was that Mapplethorpe rendered in beauty ideas that were abhorrent to them. Hickey wrote:

> Yet, the vernacular of beauty in its democratic appeal remains a potent instrument for change in this civilization. Mapplethorpe uses it, as does Warhol, as does Ruscha, to engage individuals within and without the cultural ghetto in arguments about what is good and beautiful.[7]

Hickey's notion of art corresponds well with Du Bois, who desired for black art to be rendered in beauty so the truth and complexity of black lives can shine forth convincingly. According to Du Bois, "Without Beauty, Freedom has no plea; without truth; freedom has no goal; and yet, without Freedom, Beauty is not born; without Freedom, Truth is not known; Beauty, Truth, and Freedom—but the greatest of these is Freedom."[8]

Within the Du Bois text, "Criteria of Negro Art," there is nothing that suggests a different concept of Beauty than what Hickey states here, that speaks of beauty in a way which is almost equivalent to mastery. However, Du Bois also says, "While we believe in Negro art, we do not believe in any art simply for art's sake."[9] This idea is significant, because it contains within it the weight of semiotics. Language and images carry meanings inherently. Du Bois—and Lee—see that images are always working in some way. The best an artist can do is to make their work as an individual and engage the ideas that they want to, regardless of the opinions of others, but with a mind on the weight of the same. Du Bois feels that if art is doing some work, it may as well be telling the truth. For Du Bois then, the work of art is an unconcealing of truth. As English unpacks within his introduction, Du Bois desired for art a certain character that produced uplift for his race. English highlights black art's struggle between conscripted conventions—a practice he roots within Du Bois' desire—and Alain Locke's advocacy for art that is purely formal, art for art's sake. For English's project, the moment of realization that the mask of blackness is one that is made for the purpose of defining whiteness is a game changer. It means that making work about blackness for the purpose of uplift becomes something that is a reaction to white ideas. English then wants art that operates out of an awareness but refuses to be representative of a community or limited in any way. English's project is not to eliminate conversations about race but to allow art's character to do its work, as "art is a function of change."[10]

English's project focuses on the time period that is also the context for *Bamboozled*. Lee in many ways is concerned with similar issues that English presents. In order to understand Lee's film, we must unpack why Lee calls up the ghosts he does. For the purposes of this book—because it is necessary for the project that Lee has undertaken, because he asks us to within the film—we must reconcile Lee's anger with blackface minstrelsy with his *use* of it. The impetus of the anger, therefore, must not be centered within negative depictions of black people, but in how the motivations of minstrelsy continue to operate in the contemporary moment. Some artists and cultural producers use these historical images to critique and subvert this kind of image production. Some artists and cultural producers have lost sight of the history and set up representations that reinforce stereotypical blackness.

The argument of this book is that through *Bamboozled*, Lee seeks to revisit Du Bois' notion of the color line as the main problem of the twentieth century, and that further Lee intends to unpack history through the use of fiction in order to arrive at the truth as Du Bois defines the process in *The Ordeal of Mansart's* postscript. This setting, of an art world wary of controversy, a disillusionment with the project of identity art, a mourning of beauty and a championing of pleasure paired with content is the context for what follows. Just as he calls up Du Bois, Williams, Micheaux and Ellison, Lee calls up Michael Ray Charles. Charles paintings—Spike Lee owns Charles' painting *Bamboozled*, which makes an appearance in the film—and concepts—Charles' *Forever Free* painting series provide direct inspiration for Lee's advertisements that appear in the film, particularly the Timmy Hilnigguh spot—are present and potent within it. Charles was hired by Lee to serve as a consultant. To understand Lee's purpose in creating *Bamboozled*, and Charles relationship to the film, we must unpack the work of an artist whose art garnered initially a similar critical and community reaction as Charles, and whose work was an impetus for English's project in the same way as Charles was for Lee. Her identity statement—the Negress—makes an appearance within the speech of an audience member of *Mantan: The New Millennium Minstrel Show*, Lee's show within the show. This artist is Kara Walker.

In 1994, Kara Walker emerged onto the art scene in a group show at the Drawing Center in SoHo. Walker's Negress and the signature technique of using cut paper silhouettes made their debut. The response was decidedly mixed. Many art critics, including Roberta Smith, raved about Walker's work. According to Smith, Walker convincingly communicated how "slavery visited degradation equally on all concerned and that its tragic legacy poisons life for all Americans."[11] Whether this interpretation is true remains to be seen. Walker's work—its exhibition and its meaning, as well as its purchase by white buyers—drew strong emotions in response to the installations.

Walker's favor with collectors was viewed under a veil of duality. In one sense, as Maurice Berger wrote in *The NY Times Magazine*, "The art world has been profoundly racist. Kara Walker's case is an instance of triumph, a moment where an African American artist who deals with issues of race and racism in America is actually purchased by White collectors."[12] In another sense, the ownership of these works by white buyers is a point of contention for many black Americans, given the historically racist imagery and stereotypes referenced in Walker's silhouettes. Many artists, scholars and activists within the community struggled not only with the purchase of these loaded images by white buyers, but by Walker's use of the negative stereotypes long used to denigrate people of color. In a written statement to *The International Review of African American Art*, Tina Dunkley, director of Clark Atlanta University Art collections wrote,

> If Walker is so committed along the lines of turning historical atrocities into racial parody and burlesque, then we should soon be seeing scenes like injuns and White folks fornicating along the misnamed Trail of Tears; Nazi storm troopers sodomizing emaciated Jewish children near the ovens at Auswitz (sic): and a traditionally dressed Japanese woman licking the nipple of another while her derriere is pressed tight against a California detention camp fence as a U.S. G.I. penetrates her. Otherwise, Walker sounds like Michael Jackson who sings, "It doesn't matter whether you're black or white," with no credible explanation as to how he became white.[13]

With a cast of characters drawn directly from minstrelsy, Walker's world of paper cutouts are filled with both the violent truths and fantasies of the antebellum South. Shadow figures of the mammy, Uncle Tom, the jungle bunny and the black buck, the coon and his little cousin, the pick-a-ninny, and, of course, the Negress envelop the viewer, directing the audience gaze to the degradations implied, and leaving them no safe place to look. Without apology, the atrocities of slavery and its aftermath parade before wide-eyed audiences. Worse yet, Walker's stereotypes stand complicit in the perpetration of their own degradation. The worst offenders and offended are black female figures, especially small girls. Depictions of pedophilia, bestiality, rape, white on black and black on black violence permeates Walker's work, causing many to criticize the art as inflammatory and created for nothing other than shock value.

While the controversy brewed, Walker continued to gain prestige inside the greater art community. Following the group show at the Drawing Center, Wooster Gardens presented her first solo show, ultimately offering her representation. By the end of 1995, she would begin work on an installation for the walls of the Museé d'Art Moderne, in Paris. Walker's work was purchased by the both the Walker Art Center and the Museum of Modern Art in 1997. This was an important year for Walker. At just 28 years old she had been awarded the MacArthur Fellowship, popularly known as the Genius Grant. However, despite these positive critical responses, the intensity of reactions inside the black art community was growing.

Renowned black artist Betye Saar began a campaign of letter writing, boycott and petition, requesting, among other things, that the MacArthur foundation rescind the award granted to Walker, calling her images racist, and Walker herself, young and foolish. Although, Saar also draws from stereotypical imagery, most notably, "Liberation of Aunt Jemima" (1972), Saar's assemblages of racist memorabilia worked to empower the women who had labored underneath the stereotype of mammy. To paraphrase, English, Saar looked at Walker's representations as a threat to the dignity of black representational space.[14]

The International Review of African American Art published an article criticizing Walker's methods and personally contacted her father, an abstract artist and professor at Georgia State University, asking him to make her respond to their allegations.[15] The attacks grew nastier and became less about the art, and more about the personal life of the artist. According to English, the fact that the talk around Walker's work explored such topics as "her pregnancy, hairstyle and patronage," is a proof of sorts that it is extremely difficult to convey "resistant black representations."[16] The general attitude of Walker's detractors can be heard echoing in the statements of Venise Wagner, as published in the *San Francisco Examiner*, "For this artist, the joke's on all of us."[17]

English stood amongst the defenders of Walker's installations in a series of essays contained within the beautifully presented book *Narratives of a Negress*. This catalog—published by MIT press in 2007 to coincide with the exhibition of the same name, at the Tang Teaching museum in New York—presented a series of scholarly essays on Walker's work. These read as convincing manifestos heralding their support of Walker's art, and denouncing her detractors. Several of the scholars cite connections between Walker's concept of race and its relation to the duality of identity frequently referenced in the work of black scholars, like Frantz Fanon.

Fanon believed that black and white people defined themselves in opposition to each other, that the black man was enslaved in order for the white man to be master. According to Fanon, black identity was not inherent inside the soul of the black man, but was a "White artifact." This identity was a white mask created for the black man to see himself as other. Ultimately, he concludes, this "collective unconscious … is purely the sum of prejudices, myths, collective attitudes of a given group … the collective unconscious is cultural, which means acquired."[18] English compares Fanon's mask to the identity that Walker has invented for herself in the persona of the Negress. According to English, Walker is not really the Negress. The Negress is a fictional history created by Walker, as affirmed by her own words. To quote,

> It seems like I had to actually reinvent or make up my own racist situations so I would know how to deal with them as black people in the past did. In order to have a real connection with my history, I had to be somebody's slave. But I was in control: That's the difference.[19]

This statement by Walker reflects Ellison's ideology. She seeks to encounter the past as a means for understanding her present. However, these histories are a fiction. Lies she has been told about herself. So she creates her own fiction, to let the truth ring forth. In the Ralph Ellison interview with the *Paris Review* from 1954, the interviewer asks Ellison what he wants everyone to know about *Invisible Man*, He responds, "It is not a biography."[20]

Beyond the easy sparring against the bad natured barbs directed at Walker, English employs this argument to dismantle the work of the art historian, Gwendolyn Du Bois Shaw. In 2004, Shaw wrote a book about the work, entitled *Kara Walker: Seeing the Unspeakable*. Shaw viewed the character of the Negress as Walker's self-portrait, rather than an identity statement, attributing the thoughts and desires of the Negress and her actions to Walker herself. She wrote of the Negress as a metaphor for Walker and her career. Her main support of this assertion is "Cut," in which the Negress either jumps or falls, hands sliced nearly off. The knife that executed the act of violence protrudes from within one hand, akin to the trope of the painter's brush, as the knife is Walker's weapon of choice. She compares this to a photograph taken of Walker for *Interview* magazine in which Walker executes a similar pose wearing the couture mammy costume designed by Comme des Garcons.[21] English argues that while Shaw is correct in this as a glimpse of the Negress in Walker herself, that she should be careful not to confuse the artist's identity statement with the artist's identity.[22] The arguments and raw feelings about Walker's artwork amongst the black community give credence to Darby's claim that, "This is not about the past."[23] Or, as Faulkner wrote "The past is never dead, it isn't even past."[24] Critics of Walker's work claim that her caricatures of minstrelsy function in the same way as the original. However, as Chude-Sokei has demonstrated, black performance of blackface minstrelsy often operated as a resistance, pushing back and out against the stereotypes. Clearly this understanding is not what her detractors meant but they accidentally hit upon a truth. Walker's work interrogates assumptions about black representations.

Walker's fascination with the forms and imagery of the past has roots in her own personal history. Born in the multi-racial backdrop of Stockton, California, Walker moved to Georgia around the time she turned thirteen. Her father, Larry Walker, moved the family in order to begin a teaching position at Georgia State University. Kara had a difficult time adjusting to the difference between the two communities. According to Walker,

> I became black in more senses than just the kind of multicultural acceptance that I grew up with in California. Blackness became a very loaded subject, a very loaded thing to be—all about forbidden passions and desires, and all about a history that's still living, very present ... the shame of the South and the shame of the South's past; its legacy and its contemporary troubles.[25]

She speaks of being naïve as a teenager to issues of race, describing in a candid interview with her cousin, James Hannaham, an incident in which she was on a date with her then boyfriend.

> When we got back to the car there was a flyer from the Ku Klux Klan, spelling out for him all the evils of black women, describing what sort of peril he was in, and identifying stereotypes of disease and moral degradation.... So I guess I needed a way to question how these types of issues have been represented in art previously.[26]

Walker describes this moment as an awakening, like the shattering of the mask. Walker experienced firsthand the disconnect between the reality of her person and the perception of her identity as a black woman.

For her complicated titles and narrative, Walker drew upon the text of soft-core pornographic romance novels of the South, which fetishized the black woman as Negress, as she drew upon the imagery of both the minstrel show and the silhouette to visualize her notions of this perception.

> I was really searching for a format to sort of encapsulate, to simplify complicated things.... And some of it spoke to me as: "it's a medium ... historically, it's a craft ... and it's very middle-class." It spoke to me in the same way that the minstrel show does ... it's middle class White people rendering themselves black, making themselves somewhat invisible, or taking on an alternate identity because of the anonymity ... and because the shadow also speaks about so much of our psyche. You can play out different roles when you're rendered black or halfway invisible.[27]

Walker uses a white crayon or soft pastel, drawing the images onto black paper and cutting them out with a knife. Then the cut-paper images are adhered onto one of various surfaces, canvas, wood, paper, or the gallery wall, using wax, which serves a dual purpose of ease of removal with little fear of damage, and references a link to the past through the use of historical materials.

Although over time, Walker has incorporated additional elements into her work, for example, using additional colors besides black in the paper cut outs, and light and film to deepen the space that Walker's shadows inhabit, the silhouette form still tells the same story. Featureless, anonymous caricatures indulging themselves in degradation, all of them rendered "black" by Walker's hand. Says Walker, "When stereotypes attempt to take control of their bodies, they can only do what they are made of and they are made of pathological attitudes of the Old South. Therefore, racist stereotypes occurring in my art can only partake of psychotic activities." None of the figures present in Walker's work function as full people, be they white or black. They are stuck in a dance of perversion and violence, locked in an embrace which serves to define them both yet does so only if it can reduce them as to be almost unrecognizable as human beings. The purposefulness of the silhouette in enacting this reduction through the history of its form and its associations is ingenious on Walker's part. Ultimately, it robs the figures of any identity other than what is assigned by form. The viewer is forced through interaction with the work, to be complicit in its acts. The people "seen" in

Walker's work are not explicitly rendered but implied. The shadows ask our minds supply the details, and we comply.

These grand epics of the sickness of the Old South function as history paintings, a history usually buried under a very white wash, almost optic white. Walker's goal is to illuminate the horrors of the past but also the fictive nature of the history building the South, as well as America, has done about itself. Walker cites Robert Colescott as being a major influence on her work in this regard. This influence is clear upon viewing Colescott's paintings, for example, "Eat dem taters," (1975) which satirized Van Gogh's "Potato Eaters" (1885) and the famous "George Washington Carver Crosses the Delaware: Page from an American History Textbook" (1975) a re-examining of the well-known Emmanuel Leutze painting. Both function as a social and political commentary, first through their critique of the lack of emphasis on black figures of history, and second, through their characterization of black people as lampooned stereotypes. Colescott's grinning dark figures are intended to stand not as a representation of real black people, but as a signifier of black representation in the history of visual culture. Black is operating inside both Walker's and Colescott's work as an affectation of blackface in order to critique the sources it draws upon and the constructed aspect of its forming.

Using true black to visually represent the spectrum of skin pigments culturally identified as black is a method employed by many black artists, including Kerry James Marshall. When asked why he painted his figures pure black, rather than varying shades of brown, or even a really dark brown, Marshall replied,

> They're unequivocally black. They function as rhetorical devices. In the rhetoric of social dynamics, we talk about White people, black people. We know that there are a full range of black folk that go from black to white. There are black people that look like you (referring to interviewer). Why is that? White folks define what is black and white.
>
> That's why, when I paint them black, they are absolutely black. There is no question of who they are in those pictures. You have to come to terms with their presence as a phenomenon. The blackness is the phenomenon. And then to deal with the rest of what the picture has to offer. The one thing I don't want to equivocate about is how black they are.[28]

In the same way, Walker maneuvers her way through this symbolic mine field, using the pre-existing language of race, drawing upon the visual symbols most easily recognized by the viewer, in order to elicit the most direct response. Upon examining "Cut," what is visually apparent is the stark black figure caught in mid-air, wrists sliced open, blood coming out in fantastic scrolls, like feathers. The viewer doesn't really know that the figure behind the shadow is black, but *assumes* she is black. The Negress appears from behind a veil so to speak. The veil is directly the result of the reduction.

To create a silhouette, a figure sits behind a white screen and a bright light is shone upon them, casting the shadow used to form the shape for the image. This can be executed as a drawing or in the form of a shadow play. Walker's silhouettes operate as a shadow play, with multiple figures and complex narratives. The viewer uncomfortably crosses the line into active participant, as an audience is required to receive or capture the visions. The silhouette form leaves only three visual indicators of how to view it, shape, material and color. The shape delivers the narrative of the figures. Our cultural mindset provides the indicators that allow this to happen. So, in the case of "Cut," we recognize the sharp indentation of the corseted waist, indicating the era, and the braid through its shape as a signifier of race, while the small jutting corner of fabric rising above the hem indicates an apron, telling us volumes about the class of the young woman.

Significantly, in her early work, white and black people are all rendered black. Webster's Dictionary defines black as "characterized by absence of light, thoroughly sinister or evil, indicative of condemnation or discredit, connected with or invoking the supernatural or the devil, marked by the occurrence of disaster, and characterized by hostility or angry discontent."[29] Visually, black is a void, a hole. It recedes. It operates as negative space. It is the color of shadows.

In "Old and New Identities," Stuart Hall writes,

> You have spent five, six, seven hundred years elaborating the symbolism through which Black is a negative factor. Now I don't want another term. I want that term, that negative one, that's the one I want. I want a piece of that action. I want to take it out of the way in which it has been articulated in religious discourse, in ethnographic discourse, in literary discourse, in visual discourse. I want to pluck it out of its articulation and rearticulate it in a new way. In that very struggle is a change of consciousness, a change of self-recognition, a new process of identification, the emergence into visibility of a new subject. A subject that was always there, but emerging, historically.[30]

These words might have been Walker's own for, she loads blackness with not only the stereotypes written of here, but the entire history of a place laden with the burden of past and wrong thinking. In *Virginia's Lynch Mob* (1998), a parade of figures hurry on their way to the lynching, led by a man dressed in a uniform and beating on a drum. The presence of the whistling drummer and a vulture, eating a limp eagle, represents the origins of Lynch law and the change of its use. This practice began in Virginia, with Justice Charles Lynch. He prosecuted Tory supporters who were loyal to the British crown. This prosecution was outside of the jurisdiction of the county courts, which were unable to bring charges for treason. Those who came under his punishment threatened to come after him following the end of the war, and Lynch sought solace in the legislature who directed that as he had acted to suppress acts of conspiracy, although the means were illegal, the imminence of danger justified the actions. He was found not guilty of wrong doing in thus taking the law into his own hands. The Southern states twisted its purposes, using it to kill Union supporters, abolitionists and black people: freedmen and slaves.[31] These figures inside the installation represent the folly of the law, the abuse of its terms and the years of its execution. Ominously, a young girl near the end of the procession carries a Ku Klux Klan mask, looking towards the continuity of abuse into the twentieth century. The South is sullied. Its history is blackened by the dance of violent hate and the white walls of the gallery are correspondingly stained by these inky figures. The black of Walker's figures is so black, the "white" of the white cube of the gallery becomes even whiter in comparison. Walker does not mean for this art to be easy. In *Narratives of Negress*, typed upon an index card:

> Nothing can come between a man and his ego
> Except A woman, black, with History on her
> Side, a million hungry ancestors on her should
> ers salivating at the chance for a speedy
> bloodletting.[32]

The graphic nature of this thick black paper on smooth clean walls reads as the flat page of an illustrated book, an illuminated text, shining in its perversions and claiming all of its terms. The space becomes other than what it once was.

> I wish I was a white girl....[33]

Uncompromising in its intent:

> See, I stirred something in your sedintary feet.
> spelled wrong. see. Lazy and stupid lazy and stupid[34]

English is correct in his assessment that this work is not Walker's identity, but an identity statement. This concept is the central point of the work. Walker is looking at how she feels seen. She is burning the papers in her briefcase. Walker doesn't believe this identity truly belongs to her. This fantastic circus is meant to be so very theatrical as to not be reasonably interpreted as true. And yet, the images contain enough history and enough truth that they make us uncomfortable, as well they should. Shaw comes close in her analysis, but misses the point—and Walker's purpose—when she views Walker as the Negress; as do her detractors when they put down her work as not providing portrayals of positive black types. This critique misses the point. These works are personal in the sense that they examine Walker's encounter with the South as an outsider, but with a sense of a pre-determined identity within its space, just as Bert Williams performances had done about a century before.

In the article "Spooked," Stephen Talty writes that a Southerner in the days of slavery could tell who was black and who was white by the presence of fear in the eyes of the black man when staring into the eyes of a white man.[35] That the sense of power inside a look could bring fear into a heart is a terrible thing, and though nowhere near as strong it is still present. Walker forces us look through the eyes of a narrator she has constructed to examine our fascination with race, and determine why it divides us. Race needs to be identified, in order to be examined. However, you can't portray it with a sense of individualism without dismantling its constructs. Therefore in order to examine race as an issue, we must look at the images that represent it. And the images of race are always stereotypes because they are reductive in type, reducing a sea of individuals to one character; reducing a person, to a people.

English's impassioned defense of Walker's work—and the watershed book of art theory that followed it—reflected a paradigm shift that occurred around the same time within the work of other black artists like Trenton Doyle Hancock, Mark Bradford, Kori Newkirk, Rashid Johnson and Laylah Ali whose work appeared within the exhibition *Freestyle* which Thelma Golden organized in her new post as the chief curator and director of the Studio Museum of Harlem in 2001. Golden wrote in her catalog essay that she and Glenn Ligon had discussed the new mode of working for young black artists during this time, naming it Post black. Golden's framing of this group of artists as "Post Black" verbalized a shared quality that was incalculable as style, something that went beyond aesthetics. For Golden, Post black existed inside a space which worked to broaden the context under which black artists could make artwork and through which identity and difference could be explored. As she wrote in her essay for *Freestyle*, "Their work, in all its various forms, speaks to an individual freedom that is a result of this transitional moment in the quest to define ongoing changes in the evolution of African-American imagery begun in art and ultimately to ongoing redefinition of blackness in contemporary culture." Post black was defined by Golden as a group of artists with diverse ways of working who engaged issues of race, but in a new way, and shunned the label of "Black Artist," as it had come to be defined in the 1960s. These artists made work that investigated what to do with the meta-narrative of race, of blackness, in a postmodern world.

Michael Ray Charles was a contemporary of Walker's generation, achieving his initial success in 1993. Like Walker, Charles' work was heavily criticized within the black art community, with many of the articles previously mentioned about Walker citing the images of Charles as well and condemning them both. Like Walker, Charles' initial use of racially charged imagery began in graduate school. Charles had studied advertising and design in his undergraduate work at McNeese State University in Lake Charles, Louisiana, in addition to playing basketball. His familiarity with both of these arenas would feed his investigations visually. In his interview with Art 21, Charles speaks of searching for imagery through which to talk about American-ness. A friend gave him a Sambo figurine. He began to study it, eventually making fifty copies of the figure and creating cribs for them, laying the figures out on display as stars on the American flag. The artwork marked not only the beginning of Charles foray into drawing from images of blackness in popular culture and advertising but the controversy that would plague his work as well.

In an article released in 1997 in the Houston Press called "The Art of Darkness," Shaila Dewan wrote about the controversy surrounding Charles' work claiming that many people were citing his art as a possible catalyst for racial healing. Dewan was skeptical. She wrote, "Those most affected by racism have indicated some trouble with both Charles' work and the attention it receives."[36] Unlike Walker's work, nothing is left to the imagination in the work of Michael Ray Charles. He employs the language of minstrelsy and black collectibles in his paintings which use satire and historical reference to investigate contemporary tropes. Like Walker, he juxtaposes the present and the past. Like Walker, the South is a character within the work, as are negative stereotypes, particularly the Mammy and Sambo characters. Dewan cites artist David McGee, "The thing that's so perplexing about Michael Ray Charles' work is that his images don't turn a corner."[37] But perhaps this is the point. For Charles, images of blacks in popular culture haven't turned a corner either. There is a history to the images that Charles sees as permeating contemporary media and he draws connections to them with the racist images of the past.

> I want to know about these images—how they were used, why they were used and when they are being used. There's more to my work than blackface imagery or the clown caricature. On one level, it's me trying to say what we're seeing now, in different variations, was originally rooted in these caricatures. On another level, my work goes beyond that. I am deeply motivated by various forms of communication. I like finding out how things have evolved to mean what they mean.[38]

Viewers who find Charles' work problematic and visually difficult often write or speak about fear of the damage Charles' work might cause to vulnerable youth, contending that they might form negative opinions about themselves in the process of viewing the work. Some critics cite a belief that Charles himself doesn't understand the power of his images. Unequivocally, these same viewers have no difficulty whatsoever in identifying the negative character or reading the work as a reference to this racist image making of the past. The set of difficulties present within Charles' work are the same as in Walker's work. One problem with the critical response to Charles' work is that detractors never critically investigate beyond the image to the content. The usually fine Roberta Smith praises Charles' technical skill but stops short of investigating the purpose behind the imagery; beyond conflating them to aesthetically similar art by image makers like Basquiat or Robert Colescott. Smith performs a cursory read that conflates Charles' work with the racist artifacts of Jim Crow paraphernalia that it draws from. However, Charles' work requires a slow read. Smith wants there to be a greater degree of separation between the source images and Charles' paintings. But this belittles what work Charles is trying to do.

After examining the painting owned by Lee, *Bamboozled*—which shares a title with the film and makes an appearance within the same—the image clearly is intended as an advertisement or box top layout for a sinister game. The lettering and title on the box are based off the design of a hide and seek game of the same name from the 1950s. In the center is a cartoonish image of a disembodied head with a coin slot on top, a kin to Ellison's Jolly Nigger Bank. The character, clearly a reference to the Sambo stereotype from minstrelsy, is winking. The graphic encircling the head appears to be a roulette spinner with white and black slots instead of black and red. Each of the black slots contains a letter at the end which spells out "Loose a Turn." The white slots contain a series of symbols some associated with racist symbolic language: runic writing, an inverted spade—which contains racial prescriptions as well as meaning destruction in tarot divination—the Vesica Piscis (two interlocking circles that are complimentary opposites), the center of a Celtic cross or what could be the target sight of a rifle. At the bottom of the painting appear the words "The Amazing Game of Deceit and Conquer." White dominates the game, both visually and ostensibly conceptually—as the slots ensure that betting on black is always a losing proposition—and also takes up more space. The cartoonish character makes reference to the kind of black collectible from the same era as when the Jolly Nigger Bank was produced. In addition, the words "loose a turn" are altered from the standard "lose a turn," and when examining all definitions can be said to mean to "set free a change in nature, state, form or color." Charles says within the Art 21 video that he sets within his work a Lincoln Penny. As Michael Germana notes within *Standards of Value*, the penny refers back to the coins tossed at the black Guinea within Herman Melville's *The Confidence* Man, in which the black Guinea bamboozled people into believing he was black in order to swindle the crowd of money. To bamboozle is to conceal one's true motivations through elaborate deceit behind a pretense of good intentions in order to secure gain for oneself. With the rich cultural and historical subtext and associations inherent within Charles' imagery, a deep level of critical engagement is required. The reaction to the work implies that part of the reason why Charles has not been the object of the same level of critical discourse that Walker has been afforded is because Walker's images open a similar conversation but leave space for ambiguity that allows the viewer some distance. Walker's tableaus of terror are fashioned within beautiful imagery, which while clearly connected to racial content from the first examination, simultaneously allow the viewer to defer responsibility from themselves to an imagined past so that Walker's work feels like a seduction rather than a slap and a laugh. There's a lot of work to be done to unpack Charles' paintings and it is not necessarily work that viewers—disengaged from the work by its overtly offensive content—are able to undertake within the immediate context of the viewing. The more available the history of the objects is to the viewer the more understandable the work becomes. In this sense, the difficulty of Charles' work is the same as that of *Bamboozled*, the history which allows for its proper contextualization is veiled by a repeated refusal to examine its forms which are now only understood for their negativity.

Charles also fixes the imagery with text, which can be tricky to manage in relationship to audience interpretations. Often times, the context of the viewing can alter the way the content is received and how the audience responds to the work. In some senses, the elevation processes that occur by hanging objects within a gallery can seem to create a process of approval for the words, which are more directive than images, angering the viewer.

A concrete example of this phenomenon is evident in Glenn Ligon's text based *Jokes* series. In 2008, Ligon spoke at the Tate about the historical aspect of much of his text work. He described himself as literal. His first idea was to get the texts read. Initially, he began with phrases taken from black writers and thinkers like James Baldwin and Zora Neale Hurston.[39] The sole initial goal was to render visible the words of many black thinkers and authors in the greater public sphere of contemporary art. The layers of meaning came out in the process of making.

For Ligon, the process was two-fold.[40] First, the ideas within the text and their authors were rendered with personal importance through his appropriation; simultaneously, they were problematized through their construction, words woven into myth through work. The texts are worn, as hand-me-downs, made valuable through the remembering of those who had previously worn them, and performed as paintings by Ligon, but never completely belonging to him. They are sometimes uncomfortable to wear and to read. In the *Jokes* series, Ligon solidifies moments from the stand-up routines of Richard Pryor, the controversial black comedian. Pryor unflinchingly examined race and sexuality. The paintings were physically difficult to read; the text was small and required the viewer to approach them in an intimate space in order to ascertain what was said.

On *Cocaine (Pimps)*, yellow-orange text was superimposed on a red-orange background, enhancing this illegibility. When the viewer accessed the text, the ideas would be activated, and the viewer became part of the performance of the words. The viewer was forced to read what Pryor would speak, which was more difficult than listening to Pryor onstage or on video.

Removed from the context of the stand-up routine and placed within the contemporary art museum's white cube, the viewer had to not only confront the text of the joke but also decide what to publicly do with it. The viewer was forced to confront what the joke meant hanging in the wind by itself without situational support. How should the viewer respond to?

> Niggers be holding them dicks too…
> White people go "Why you guys hold your things?"
> Say "You done took everything else motherfucker."[41]

Ligon related a story of a docent at the Whitney who led patrons on tours through the *Black Male* exhibition. The docent did not want to read the jokes, because he didn't want to say some of the words that the jokes contained. Inevitably, when they would come to the part of the tour where they confronted Ligon's work, someone would ask the docent to read the joke. The docent would continue to talk about the work, and try to ignore or assuage the requests, but due to the intimate nature of the read and the size of the groups in the tour, the request to read would become more insistent. During the particular instance relayed by Ligon in his talk, the crowd pushed past the docent to read the joke. When they realized what it said, the crowd became agitated. One member of the crowd, when asked if he didn't appreciate Richard Pryor's stand-up, related that yes, he did, but Richard Pryor in his living room is one thing, and on the wall at the Whitney is another.[42,43]

Golden tells a similar story of a woman who approached her at the *Black Male* show, expressing her disappointment at the kinds of images of blackness presented at the exhibition. The woman cited the work of prominent black artist Robert Colescott's *George Washington Carver Crossing the Delaware: Page from an American History Textbook* (1975) as containing the kind of images of the black male that black people had been fighting against for centuries. The woman did not see the critique of the portrayal of blackness that Colescott exacted or the complexity of the image's history, only the negative stereotypes that it drew upon.[44]

This issue with history is a double-edged sword for Charles, and ultimately for Lee. Because people have forgotten—or in some cases, misremembered—the history of the black collectibles and minstrelsy, and the attempts at resistance that many black minstrelsy performers incorporated into their performances, the interpretations of these works are flattened and discarded as one-liners. What Ligon relates about the bad feeling in relation to the *Jokes* series is multiplied in relationship to Charles' images because many people can only view them as a signifier for one idea.

When Dewan asked Charles in a phone interview about his work, whether it promoted racial healing—a claim that another article had made about his work—he responded, "Did I say that?" To which she had to respond that he had not. She then asked, "Does it heal?" Unequivocally, Charles responded, "No."[45] Clearly, the point of Charles' work is to make people uncomfortable. The images unsettle us, and force us to question what other images are functioning in the same way. If minstrelsy is American, and if these objects are Americana, what does it mean when we say that images are "American" today; should we laugh at the comedic types of "the interlocutor and Mr. Bones" as they appear on *Saturday Night Live*? Is it hypocritical for us to condone through our viewing the types of minstrelsy if they no longer wear blackface, even if they do the same work that minstrelsy did? Or should we be more offended by imagery that forces us to confront the difficulties of minstrelsy as current and ever present? In other words, why are the images of the past that are loaded with racist content more bothersome to us than the same kinds of images in the present? Is it possible to ask that question without resurrecting the images of the past? We should be offended by negative imagery that works to be reductive towards any people group, but we should also think critically about how images operate in their complexity.

5
Spike Lee

> *Liberty trains for liberty. Responsibility is the first*
> *step in responsibility.* —W. E. B. Du Bois

Shelton Jackson Lee was born in Atlanta, Georgia, on March 20, 1957. His father Bill Lee was a jazz musician. Lee's mother Jacqueline was a teacher of black arts and literature. Jacqueline—whose maiden name was Shelton—gave Lee the nickname Spike. When Spike was young, his family moved to the Fort Greene section of Brooklyn. In Fort Greene, Spike enjoyed a relatively upper-middle-class upbringing. Lee attended John Dewey High school, graduating in 1975. He first demonstrated a passion for filmmaking when enrolled at the historically black, Morehouse College in Atlanta where his father and grandfather had also attended. Lee would earn a bachelor's degree in mass communications from Morehouse before returning to New York; eventually enrolling in the NYU Tisch School of the Arts, earning a master in fine arts. His student film "Joe's Bed-Stuy Barbershop: We Cut Heads" was the first student film ever showcased in the Lincoln Center's prestigious film series "New Directors, New Films."

The success of this short encouraged Lee to seek agency representation, although this move did not garner the attention—or the funding—he had hoped. Eventually, he was able to secure the financial backing necessary to create his first feature-length production *She's Gotta Have It*, a comedy about a young black woman, Nola Darling, living in Brooklyn and entertaining the advances of three suitors. Nola finds herself attracted to each of the three men, and interested in the power and freedom of an unrestrained manner of dating, which has standardly been characterized as masculine. Nola's voice within the film is strong. Lee captures quite well the struggle women in general—and black women in particular—have when expressing their sexuality directly and when resisting the pressure to define their fulfillment in life through their romantic status. Nola's resistance to her suitors' attempts to make her commit to one of them represents a resistance against this pressure.

And there is much about this film that advocates a progressive view of women's sexuality. However, this progressive stance on a feminist view of female sexuality is undermined by Jamie's rape of Nola and her subsequent pursuit of Jamie. And—as feminist critical theorists like bell hooks have pointed out—Nola's person and experiences are not represented beyond her sexuality. This writing of Nola by Lee establishes a pattern of his characterizations of women. Quite often, Lee's strong and able women wind up in situations in which their power or agency is limited. Outspoken Tina—waiting for Mookie to be with her and care for their son, trapped in her mother's apartment—in *Do the Right Thing* and Sloan—diminished and unheard by both Delacroix and Manray—in *Bamboozled* are examples of this limitation. *Girl 6* would highlight an unlikely vision of a telephone sex worker who likes her job, a lot. This last reads more as a male fantasy of the woman on the other end of a telephone sex line than it does of the women who work these jobs in real life even though the parallels it draws to the experiences of women in Hollywood on the casting couch is one that is true enough.

She's Gotta Have It won the Prix de Jeunesse award at the Cannes Film Festival in 1986. This recognition would open the doors to studio backing and development for *School Daze*. Island Pictures, the distributor for *She's Gotta Have It,* was set to produce the film but wanted to limit Lee with a budget of $4 million dollars, in comparison with the $175,000 budget that Lee had used to make the previous film. That Lee was able to court an offer from Columbia Pictures with an open-ended budget was a testimony to the buzz that surrounded his early work. Lee intended to shoot the film—which takes place at the fictional historically black, Mission College—at his alma mater Morehouse, but early on in the production, the college withdrew their offer of use after Lee refused to show them a script for the film. The school executives had heard that *She's Gotta Have It* was risqué and feared what a similarly themed film might do to the reputation of black colleges. According to Lee, "They had heard that 'She's Gotta Have It' was a pornographic film.... We wanted to give a benefit screening (She's Gotta Have It) for Morehouse, but they turned it down."[1] Lee noticed within negotiations that Morehouse was slow to sign the agreement to shoot there, and decided to go ahead with shooting until Morehouse either signed the contract or kicked them off the property. They were kicked off three weeks after beginning. This incident was not the only rejection the film suffered. The United Negro College Fund canceled a benefit screening for *School Daze* as well. *School Daze* dealt with cultural divisions between the wannabes and the jigaboos that represented two groups of students, light-skinned blacks characterized as mimicking white behavior, dress, and attitudes versus the dark-skinned blacks characterized as maintaining a connection to what Lee refers to as Afro-American culture. Says Lee, "I can think that anybody can see that my allegiances are with the jigaboos, but I do not hate the wannabe faction. And I am sympathetic. I feel that they're naïve and they just don't know, but not one particular group is held up as heroes."[2] In addition, the film appears somewhat critical of the college with administrators who are inept. The film is confrontational. "I make confrontational films. They're supposed to do that.... My job as a filmmaker, I feel, is to present stuff, people don't even acknowledge that it exists. How are you even gonna make any moves to remedy it?"[3] Lee strives in all his films to get to the pulse of the issues he seeks to convey.

Perhaps nowhere is this more evident than within Lee's third feature film, *Do the Right Thing*. Considered to be one of the most important films of all time, and chosen by the National Film Preservation Board to be preserved as such, this film is arguably Lee's most masterful, and it definitely hits its target, painting a powerful portrait of the racial tensions of the late 1980s through its depiction of the relationships between neighbors living and working together on one block in Bed-Stuy. At the 25th anniversary screening of the film, Luis Ramos said to the *New Yorker*,

> ... There's a commonality about the black and Latino experience in New York in the eighties and nineties. I knew as much about Alabama by the time I was thirteen as I did Puerto Rico. And the same thing with Italian culture. You're forced to grow up with each other in New York City. And learn. And that's something that "Do the Right Thing" captures really well. You got your Puerto Ricans, Koreans, and blacks, and Italians, and we're all in this together—until we're not. And that's the legacy of "Do the Right Thing." We're all in this together, until we're not.[4]

Lee intertwines the lives in characters from a variety of socio-economic layers and documents nuanced interactions between ethnic groups. The neighborhood is populated primarily by black people and Puerto Ricans. The businesses are owned by the Korean couple and of course, Sal. However, Sal and his sons don't live on the block. Sal's son Pino—played by John Turturro—tries to persuade him to move the pizzeria into the neighborhood they live in, but Sal doesn't want to leave, citing the prevalence of pizzerias within their own neighborhood. On this block, they are a big fish in a small pond; a beloved neighborhood fixture. The one white gentleman who is shown to live on the block is a yuppie who has purchased a brownstone, and lives on the block but not within it, one almost feels that Lee is pointing to how Sal belongs to the neighborhood by contrasting him with this brownstone owner. There are two neighborhoods, one geographic and the other cultural.

The interactions between characters are fraught with subtext, easy and integrated in some aspects, but tenuous in others. Sal employs Mookie and is attracted to Mookie's younger sister, Jade, which Mookie doesn't like. Otherwise, Mookie has a genial relationship with Sal and a good friendship with Sal's younger son Vito. However, Pino, Sal's older son, is racist and openly resentful of Sal's friendly interactions with Mookie and Da Mayor and disturbed by his father's flirting with Jade. Jade berates Mookie for not taking greater care with his responsibilities to Tina—Mookie's girlfriend who is Puerto Rican—and his young son. Da Mayor oscillates between the groups of people negotiating the spaces between with amiable, if somewhat intoxicated, finesse. The closest he comes to anger is when the Korean fruit and vegetable market no longer carries Miller High Life. Even within his sharp-tongued back and forth with Mother Sister, he is beleagueredly affectionate. His weariness comes through, however, in his exchange with the teenagers who call him a drunk.

> What do you know 'bout me? Y'all can't even pee straight. What do you know? Until you have stood in the doorway and heard the hunger of your five children, unable to do a damn thing about it, you don't know shit. You don't know my pain, you don't know me. Don't call me a bum, don't call me a drunk, you don't know me, and it's disrespectful.[5]

Da Mayor cleans Sal's stoop, saves the young boy from getting hit by a car, saves Sal, Vito, and Pino from harm's way during the riot. He comforts Mother Sister after Radio Raheem is murdered. However, Da Mayor drinks from the burden of no escape for the neighborhood; he drinks from the things he has seen, and so he can keep on doing the right thing, despite the bitter circumstances. His statements about his children link him to Mookie. Da Mayor cleans the stoop for Sal, Mookie trashes it. Sal pays both of them for it. When Mookie heaves the trashcan through Sal's plate-glass window, he believes he is taking Da Mayor's advice, always do the right thing.

For his part, Sal looks at the pizzeria as his place; his legacy for his sons, built from his sweat. Buggin' Out sees the pizzeria as profitable because of the patronage of the black people of the neighborhood. He wants brothers on the walls. Buggin' Out views Sal's refusal to acquiesce to this request as a refusal to acknowledge how the business was built through the money of the neighborhood's black residents. This stance leads to Sal throwing him out of his place and Buggin' Out retaliates in anger. Boycott Sal's. Mookie plays like Da Mayor, trying to smooth things over but ultimately, by inciting the riot, does what he sees as the right thing, and Sal recognizes it, "You do what you gotta do." In this line, spoken in shock and in defeat, and later within his genuine anger at Mookie giving way to bluster the following morning in the aftermath of the riot, we see that Sal understands the neighborhood because he is part of the neighborhood. The police in this movie operate as a callous institutional machine dispensing brutality and indifference in place of justice. Sometimes they quell the tensions—as when they move along the white car owner whose car is flooded by the fire hydrant—and sometimes they fan the flames. The trashing of Sal's Pizzeria for Mookie is not about Sal, but about Radio Raheem, and about expressing anger and outrage in a way that honors his memory, and makes his voice heard. By naming the real-life victims of violence at the end of the film, Lee forces us to think more broadly about the circumstances for the reactions within the affected communities.

American protest through the destruction of property is as old as the first Tea Party in Boston. The genuine injustices endured by black Americans have been and continue to be so egregious that rising up makes sense. It is what our Founding Fathers did. Lee's film is so powerful not because it draws a clear line between black and white but because it does not. Lee presents archetypes and interrogates their easy read; forcing us to rethink our presuppositions and assumptions about how these types function. Lee critically engages race and demonstrates both its constructed tangibility and its inadequacies in describing how people relate within communities. The chasm between black and white and between property owner and renter is minutiae when held up under the light of Radio Raheem's unjust death. All of the neighbors who witness his death are rocked by its unfolding. It is not Buggin' Out—the character easily brought to the boiling point, who is itching for a fight within the film—who ultimately ignites the riot on that street that night. Reasonable, personable and well-liked Mookie begins it. Didactically, this choice proves that the decision to riot is reasonable and measured. Following the brutal killing—which escalates from an attempt to subdue Raheem to strangulation as quickly as the fight had unfolded in Sal's—the scuffle within the neighborhood, personal disagreements and tensions became a fraught symbol of greater conflicts. As Da Mayor rebukes the youth who would judge him without understanding where he comes from, Lee shows us where Mookie comes from, and why he does what he does, so we can see his actions not as a sound bite or a headline, but as the sane actions of a reasonable man who sees no other choice.

The events of that one day on that one block of Bed-Stuy unfold under a perfect storm of factors with plenty of shares in the blame to be handed around, as well as plenty of sympathy. We witness Sal working hard to build his business and his pride in his Italian heritage. We understand that Radio Raheem cares about his music solely and is equally angry at all who would tell him to turn it down or off. We see that Buggin' Out has a point, despite the fact that he is always bugging out. The things that offend him are not pulled out of thin air, but they are perhaps things better to not bug out about. Mookie is the man who does what he's got to do. He has to get paid. He has to go see his son. He has to throw a trashcan through the window of Sal's because that excessive force exercised upon the body of Radio Raheem by that cop, his adrenaline pumped, his partner cautioning him to stop, "That's enough!"; it undeniably crosses a line. Everyone who is there to bear witness recognizes it. The cop may not be a bad man, but he becomes a bad cop when he ceases to dispense justice and keep the peace because his presence of mind is not dispassionate enough to hear that he is killing the young man, or he does not care that he is killing the young man. In 1988, and in 1991, and in 2014, it is still true that the police deliver injustice onto the bodies of young black men. That it happens at all is a problem. That it happens so frequently is an anathema. To say that the American government seeks to limit the acts of resistance of its citizens is not an unreasonable claim. This task is the job of government, to provide order tempered with justice. But the order must be tempered with justice, otherwise wouldn't our founding fathers argue that in breaking their contract with us that citizens of the United States have a right to resist?

Drawing parallels between how colonists in the British colonies reacted if the body of a colonist were rendered lifeless by a British soldier in the 1770s seems not unreasonable. It speaks to the question of whether or not there remains a desire to limit the actions of black Americans' resistance by characterizing it as uncivilized. One need look no farther than the events that unfolded within the Boston Massacre, an exchange which many historians cite as the first skirmish of the American Revolution. On March 5, 1770, 4000 British soldiers occupied the city of Boston—which boasted approximately 15,000 inhabitants. The soldiers occupied the city to enforce the taxation which the citizens of Boston found to be unfair because they lacked representation in British Parliament. Tension between the British forces and the Boston citizens were palpable. On that evening, a group of merchant sailors, apprentices and laborers confronted the soldiers, harassing them and throwing snowballs and rocks. In the chaos, one soldier, Hugh Montgomery, accidentally discharged his weapon triggering the other soldiers to fire upon the crowd. After the dust cleared, five colonists were dead, and three injured, including Crispus Attucks, a black sailor popularly considered the first martyr of the American Revolution. Paul Revere created an engraving of the incident that became one of the most famous pieces of propaganda for the war. The engraving is an emotional representation of the event rather than a factual one, intended to stir up anti–British sentiment. Revere depicted the British Army standing forward aggressively, formed in a line as if in battle. The working class people which made up the crowd are depicted clothed in finery, in an effort to hide their class. Crispus Attucks was depicted in most printings of the engraving as white, in order to produce broader sympathy to the cause across all the colonies. The story is often talked about in relationship to the defense of the soldiers undertaken by John Adams, a patriot and future president who defended them in order to uphold the value of a fair trial. The verdict of that trial, which found Captain Thomas Preston and the majority of his men not guilty, also found two of the soldiers, Montgomery and Matthew Kilroy, guilty of manslaughter. What this situation demonstrates is, first, that retelling of circumstances are often manipulated to serve the goals of those who are looking to form public perception of the events, and that the truth is often muddier than it is presented to be. Second, the narrative of rebellion in American history is framed as acceptable only within certain circumstances. How we can exercise our rights to defend liberty is highly dependent upon who we are and what social capital we possess. Poverty and race influence how the general American public perceive the resistant actions of its citizens, and what responses they feel compelled to undertake. For example, the first comprehensive Slave Code in the colonies was the Virginia Slave Code of 1705, which arose after the events of Bacon's Rebellion proved the effectiveness of the organization of black and white forces against the British government. These codes became the model for the codes of other states that were to follow, eliminating any differentiation between black indentured servants who were supposed to earn their freedom after a certain length of service and slaves, separating court systems, making it illegal for blacks to bear arms, and making it legal for masters to kill their slaves in disciplining them. Stating,

> All servants imported and brought into the country ... who were not Christian in their native country ... shall be accounted and be slaves. All Negro, mulatto and Indian slaves within this dominion ... shall be held as real estate. If any slave resist his master ... correcting such slave, and shall happen to be killed in such correction ... the master shall be free of all punishment ... as if such accident never happened.[6]

In addition, slaves had to ask permission to leave the plantation. If caught associating with whites, they could be maimed or whipped. These laws remained in effect until the 1850s. Following the emancipation and the Civil War, in 1874, the first of the Jim Crow laws took effect and remained in large part the law of the land until the Civil Rights legislation was enacted in the 1960s.

Means that were deemed as available and accessible to well-educated white men are considered by most to be the mark of savagery when employed by black Americans throughout our country's history. In an editorial in *The Crisis*, W. E. B. Du Bois advocated for black resistance following the Chicago race riots of 1919, saying,

> For three centuries we have suffered and cowered. No race ever gave Passive Resistance and Submission to Evil longer, more piteous trial. Today we raise the terrible weapon of Self-Defense. When the murderer comes, he shall no longer strike us in the back. When the armed lynchers gather, we too must gather armed. When the mob moves, we propose to meet it with bricks and clubs and guns ... whether the line between just resistance is hard or easy, we must draw it carefully, not in wild resentment, but in grim and sober consideration.[7]

Thus are the actions of Mookie in the film. Lee plays the role of Mookie to identify for us where his sympathies lie. Lee is not merely calling for resistance; he is unpacking the reasoning of resistance. To achieve this goal, he puts all of the film's representations work overtime. Lee packs within films as much content as they can hold. The famous dance sequence at the beginning of *Do the Right Thing*—whose music featured Public Enemy's "Fight the Power," the same group and song that dominated Radio Raheem's boombox—shows Rosie Perez in her movie debut. Perez was known as the girl from Soul Train, where she was a regular performer. The opening sequence of *Bye Bye Birdie* inspired the dance. In Bosley Crowther's *New York Times* movie review, he writes that *Bye Bye Birdie* "is supposed to be about American kids."[8] That musical—which references 1950s and 1960s dance culture, and rock'n'roll, sending up personalities like Ed Sullivan—connects very well to the focus of Lee's film and its emphasis on the American youth culture of a different decade.

Lee's choices are consistently smart and loaded. *Jungle Fever* is another example of this. This story is a modern-day updating of Micheaux's explo-

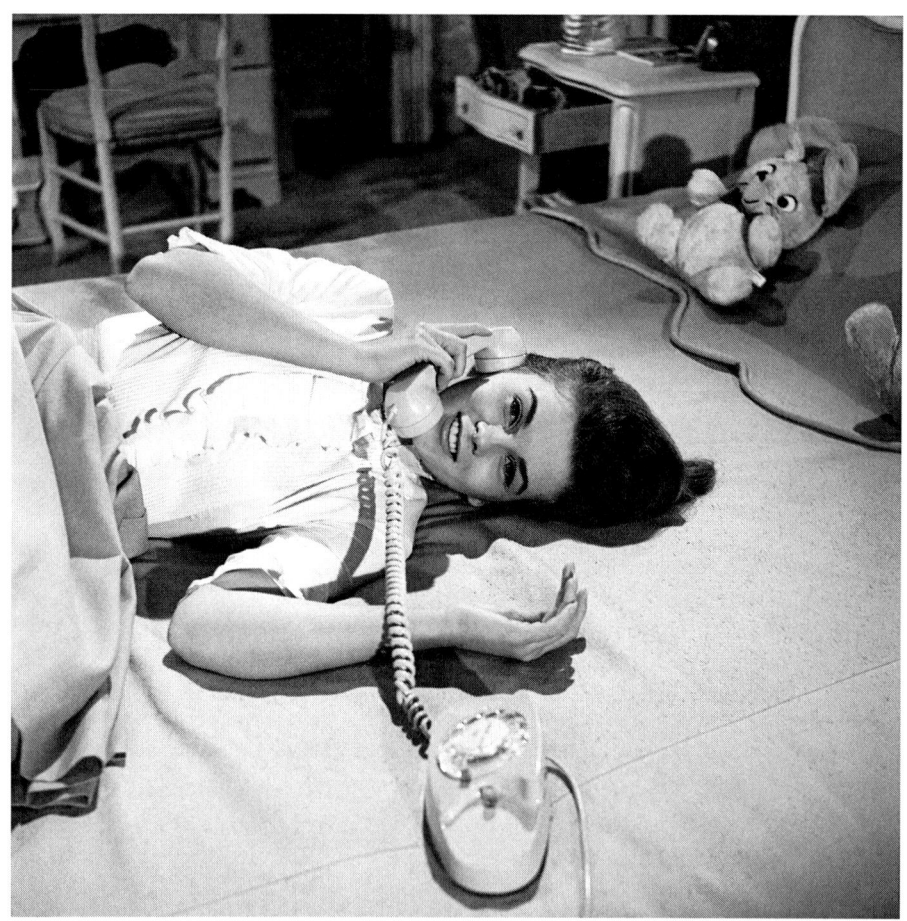

Ann-Margret as Kim McAfee in George Sydney's *Bye Bye Birdie* (1963).

rations of interracial coupling. The plot arc is: married black male architect has a sexy white secretary and cheats on his light-skinned black wife. Lee uses this plot to unpack the series of myths that surround black men and hite women in relationship to miscegenation. The first of these myths is the black male as powerfully sexual and the white woman as ideally beautiful. Other characters within the film suggest that Flipper Purify—played by Wesley Snipes—is specifically attracted to Angie Tucci for her whiteness. Angela represents to him, a level of achievement unavailable to unsuccessful black men. Their relationship serves as a marker for his professional prowess. In Flipper's conversations about the affair with his friend Cyrus—played by Lee—it is evident that he knows that her whiteness is an issue, and the implication of their talk is that it would not be a big deal if this affair was with a black woman. Flipper's wife Drew believes that he selected her as a bride because she was light skinned. She implies in conversation within the film that she was worried what this meant at the time, but she ignored it.

Angie wants Flipper because he is black. To her, an affair with Flipper represents rebellion and passion, a very different relationship than the traditional courtship she has with Paulie. When she breaks off their engagement, Angie says that she wants something more than their neighborhood. She wants to get out. Angie doesn't recognize that Paulie also holds this desire and wants to pursue a city college degree. Paulie also holds more progressive political views than the other guys that hang around inside the shop. Angie sees these qualities as inherent within Flipper because his body and ethnicity are foreign to her. She looks at the surface rather than the soul. When this mismatched couple stands alone, then the excitement of their choice to pursue an interracial relationship wanes. Flipper and Angie—isolated from their communities—realize that they have no common ground to build upon.

The most affecting scene within the film is the conversation between Drew and her friends about the relations between black men and black women. Lee asked the actresses to speak freely and candidly about the topic through their own viewpoints, with a little supplementary guidance from Lee based on the direction of the film. Because the dialogue is for the large part improvised, the scene reads as natural and heartfelt. Paraphrasing: "Good black men are hard to find, and harder to keep. Away from White women, who are out to do what they can to get themselves a good black man. But no one is looking or thinking about working class black men who drive buses or collect garbage or deliver mail. The best solution is to date any man of any color that is kind and loves me. The best solution is to date within the race but not worry about what kind of jobs or education they might have. Black men do not want women who are smarter or earn more though."[9] It's an amazing scene in a movie that presupposes quite a bit but addresses again issues pulled from within the context of the times.

As in *Malcolm X*, *Do the Right Thing*, and *Bamboozled*, Lee uses the film's opening to give us a clue to the overall content. Stevie Wonder tells us that he's got *Jungle Fever* and Lee focuses on an image of Yusuf K. Hawkins who was shot after being mistakenly identified as the lover of an Italian girl with a reputation for dating black men. The murder occurred within the Bensonhurst section of Brooklyn where Angie lives within the film. Thus, Lee identifies the correlation between his film and these real-life events. This theme of miscegenation—as well as the rumor of its possibility—are part of a historical trajectory of fear that reaches backward towards the past that birthed *Birth of a Nation*. This trajectory is loaded with the very real consequences for black men resulting in excessive and violent reactions by racist whites, like Hawkins' murder; like the disfiguring beating and lynching murder of Emmett Till, the 14-year-old black boy who may or may not have flirted with a white woman. So while, as in Micheaux's *Homesteader*, the presentation of an interracial romance within *Jungle Fever* chips away at the taboo—and we see and condemn the reactions of those that surround the couple as racist or perhaps at best, problematic, but not unexamined—Lee also presents the context which frames these reactions. Both of these individuals betray their communities and families through the breaking of vows and promises. Lee doesn't allow this movie to be a simple declarative, "Love conquers all."[10] Because, importantly, this romance isn't love. The chemistry between Flipper and Angie onscreen is not strong. This choice seems purposeful. Lee doesn't want us to believe in their romance. He wants to show us how things break down within communities when people choose their partners based on solely the Otherness of the partner instead of the commonality; a bit of an anti-Romeo and Juliet. This romance is no West Side Story. This film cements Lee's reputation as filmmaker who pushes the limits of our ways of talking and thinking about race. It demonstrates a need for all of the things that we think and feel about race to be brought into the light and examined.

The release of *Malcolm X* in 1992 was the climax of this early racially loaded filmmaking practice Lee engaged in, both through its controversial opening and controversial subject. It was Lee's first historical epic, and the film was broad and affecting, painting a portrait of Malcolm X that was both smoldering with its intensity and optimistic in its portrayal of a vision of inclusion at the films ending which demonstrated a different understanding of Malcolm X's worldview than what is sometimes popularly characterized.

The film for Lee represented a labor of love. *X* also was mired with difficulty in its making. Lee had trouble securing the necessary financial backing, turning to friends within the black community to make up the shortfall. Lee's version of Malcolm X's Harlem Rally speech contained the vignette, which Lee would reference within *Bamboozled*'s characterization of Denzel Washington as an actor who would not blacken up for the camera. Obama would

Top: Spike Lee as Shorty (left) and Denzel Washington as Malcolm X in Lee's *Malcolm X* (1992). *Bottom:* Denzel Washington as Malcolm X in Spike Lee's *Malcolm X* (1992). Harlem Rally Scene.

quote the film when addressing rumors of his agreement with the Rev. Jeremiah Wright in his presidential campaign of 2008.

Several vignettes of life in New York City followed. Crooklyn was a semi-autobiographical film Lee co-wrote with his sisters, an homage to the Brooklyn Lee remembered from his youth. Summer of Sam painted a very different portrait of a New York gripped by heat and fear during the summer when the serial killer Son of Sam walked the streets and what was different seemed frightening in its difference. In 2002, Lee released the *25th Hour*, which starred Edward Norton as a man about to go to prison. The film spotlighted his final hours as a free man, focusing on how he spent his time. This film contained the famous monologue rant that painted a vivid picture of life in New York City in 2001 and its varied inhabitants. No one was safe from the raging ire of Montgomery Brogan. But what begins as the worst thoughts that New Yorkers have about each other narrows in on the personal as Brogan critiques his friends and family then finally himself.

> From the row-houses of Astoria to the penthouses on Park Avenue, from the projects in the Bronx to the lofts in Soho. From the tenements in Alphabet City to the brownstones in Park Slope to the split-levels in Staten Island. Let an earthquake crumble it, let the fires rage, let it burn to fucking ash and then let the waters rise and submerge this whole rat-infested place. [pause] No. No, fuck you, Montgomery Brogan. You had it all, and you threw it away, you dumb fuck!¹¹

This rant, in the end, is Lee's tribute to the city, and his acknowledgment of its faults in the wake of the events of 9/11. For in Lee's films, New York is a character, not just a backdrop. The comparisons that many have made between Lee and Woody Allen in this respect may be true, both directors understand their New York. But there is something in Lee's films that moves beyond narcissistic self-portraiture and love of home. The greatest of Lee's films showcase a complex understanding of this place, New York, in its quintessential Americanness; pointing to a love and hate of the country; opening up the can of the optic whiteness of it all to demonstrate the drops of color. Lee holds up for display the messiness of an America not as a melting pot, but a lasagna—not thoroughly integrated but one—impossible to extricate the parts from the whole.

Edward Norton as Monty Brogan in Spike Lee's *25th Hour* (2002).

The best of his films demonstrate his political sensibilities and provide an outlet for his voice as a seething angry visionary.

Nowhere does this seething vision display itself more prominently than within *Bamboozled*. It is within this masterpiece that Lee conveys to the world the standard of responsibility that he holds for the rest of his films; according to Du Bois' program of uplift for the race. "Don't these artists have responsibility for what they do?"[12] For Lee is angered by the forgetting of history, the continuing buffoonery, and thoughtless image making, though not necessarily negative depictions of black people. He is mad as hell, and he's not going to take it anymore.

6
The Problem of the Color Line

What's wrong with some color in your family tree?
—Public Enemy, *Fear of a Black Planet*

W. E. B. Du Bois argued passionately for the higher education of talented black people as a primary means of uplift in his important book, *The Souls of Black Folk* (1903). The popularity of this text would propel him to the forefront of the civil rights movement for black Americans in the first half of the twentieth century. In 1905, he would co-found the Niagara Movement. The Niagara Movement was a civil rights organization formed from people who could be members of the Talented Tenth; teachers, clergy, and business owners, mostly men, but a few women as well. The organization formed in part as a reaction to the general policies of Booker T. Washington and other like-minded reformers. Du Bois and the other members of the Niagara Movement strove unequivocally for equal rights, a stance which set them apart from other organizations at that time, many of which supported a wait and see attitude that heavily relied on programs of compromise, or accommodation. This organization met annually until 1908. In August of that year, race riots erupted in Springfield, Il; the hometown of Abraham Lincoln. The events of that riot would undermine the efficacy of the Niagara Movement's platform, making it clear stronger methods were needed. Springfield combusted within burning racial tension; exploding into violence resulting from white fear. The riots began with the transfer of a black prisoner who had been accused of rape. The charges against the man eventually were withdrawn—considered by many historians to have been false accusations—but the incident left tragedy in its wake. The rioters burned homes of a host of innocent black families, looted stores and businesses, shot several bystanders, and lynched two older black men, Scott Burton and William Donnigan. Donnigan's death was doubly symbolic for the crowd. First, he had lived in Springfield since he was 17 years old, building a substantial cobbling business as a shoemaker, and then eventually amassing significant wealth through the purchase of real estate. The mob likely felt resentment at his successes. In addition, Donnigan had married a white woman who was 30 years his junior. This fact played into the fears of miscegenation that had propelled the crowd to violence in the first place. These events clearly demonstrated that racist attitudes were not only a problem within the American South but within the North as well.

The members of the Niagara Movement felt that a stronger platform with an interracial coalition was needed to usher in change. William English Whiting wrote in his affecting article *The Race War in the North*, "Yet who realizes the seriousness of the situation, and what large and powerful body of citizens is ready to come to their aid?"[1] Du Bois and a coalition of prominent black and white civil rights advocates of the day formed the National Association for the Advancement of Colored People, or NAACP; answering this call.

During his tenure within this institution, Du Bois served as a vocal editor for *The Crisis*—the NAACP's journal publication—and a leader of the political arm of the organization; working hard through both propaganda and advocacy to pass legislation that would make lynching illegal. Over this time period, Du Bois struggled to rally support for events like the Pan-African Conference, a forum for black leadership to discuss problems of black people worldwide. Du Bois intended that the Pan-African Conference would serve as a coalition exerting influence upon world leaders through its strength in numbers, but very few showed up to the meetings. Du Bois became further frustrated by the apparent success of the more radical reformer Marcus Garvey in coalescing support for his pageants and endeavors. Du Bois publicly condemned Garvey's extreme separatist strategies as wrong-headed, and insulted the man himself, whom Du Bois greatly disliked. Du Bois wrote that Garvey was "inordinately vain and egotistic, jealous of his power, impatient of details, a poor judge of human nature, and had the common weakness of untrained devotees that no dependence could be put on his statements of fact."[2] Du Bois felt resentful of Garvey's critique of black American leaders like Washington and Frederick Douglass. He viewed Garvey as ignorant in his presumptions about the issue of the American color line which Du Bois believed had a particular character and history that Garvey eschewed. He did however begrudgingly admit that Garvey was a great orator—something Ellison would echo within *Invisible Man*—and over time Du Bois' own ideas would reflect touches of the doctrines he rejected from both Garvey and Washington.

Following his first visit to Africa, Du Bois increasingly viewed black American experiences as linked to the growing crises experienced by many people of the black diaspora and on the African continent as a direct result of colonial rule. Ultimately, these influences caused Du Bois to change his mind about the path towards integration and supporting black capitalism. That his position was changing over time became increasingly clear. The writings from his early tenure with the NAACP exercise a faith in the ability of white and black Americans alike to view their fate as intertwined. According to Du Bois in 1911, "Hope for the future lies in the perception by the intelligent American laborer of his common industrial cause with the Negro, in the physical virility, hard work, and dogged determination of the American Negro, as well as in the sympathetic attitude of the better class of Americans."[3]

And yet, passages like this highlight Du Bois' Marxist views as well, citing these later developments as part of a greater trajectory. Du Bois expressed growing disillusionment, as many of his own educational and political platforms failed to result in more rapid tangible change for his black American fellows. He would travel to Russia in 1927 and study the Russian Revolution; becoming inspired by the socialist notion of a classless society as a better model towards integration. After reaching a critical mass in his relationship with the NAACP in 1934, Du Bois would leave the organization rather than attempt to reform the board which he now strongly felt should be under entirely black leadership. He instead advocated independently for black Nationalism with Marxist leanings, conceding in a speech in 1948, "Karl Marx stressed the fact that not merely the upper class but the mass of men were the real people of the world."[4] Du Bois clashed with other leaders within the NAACP over the best way to advocate for Civil Rights, and what the direction for black citizens of the country should look like, ideally. His reading of Marx affirmed the role of black men as proletariats, exploited workers. Where initially he found this identification as a worker to be a commonality between black and white laborers, Du Bois would eventually perceive that persuading white laborers to invest in the concept of equality was folly; so greatly pitted were these groups against each other in American historical rhetoric. Du Bois came to view the efforts of a standard model of integration as futile because of the underlying economic impetus of the disenfranchisement of the black citizenry.

After leaving the NAACP, Du Bois taught for the second time at Atlanta University and wrote two books during this period, one of which would be his masterwork of history and research, *Black Reconstruction in America*. In it, Du Bois would plainly state, "One fact and one alone explains the attitude of most recent writers toward Reconstruction; they cannot conceive Negroes as men."[5] The difference between this viewpoint and the one expressed in 1911 directs the reader to a clear shift in Du Bois' worldview away from the hope of reconciliation between white and black laborers in America, and the sympathetic attitudes of some, towards a more cynical view of what could realistically be implemented. Still, Du Bois turned to a platform of education, attempting to right the mis-remembrances and mischaracterizations that created the rift between history and truth.

In the book, Du Bois wrote about the gross inaccuracies inherent within most United States History textbooks published at the time of its writing. *Black Reconstruction*, a treatise of over 700 pages, painstakingly reviewed the history leading up to and the role of black Americans during the period of Reconstruction which followed the Civil War. For Du Bois, black contribution to the building of the United States of America as a country and as an economic force and resource were crucial. The project of whiteness and whitecentric U.S. History as a discipline undermined black history and black significance isolating it from the greater narrative. Unsung heroes and heroines remained heretofore unknown and hidden from student audiences, white and black alike. As Lee would do a half-century later, Du Bois held education up as a necessary precursor to equality.

Du Bois was in a unique position to argue for this platform. He was the first black American to receive a Ph.D. in history from Harvard. Du Bois revolutionized the discipline of history, as well as transforming American sociology. He organized reforming groups to undo the damage caused by the historical misrepresentation of black Americans by generations of white cultural producers. In his writing and in his public conduct, Du Bois combatted white efforts to maintain an economic order in which black bodies did work but received no credit for their labor. Ironically, Du Bois—the first major American empirical sociologist to publish a substantial work in 1899's *The Philadelphia Negro*—would remain unrecognized by his field for that accomplishment. Instead, that honor would be long ascribed to W.I. Thomas and Florian Znaniecki's 1918 work *The Polish Peasant in Europe and America*. Perhaps this painstakingly slow journey of progress and Du Bois' long-held belief in art as a champion of truth brought him to the point of writing the same story contained within *Black Reconstruction* as a work of fiction.

The Black Flame Trilogy is a trio of novels that draws upon historical fact to create a fictional narrative, which unpacks the experience of blackness in America beginning with the Reconstruction. The Mansart family is headed by Manuel and contains members who symbolically stand in for different types and/or figures in American history. Brent Edwards has argued that the types contained within the text reflect the differing aspects of Du Bois' personality. This assertion is likely true but does not negate their historical association. Manuel is an educated man and a teacher. The character types that surround him demonstrate the historical difficulties black people have encountered and the strategies that have been employed as people—black and white—attempt to deal with the problem of the color line. As Du Bois writes within the postscript, "I am trying by the method of historical fiction to complete the cycle of history which has for a half-century engaged my thought, research, and action."[6] So, at the end of his life, Du Bois undertook a project of fiction as his final means to secure the audience for ideas he had presented in a straightforward manner through critical engagement and debate. Here, Du Bois continues his project in a way that brings the Truth as he understands it through a side door; one perhaps less vigilantly guarded. Not covertly—he very explicitly states his intent—but in a way which heightens sympathy for his ideas.

This first novel of the trilogy was published in 1959, seven years after the publication of Ellison's *Invisible Man*. It seems likely that Du Bois encountered the Ellison work, especially given the form *The Black Flame* takes, following so quickly on the heels of *Black Reconstruction* and undoubtedly noting the success of Ellison's seminal work. It is likely as well that Du Bois saw the allusions that Ellison made within the work to double-consciousness through the form of invisibility and the narrator's awareness of his own invisibility. Whether this connection is a direct correlation or not, is not necessarily important for the purposes of establishing a greater understanding of both of these projects' relationship to *Bamboozled*. The influence of both these texts is clearly felt in Lee's narrative. The theoretical bent of the film is decidedly Du Bosian. As discussed in Chapter 3, Ellison uses allusion but is hesitant to draw one to one comparisons between characters in *Invisible Man* and historical figures, despite the connections that seem obvious to readers. Du Bois, on the other hand, is intentionally connecting the dots. His project is specifically historical in its premise. As Lee in *Bamboozled* creates the voice for his historical narrative through Jada Pinkett Smith's Sloan Hopkins, Du Bois inserts himself into his narrative through the most progressive character in the novel, Jean Du Bignon. As he wrote, "But Jean Du Bignon was in some ways different or at least seemed so. In spite of her comeliness, she was not beautiful, and her total impression was not of sex but sense."[7] Du Bignon's name is French and reflects the form of Du Bois own. She teaches Mansart how to be a leader in the novel, just as Sloan attempts to do with Manray. In the character of Jean Du Bignon, we find Du Bois within his narrative, and through the connection find Lee—and Du Bois—within *Bamboozled*. For, Sloan represents the project of history. *Bamboozled* and *The Black Flame Trilogy* both specifically employ direct character types that represent and present history. This practice demonstrates the connection between these two endeavors and broadens the evidence of Du Bois' influence on the film. Lee marks their project as the same. In the process, he opens the film up to a broader discourse.

7
Bamboozled's Reception

> Get on the Bus, Summer of Sam, Bamboozled *are all easily slotted (and forgotten), as big-budget agit-pop-movies regularly praised by* The New York Times *assuredly don't agitate anyone.*—Armond White, *Cineaste*
>
> *I think it is very important that films make people look at what they've forgotten.*—Spike Lee

On October 10, 2000, four days after *Bamboozled*'s theatrical release, Armond White published a scathing review entitled, "More Trash from Spike Lee." In it, White dismissed Lee, framing him as a man who didn't understand the material he satirized. "Lee's scattershot approach, and his confusion about the meaning of blackface routines and blackface metaphors, make no advance."[1]

White pointed to what he viewed as Lee's own participation in and complicity with the industry that churns out the stereotypes condemned within the film, citing Lee as arguably the most prolific purveyor of these negative types. "…you could make a strong argument that no single mediamaker[sic] in the past decade has fostered more black stereotypes than Lee."[2] White castigated Lee with cutting, personal language. According to White, Lee was behind the times, exploitative, confounding, a Puddin'head.[3] White did not really review *Bamboozled* the film but, rather, critiqued Lee the man, his cultural capital and his right to speak out on race and racial stereotypes in the media. White took Lee to task for invoking blackface at all and for equating contemporary forms like low-brow television and sketch comedy with minstrelsy, despite their direct descent from vaudevillian sensibilities. As in the negative responses to Michael Ray Charles and Kara Walker, overall, White deflected his response from a direct engagement of the work to a critique of the author.

At first glance, White's piece is typical of most reviews of *Bamboozled* contemporary to its theatrical release. Both positive and negative reviewers cite Lee as scathing but miscalculating. For instance, *Rolling Stone*'s Peter Travers gave the movie four stars, but still called it "a frustratingly uneven satire" albeit "with undeniably sharp teeth." Roger Ebert argued that Lee missed his mark by invoking blackface and minstrelsy, stating that he should have satirized the television programming that bothered him more directly to be effective. White agreed with this point, writing, "If he had an honest or up-to-date approach to the problem of self-abasement and media corruption—if Lee simply knew the frustration of trying to get a project approved—he wouldn't resort to the age-old calumny of actual blackface routines and minstrel shows."[4] White implies here that Lee's invocation deceives the viewer. That the use of blackface within the film is lazy and uninformed and that Lee's success prevents him from viewing those he critiques with clarity. However, White's statement is inaccurate in several ways.

First, Lee's approach—mining historical imagery—mirrors that of his Post black contemporaries. The inclusion of Michael Ray Charles' work within the film demonstrates Lee's purposefulness in making that connection. Kara Walker's first show was in 1994, a mere six years prior to *Bamboozled*'s release. Lee's approach definitely has a connection to the past, but it rises from contemporary practices and methodology.

Second, Manray and Womack—the principal characters who wear blackface in *Bamboozled*—are arguably its most sympathetic characters and the ones who behave the most ethically. Manray and Womack stand in for black performers who enact self-abasement out of desperation for work and/or lack of opportunity. White calls out Lee for misusing and debasing Savion Glover by casting him as Manray and flattens Lee's treatment of him in the film. White begins with the unacceptability of blackface, disallowing any difference of use while simultaneously criticizing Lee for limited portrayals of blackness. White wants Lee to create a different discourse than the one *Bamboozled* has started rather than evaluate what work *Bamboozled* does. White ironically performs a debasement of Glover in saying that his role in the film only operates as such, in a similar flattening to that of Bert Williams' performances by generations of blacks that sought to distance themselves from the burnt cork. Lee doesn't truly debase Glover within the film; he frames him very sympathetically.

Third, Lee has had notorious difficulty getting many of his films funded. Both *Do the Right Thing* and *Malcolm X* required extraordinary measures to secure funding. Paramount's support for the *Do the Right Thing* faltered because of the explosive content. According to Lee's diary from the period, the company became concerned about how viewers might react to the film particularly the final scene in which neighborhood residents level Sal's Pizzeria in response to the unjust murder of Radio Raheem at the hands of police. "How would audiences feel leaving the theater? Will blacks want to go on a rampage? Will whites feel uncomfortable?"[5] Eventually, Universal Pictures stepped in, talking Lee down from a $10,000,000 budget to a mere $6,500,000 in exchange for their promise not to interfere. And Lee was forced to turn to prominent black celebrities for funding on *Malcolm X* after the bond company underwriting the film refused to write the necessary checks to complete filming after the picture went over budget. According to Lee, "When we began the film, we never had the amount of money we needed"[6] More recently, the local government threatened to rescind tax breaks for Lee when *Chi-raq's* title was revealed, claiming it would do damage to Chicago's reputation.

Bamboozled was no exception. According to his interview with Charlie Rose, Lee approached more than ten studios before New Line agreed to take *Bamboozled* on.[7] Travers notes that the $10,000,000 budget was the limit of what he was able to secure for the project.[8] Given the positive critical response many of Lee's films have garnered—an average of 71 percent for rated films on Rotten Tomatoes—the level of difficulty he encountered securing financing should be surprising. As *New York Times'* Thomas Chatterton Williams puts it, "In 31 years, Lee has achieved a rate of productivity that is rivaled in America only by Woody Allen. His body of work is prodigious: 22 feature movies,[9] of which at least three are absolutely first-rate; a half-dozen more are flawed classics, and all of them are at least sporadically brilliant, artistically daring and always intellectually ambitious."[10] Williams' comparison to Allen is a fruitful contrast for demonstrating the independence and risk inherent within Lee's work ethic, which belies White's statement that Lee's status as an auteur is tested by his financing. Both Lee and Allen have produced films at a rate of around at least one per year. However, while Lee is renowned as unrelenting in pursuing his personal vision despite all obstacles, Allen has established quite a different reputation. When recounting the last several decades of Allen's career, Christopher Orr noted in "The Remarkably Lazy Woody Allen,"

> Allen's moviemaking technique is something more akin to an assembly line. From beginning to end, the enterprise is designed to maximize efficiency, all but inevitably at the cost of quality. Screenwriting, casting, shooting—at almost every stage of the process, Allen performs, to judge from [biographer Eric] Lax's account, a fraction of the labor customarily expected of a director.[11]

Orr goes on to describe Allen's process securing funding with a few lines scrawled on paper. Major studio distribution without any input from the same, a carte blanche. Despite his declining quality of work, Allen coasts on the reputation of films he made a generation ago, while Lee continues to make challenging films that are difficult to fund. Lee uses the capital of his reputation to make films that widen the marketplace for other black filmmakers and hires and promotes black talent in the process. If Lee secures funding that rivals other directors financial security while maintaining his own voice, that's part of the end goal.

Yet, White asserts that Lee hasn't been an independent filmmaker since

1986—after Columbia Pictures produced School Daze in 1988—using this fact as proof for Lee's improper positionality without detailing why it prevents Lee from lofting a critique. His argument is very similar to the one launched by Jerome Christensen, who took issue with Lee's Mars Blackmon ads for Air Jordans. Christensen sought for Lee to make films without corporate influence, referring to the product placement within *Do the Right Thing* as "product fetishism."[12] Andrew Dewaard points out within "Joints and Jams" in *The Spike Lee Reader* that completely dismissing Lee's films because of their funding is a problematic tactic in part because of the pragmatic need for the funding. "In a highly commercial industry, Lee not only uses commercial means for his own building an impressive career out of his many various forms of 'joints,' he criticizes and reappropriates this very same commercialism, at times 'jamming' the system from within."[13] In Dewaard's conclusion, he notes that the lines between the big studios and independents are not as hard as they might seem, which makes defining what is independent trickier.

Independence in film is somewhat malleable. The strictest understanding of the term—any film made without money from a major studio—isn't adhered to, as critics like Dewaard often use it to mark the work of auteurs. This perspective emphasizes the rift between the way independent films are envisioned and the way big studio films are created. A big studio film holds box office earnings as the largest consideration. Independent films are invested in giving voice to unique points of view. Generally, these two objectives do not coincide. However, following the wave of successful independents in the 1990s, the big studios saw financial opportunity within the independent model and created their own brands that mimicked the selection process and budgets of smaller studios, expanding the type of movies that were getting made within their walls. In addition, many independents—while operating as separate entities—reached distribution agreements with major studios.

New Line itself is a member of the Independent Film & Television Alliance and was at it's start an independent studio who built its cult reputation through films like John Water's *Polyester* and *Nightmare on Elm Street*. Although New Line is now a division of Warner Brothers, even after its initial acquisition by Turner Broadcasting it operated as a separate entity, albeit with slightly deeper pockets. Several independent film companies of the 1990s shared this fate, Miramax operated in this way under Disney. So while White is technically correct, he's using the term in a way that implies Lee's projects receive strong favor from major studios and that his success and productivity necessarily preclude him from understanding the roadblocks most black filmmakers experience trying to get a project made. While it is definitely reasonable to state that Lee has an easier time getting his projects made than many relatively unknown black directors, it isn't necessarily the same thing as saying that Lee hasn't experienced the frustration of trying to get a project approved. Given his critical reputation, Lee should not have the level of difficulty he does. In part, he experiences that level of difficulty because he chooses to make projects like *Bamboozled*. Lee stubbornly remains the angriest auteur.[14] This stance is arguably what makes him an independent filmmaker. Like all of Lee's films, *Bamboozled* was made with an independent mindset, which is perhaps more important than the money trail. According to cultural anthropologist Sherry Ortner:

> [One] promise of anthropology has been to serve as a form of cultural critique for ourselves. In using portraits of other cultural patterns to reflect self-critically on our own ways, anthropology disrupts common sense and makes us reexamine our taken-for-granted assumptions.... It is not a stretch to transpose this idea to the world of independent film, which often uses many of the same de-familiarizing strategies of anthropology and ethnography to "disrupt common sense and make us reexamine our taken-for-granted assumptions." Specifically, many independent films embrace a kind of harsh realism, making films that display the dark realities of contemporary life, and that make demands on the viewer to viscerally experience and come to grips with those realities.[15]

Ortner's definition supports defining this film—if not Lee's body of work—as independent, regardless of the financing. White's dismissal of Lee's authority to speak prevents his serious consideration of Lee's arguments within the film. It is possible that White formulated these arguments in order to avoid addressing in depth the work blackface does within *Bamboozled*. The evidence for this claim is found within two passages of White's review that set *Bamboozled* within the historical framework of black culture in New York in the 1980s. This framework is indeed crucial for unpacking *Bamboozled*, but White makes use of it disingenuously. White's review provides the framing for Lee's arguments as an aside and does not unpack the framework's impact on the vision of the film, nor its impact on White's review. According to White, the root of those arguments lies within a critical disagreement about the arts in New York during the time Lee's star was on the rise:

> Lee's willingness to disparage anything black celebrities do grew out
>
> of the license and arrogance of a group of New York–based black writers and performers newly acquired during hiphop's advent. (Remember those 80s *Village Voice* pieces discrediting Michael Jackson, Wynton Marsalis, then celebrating Lee?)[16]

For White, *Bamboozled* is a politically positioned documentation of an argument long solved.

> Though contemporary, *Bamboozled* relies on an ossified form of Afrocentricity. It goes back to late–80s skepticism about black celebrity and showbiz ascension. Black Urban Professionalism is critiqued (hell, it's exercised about) as if it were an unprecedented social phenomenon. Because we're past all that now, *Bamboozled* at first feels confounding.[17]

These passages point to an important distinction between White's review and the reviews of other popular critics. White views *Bamboozled*'s argument as framed within a completed political discourse, advocating a view he already disagrees with. Thus, the more personal and less critical review. These review passages are shorthand for an existing conversation that has been and is still ongoing, not closed as White would have readers believe. This argument stems from similar conversations that surrounded Post black art with regard to how identity is discussed and framed. White is pointing towards black respectability politics and presenting Lee as someone who expects a certain vision of blackness. But he never pins down firmly how *Bamboozled* operates to advance any particular vision of blackness, nor does he define the vision of blackness that he claims *Bamboozled* asserts. White implies instead that Lee himself is that vision and in the course of personalizing the critique, White performs the same injustices against Lee he says are inherent within *Bamboozled*. He reduces Lee to a type. White glosses over how *Bamboozled* functions, insisting it does not. So while White's review astutely identifies the scope of Lee's discourse and Lee as an historical actor in the conversation, it is less than transparent in marking White himself as the same.

Many arguments with similar premises to White's reviews critique *Bamboozled* outside of that historical conversation. For example, Ebert's review mischaracterized Lee as underestimating the power of blackface as a symbol, comparing him to Ted Danson and Whoopi Goldberg. Ebert viewed Lee as having misread the audience's ability to get past blackface's predominant meaning. In a generalized way, Ebert's view of blackface is nonfunctional. Therefore, for Ebert, all uses of blackface result in the same outcome—a shutting down of receptivity—and can be compared in their folly.

On the other hand, White receives a specific message and applies it to a specific grievance. White cited references in Village Voice articles about music in the 1980s that belittled a certain style of blackness and similar articles that elevated Lee's stature in the arts. For White, *Bamboozled*'s arguments prop Lee up as a cultural icon at the expense of other black entertainers. This misperception stems from a culture war that has generations of iterations beginning with the debate between Booker T. Washington and W. E. B. Du Bois and continuing in the sparring of Ralph Ellison and Amiri Baraka. This debate is the one outlined in the historical framing within *How to See a Work of Art in Total Darkness*. Lee invokes this history by referencing Ralph Ellison's *Invisible Man* within the film. A point White has to be aware of as he uses Stanley Crouch as an example when talking about race men and women. "Despite many recent examples of well-remunerated race men and women–from Stanley Crouch to Lauryn Hill, Terry McMillan to Russell Simmons–Lee has no other regard for public figures' personal responsibility, racial authenticity or inauthenticity except to judge it as blackface minstrelsy."[18] This language indicates to the reader White's association of the content of *Bamboozled* with the greater historical conversation and ties the project to the work of Du Bois through the language he uses. And by invoking Crouch, White refers back to the verbal sparring of the 1980s. A fan of Marsalis, Crouch used his podium as a critic and journalist to criticize Lee, a point White doubtless wants to remind the reader.

Crouch's political and cultural views evolved from the more militant expressions of black Radicalism towards an elevation of black forms as formative of American culture, a point which demonstrates Ellison's influence on his thinking and writing:

> The intellectual tradition that Crouch aligns himself with is anchored in the works of Ralph Ellison and Albert Murray. Its most powerful expressions are Ellison's "Invisible Man" and his essays in "Shadow and Act" and "Going to the Territory," and Murray's "The Omni-Americans." Fleshing out James Baldwin's observation that "the story of the Negro in America is the story of America," these writers argue that African-Americans are the moral center of the country's hybrid culture; Ellison, indeed, went as far as to assert-in his 1970 essay "What America Would Be Like Without Blacks"—that America "could not survive being deprived of their presence."[19,20]

Doubtless, White understood that in invoking Crouch he brought to the forefront these ideas, meaning to shame Lee for *Bamboozled*'s message. However, what message did White believe the film contained? This film which White described as easily slotted and forgotten has spawned several decades of conversation beginning with 2003's symposium "Minding the Messenger: A Symposium on Bamboozled," which included Crouch, and continuing through present day with two recent books released in 2015 and 2016 and a symposium on race at the University of Ohio which included a screening of the film in March of this year. *Bamboozled*'s influence seems to be growing, and the film feels ever more prescient after the close of the Obama presidency, as the issue of race permeates Trump's America, more scholars return to this angry film, which has not faded in its influence but grown. Jordan Peele's excellent *Get Out* broaches comfortability and the necessity not to relax vigilance over racism.

Peele produced Lee's most recent effort, *BlacKkKlansman* screened at Cannes to an 8 minute standing ovation. In no small measure of irony, *Vox* reviewer Alissa Wilkinson criticized the film for not taking the opportunity *BlacKkKlansman* afforded to say more about the careless image making of films that are not as overtly racist as *Birth of a Nation* but nonetheless do work to promote stereotypes that allow audiences to minimize groups of people.

> There's a host of reasons that images are powerful, but when we participate in them uncritically, they can cause real damage to real lives. A film that traffics in depiction of stereotypes contains the rich possibility of exploring that with its audience, showing how they, too, are culpable.[21]

Top: Daniel Kaluuya as Chris Washington (center) in Jordan Peele's *Get Out* (2017). *Bottom:* Spike Lee's *BlacKkKlansman*, with Spike Lee (left) and John David Washington as Ron Stallworth 2018.

The film Wilkinson describes is *Bamboozled*. It's effectiveness in highlighting that culpability for most of its audience members explains its staying power and the intense reactions to its message. *BlacKkKlansman's* purpose is related but different. *BlacKkKlansman* marks the trajectory of how we got from Bamboozled to 2018. In it, Lee creates for the audience the kind of characters he desires for films. Police who stand against corruption in their ranks. Authority that recognizes in the insidiousness of the White Power movement.

And a black cop who manages to strike a balance between the black and the Blue. Like *Bamboozled*, the film is also an historical document but one from a different time that seeks a different end. *BlacKkKlansman* proposes a way forward from the place where *Bamboozled* has told us we are. To paraphrase the film, Archie Bunker made White people want to not be racist, but didn't attempt to hide that racism existed. *BlacKkKlansman* operates in a similar way to *All in the Family*. It sits next to racism and uses humor and subtlety to convince us of its immoral character. But *BlacKkKlansman* was released following nearly two years of the polarizing presidency of a man who refused for some time to disavow David Duke's endorsement and refused to condemn the White Nationalists in Charlottesville. In the year 2000, control over image making was looser, and there was even less opportunity for black representation in media. Racism was an undercurrent rather than a topic in the news. The conversations were of a different character.

The first half of this text served to establish the context for *Bamboozled* as an historical document. The second half will attempt to unpack the work of the film itself, its references and symbols. Claims will be staked. Analyses postulated. We will examine what angers and frightens us to find the forgotten things.

8
Symbolic Naming and Casting Practices

From back then until now, We see no comedy; We have been a misrepresented people.—Stevie Wonder, "Misrepresented People"

According to Stuart Hall, "Representation doesn't occur after the event; representation is constitutive of the event.... It is one of the conditions of its existence, and therefore representation is not outside the event, not after the event, but within the event itself."[1] To undertake the act of re-presenting images, language, or stereotypes is to either reinforce the status quo or subvert it in some manner through which change can be affected. The act of representation always does work. The question is not whether or not work is being done through images and representations but rather what work are images and representations doing? In the case of *Bamboozled*, what types of representations are present?

This chapter deals with two forms of representation: naming practices, and casting practices. Spike Lee named and cast the characters in this film according to their cultural weight. Each role is densely packed to ensure the clarity of his message to the audience. In part, Lee imbues the characters in the film with historical significance to make visible black authors, artists, performers, and thinkers to a new generation. But Lee also wants to communicate his understanding—that mirrors Hall's understanding—of the way language and images operate, as presentations that either reinforce existing ideas and stereotypes or alter their meaning through difference of use. The names we give things bear meaning, and as icons, actors bring cultural capital to their roles. Lee is clearly thinking about this within the film. When Pierre Delacroix talks about casting *Mantan: The New Millennium Minstrel Show*, he says, "to ask Denzel to put on blackface is foolish."[2]

The clip that Lee shows behind this narration is Denzel Washington performing as Malcolm X saying, "You've been bamboozled."[3] There are several possible implications to this juxtaposition. Lee could be implying that asking Denzel to play Malcolm X is, in the minds of some, Denzel blackening up. He could be implying that Denzel who takes on serious roles with heavy political significance would not blacken up, but would object. Lee could also be emphasizing that Delacroix is fooling himself and us. Likely, Lee is flirting with all these ideas and deliberately maintains ambiguity in order to make us uncomfortable. Definitely, he is using the cultural capital of Denzel Washington as an icon of black celebrity and integrity, just as he later lampoons the Oscar acceptance speech of Cuba Gooding, Jr., for *Jerry Maguire*, as buffoonery. Undoubtedly, the roles in the film are named and cast in the same spirit, and though the story is fictive, like any satirical work, it intersects with real life.

Like Du Bois' *The Ordeal of Mansart*, Lee uses fiction to point to a truth that a straightforward recounting of history cannot. As Du Bois writes,

> The basis of this book is documented and verifiable fact, but the book is not history. On the contrary, I have used fiction to interpret those historical facts which otherwise would not be clear. Beyond this, I have in some cases resorted to pure imagination in order to make unknown and unknowable history relate an ordered tale to the reader [...]
>
> It may well be asked, and as one who has done some historical research I join in the asking, why should one tamper with history at all in order to write truth? The answer, of course, is Never, if exact truth can otherwise be ascertained. But every historian is painfully aware how little the scientist today can know accurately of the past; how dependence on documents and memory leaves us all with the tale of the past half told or less. The temptation then comes to pretend we know far more than we do and to set down as accurate history that which is not demonstrably true. To me, it seems wiser and fairer to interpret historical truth by the use of creative imagination, provided the method is acknowledged and clear.[4]

These methods are clearly a part of Lee's modus operandi. Lee's films always condense their greater message within the opening sequences. These sequences serve as the one of the one-two punch enclosed by his films' endings. Things always come full circle. In *School Daze*, the opening credits roll over images documenting black history and Civil Rights; cementing connections between American cultural behaviors and freedom for Africans through the imagery of the slave ship plans—which reference not only the African ancestry of black Americans and the circumstances of their arrival, but an object that historically served as a catalyst for widespread international abolition. The credits also contextually highlight the Civil Rights movement's emphasis on education through the varsity letter font. Within the film, fictional Mission College has not disinvested from South Africa despite continuing apartheid. Dap's protests underscore that the conflicts between the wannabes and the jigaboos are mirrored between the Mission students and the townies; also black Americans and South Africans; broadening the scope of the movie. The comfortability or complacency felt by many of the school's students and faculty and the warm ignorance to greater issues for black people outside the Mission's borders requires the wake up demanded at the film's close. In *Do the Right Thing*, Public Enemy's *Fight the Power*—the song Radio Raheem wants to blast on his boombox—is allowed uninterrupted play. In the *25th Hour*, New York City and haunting blue light create abstract forms like paintings until fixing upon the source of the light; the empty spaces formerly occupied by the Twin Towers.

Bamboozled opens by clearly marking the contents of the film a satire. Lee provides a definition to outline his intent. "Satire, one A. A literary work in which human vice or folly is ridiculed or attacked scornfully. The branch of literature that composes such work—irony, derision or caustic wit.... Used to attack or expose folly, vice, or stupidity."[5] And behind Delacroix's recitation of this definition, Stevie Wonder sings of history and misrepresentation. Lee is taking Du Bois' advice and following Du Bois' parameters. He is dealing with a thick history rather than merely a contemporary moment. And like Williams, Micheaux, and Ellison before him, Lee finds a complex vision of history and his characters more satisfying. As Delacroix says in the film, black Americans "are not one monolithic group of people."[6] Lee presents a wide range of characters and personalities that stand in for a range of cultural blackness but simultaneously complicates these characters beyond caricature. Additionally, he marks them as historical referents by encoding them as signs through his naming and casting practices. As a result, the film's language also performs social critique; as invested in exposing folly through satirical form as in heralding the work of cultural figures of the recent past. Lee cautions about the power symbols and language wield in creating identity. As Wonder sings, "You must never be a misrepresented people."[7] This chapter will exam-

Opening credits of Spike Lee's *25th Hour* (2002).

ine the naming practices of the major characters within the film: Thomas Dunwitty, Pierre Delacroix, Manray and Womack, the Mau Maus and Big Blak Afrika, and Sloan Hopkins; in individual sections, also touching upon selected minor characters. In this process, casting practices will also be examined, where appropriate.

Thomas Dunwitty

The names for the characters in *Bamboozled* operate as didactics, shorthand to assign specific characteristics. This practice mirrors that of the 1728 comedic *Beggar's Opera*, which features names that operate as puns: Molly Brazen, Sukey Tawdrey, Mrs. Vixen, and Wat Dreary. The most overt example of this within *Bamboozled* is in the character Thomas Dunwitty as portrayed by Michael Rapaport. That Lee names Dunwitty in the same way as the operetta that helped birth the genres of burlesque, vaudeville, musical variety, and minstrelsy is not coincidental. As John Shepard and David Horn state, "In using native low-brow characters to mock imported high-brow culture, minstrelsy carried on a tradition that can be traced back to *Beggar's Opera*..."[8] Minstrelsy was a gross caricature of both the black culture it claimed to rise from and the white audiences it appealed to. As representations of black culture, the forms were inaccurate and highly exaggerated, but characters like the Zip Coon satirized white culture as well, putting on airs that offered a farcical misrepresentation of high culture. According to Eric Lott, minstrelsy for working-class white audiences was less about believing in the authenticity of this vision of blackness, and more about defining their own cultural space.[9] If white minstrel performers could put blackness on, then they could also remove it. Working class whites could appreciate base humor and antics within minstrelsy that upper-class whites looked down upon without owning the forms as their own. Dunwitty represents the repetitious practice of a Romantic racism that reduces black cultural forms while trying to lay claim to the same. Dunwitty is a wigga type, marking not only a space where poor white trash and blackness engage but where the authenticity of identity is questioned. Dunwitty is Micheaux's villain Griddlestone, but he is also Norman Mailer, like "White Negroes," searching for the power he perceives in the primitive of the urban black. As Lee notes in the commentary, "There's a difference between liking a culture and appreciating that culture, and bogarting that culture, taking over that culture."[10] Dunwitty specifically cites Quentin Tarantino as being correct, "Nigger is just a word."[11] and Rapaport, who appears in Tarantino's film *True Romance,* stands in for Tarantino. The offensiveness of Dunwitty is his assumption that he understands blackness better than Delacroix and that blackness is equated with buffoonery.

From left: Brad Pitt as Floyd, Michael Rapaport as Dick Ritchie, Christian Slater as Clarence Worley, and Patricia Arquette as Alabama Whitman in Tony Scott's *True Romance* (1993).

Dunwitty seeks the same sort of conceptualizations of blackness for the network. He wants earthy, comedic representations that are *fresh* and *dope*. He wants everything done witty. In the staff meeting and then later in a private exchange between the two men, Dunwitty expresses his desire for Delacroix to be a black voice and his disappointment in Delacroix's performance in this capacity is clear. Dunwitty instructs Delacroix to come up with a point of view which "digs deep" into his "Black roots." This indicates that Dunwitty views cultural blackness as natural and inherent, and uncomplicated. For Dunwitty, Delacroix has a genetic connection to a past that is or should be accessible to him in a real way whether or not that past is one Delacroix has personally experienced. To do as Dunwitty has asked Delacroix must draw from a place beyond his own identity to a history that cannot really belong to him. Because Dunwitty views blackness as easily knowable, he assigns authenticity only to his own limited conceptualizations. Dunwitty works hard to reinforce his ideas about cultural blackness, all the while seeing himself as a preserver and connoisseur of black culture, "I'm Blacker than you. I'm keepin' it real."[12] Lee uses Dunwitty's name to connect these actions to historical practices of exploitation and misrepresentation of black culture by white cultural figures.

Peerless Dothan/Pierre Delacroix

Played by Damon Wayans, Delacroix is the token black member of the creative team at the Continental Network System. He represents a satirical interpretation of Micheaux's race hero and Alain Locke's New Negro. He is part of Du Bois' Talented Tenth. The narrator of the film, Delacroix operates in an ambiguous space—like Lee, whose presence looms in the background, and who is part of the cultural body he dissects—self-aware and complicit, yet doubting his complicity. *Mantan: The New Millennium Minstrel Show* is birthed as the brainchild of Delacroix, only half in jest and protest, with little spurring needed by his racist boss Dunwitty. Initially, Delacroix introduces the idea for the show as a commentary on his conversation with Dunwitty. He is angry over being chastised for writing pilots that focus on positive images of the middle-class black experience. After the meeting, Delacroix states to Sloan Hopkins that he intends to write a script so offensive that he will be fired, as his financial and contractual obligations do not allow him to quit. Sloan expresses concern over his judgment, and it is difficult not to agree with her. However, after Dunwitty receives the show enthusiastically, Delacroix's anger is stunted and confused. He does nothing to stop the momentum of the show as it is adopted by the network. Rather, his fervor for writing the racist material is fueled by its acceptance. Delacroix becomes heavily invested in this critical validation and will deny his very identity in order to secure it.

This striving for acceptance does not originate with his taste of success, however, but prior to the start of the film. When we meet Delacroix, he has already made a series of concessions as an attempt to fit into a culture where he is an outsider. His mother reveals that he has changed his name by calling him Peerless. He is Peerless Dothan. His first name is a pun like Dunwitty. He is without a community of peers; an *Invisible Man*. His last name is both a city in the South—Dothan, Alabama—and the biblical city where Joseph's brothers sold him into slavery. This last name indicates both a refusal of his past and an indication of his character, as he sells out Manray to Dunwitty and CNS in order to prevent financial loss. He has styled himself into something unreal and affected. His father, Junebug, points out his phoniness, "Nigger, where the fuck did you get that accent?"[13] This moment is complex in its signification. While Junebug confirms suspicions regarding the inauthenticity of Delacroix's speech, he also uses denigrating language to effectively deconstruct the performative identity Delacroix has been building. This lack of acceptance undermines Delacroix's self-determination. Junebug holds his own vision of blackness in the same way that Dunwitty does, and he is just as heavily invested in Delacroix's adherence to that vision. Junebug sees through a veil of the prejudice he has endured. He describes speaking racial epithets to himself in the mirror to "keep his teeth white[14]" and presumably his skin black. His name is tied to the South, as a Southern slang for May beetle, and carries implications of prison—possibly either literal or figurative—as Junebug is also slang for "a prisoner who is considered to be a slave or a footman for others," according to *A Prisoner's Dictionary*.[15] Lee's casting of Paul Mooney for the role is significant as a generational marker. Mooney was a standup comedian during the 1970s to the present day and wrote for Richard Pryor, amongst others. By the end of the 1980s, Mooney's career as a writer had expanded to include writing credits for *Good Times*, *Sanford & Son* and *Saturday Night Live*. In the 1990s, he contributed to *In Living Color*. He was still writing for television after the turn of the twenty-first century, partnering with Dave Chapelle for sketches on *Chapelle's Show*. His stand-up performance in *Race* from 1993 is a masterful example of satirical "White people" jokes. Until a verbal skirmish with Michael Richards in 2006, he regularly used the N-word in his comedy routines, believing that he had been called the word enough that it belonged to him. Junebug onstage is Mooney. Lee's emphasis highlights an unadulterated talent in this scene in the same way that Manray's final performance is a pure presentation of the talent of Savion Glover. Offstage we witness through Delacroix's gaze that Junebug is bitingly funny, yet horribly sad, boxed within presets he embraces, limited by external and internal expectations. To some degree, Delacroix's movement away from what he views as the failures of his father is understandable, and yet, there is a sense that Delacroix is throwing away too much, and has lost a part of himself in the process. Junebug jokes have a teeth and pose a danger to racist attitudes that Delacroix's do not.

The name change indicates a denial of his background. Delacroix separates himself from his mother and father marking them as beneath himself, as he did earlier with Manray and Womack. Yet, Delacroix remembers all the names of the (white) people in his office. He walks down the halls greeting coworkers who do not respond or seemingly even acknowledge his presence. Delacroix's performative identity as a successful black executive is as inauthentic as Melville's Black Guinea's minstrel performance.[16] He is playing a role. Yessing them to death, like the narrator's grandfather in *Invisible Man*. Delacroix uses the word Negro in place of black to indicate his migration from this past. He sees himself as a pioneer who is leaving behind a rural Southern blackness for a new urban/metropolitan identity. This phrasing designates Delacroix's understanding of his own blackness as relating to the ideas of uplift for the race contained within theoretical texts like Alain Locke's *New Negro* during the Harlem Renaissance in the 1920s rather than with the militant understanding of blackness that arises from groups like the black Panthers in the 1960s, a vision his father doubtless finds more authentic. However, Delacroix's understanding of self is mostly affectation. When CNS publicist Myrna Goldfarb states that Delacroix's blackness will serve as an argument against *Mantan* being racist, Sloan says, about Delacroix. "That's where you're wrong. He's not black, he's a Negro."[17] Sloan points to the irony of both assertions, but also uses the phrase to put down Delacroix by making reference to Malcolm X's use of the word in his rally in Harlem, "The only black man on earth who is called a Negro is one who has no knowledge of his history. The only black man on earth who is called a Negro is one who doesn't know where he came from. That's the one in America."[18]

As played by Damon Wayans, Delacroix's improbable accent and his strange dandyish gestures render him a Zip Coon. Delacroix only manages to perform a parody of a middle-class black man because he has a limited understanding of this experience. Because Delacroix is already performing, it is not difficult for him to buy into the validation he is given for the terrible greatness of *Mantan,* eventually accepting the accolades sincerely, "Well, it *is* pretty good."[19] Near the end of the film, he dons blackface, as does every character in this film who adopts a prescribed cultural blackness in place of authentic identity. Blackening up—either through blackface or the plastic blackface Halloween masks—is rendered by Lee upon all characters who express affectations of expected "Black" behavior, whether that is the positive affectation of uplift, as first touted by Delacroix in his list of show pilots or the supposedly authentic black behavior of the Mau Maus. The struggle over what constitutes authentic blackness is a central theme of the film.

Delacroix's name comes from the French Romantic and Orientalist painter Eugene Delacroix. The painter traveled to Northern Africa in the mid–1800s in order to escape Parisian culture and be inspired by what he referred to as a more primitive setting. He exoticized the people of Northern Africa and objectified them. His images were considered highly authentic because of his unusual access to Algerian Muslims. Authenticity presumes knowledge. A similar sort authority of authenticity is prescribed to Pierre Delacroix because of his blackness. However, as Deborah Root points out in regard to Eugene Delacroix's art, this type of authentication is suspect. "Exotic images and cultural fragments do not drop from the sky but are selected and named within specific historical contexts; certain fragments of a cultural aesthetic are selected and rendered exotic while others are rejected."[20] This mirrors the way that Delacroix marks Manray and Womack as culturally black within the film. Dunwitty is looking for a coon show; Delacroix looks at Manray and sees a coon show. The reduction that Dunwitty performs upon Delacroix, Delacroix performs upon Manray and Womack. Delacroix assigns them the names Mantan and Sleep'n'Eat after Mantan Mooreland and the original Sleep'n'Eat as portrayed by Willie Best. He extends a courtesy of asking Manray for permission because of his perception of Manray's talent but does not afford Womack the same courtesy, dismissing Womack's authority to choose for himself.

Manray/Mantan and Womack/Sleep'n'Eat

Manray receives his name from the avant-garde Dada artist Manray from the early twentieth century. This theoretically encapsulates Manray within the time frame occupied by performers like Mooreland, as well as Bert Williams. Underscoring this connection, Sloan shows portions of "Natural Born Gambler" to Manray and Womack as they prepare for the show. In this way, Lee stresses that the manipulation of Manray and Womack mirrors the lack of agency afforded performers like Williams. Their acceptance of the roles Delacroix offers does not indicate that they are ignorant or lazy—as Delacroix later characterizes them in front of Dunwitty—but that they are desperate, truly in financial straits. Their poverty stands in stark contrast to Delacroix's claims that finances prevent him from quitting his job despite the moral imperative he claims to feel. This comparison highlights Delacroix's investment in his own comfort. Lee contrasts Delacroix's work ethics with the pair from the opening scene of the film. Womack and Manray are at work hoofing before Delacroix arrives at the office building at the beginning of the film, because "if we snooze, we lose."[21]

The performance routines of figures like Bill Robinson, Willie Best, and Bert Williams are also resurrected for the show within the show. Lee first references the history with respect unfolding it with Sloan's gentle historical exposition, before contrasting the racist cultural practices of minstrelsy with the racist cultural practices of today. When Mantan and Sleep'n'Eat step out and say, "We're two real coons," they are calling up the tagline of Williams and his partner, George Walker. Says Lee, "I think as an artist, you really have to understand, whether you're black or white or whatever, that you're not the first person. There were many people before you that were doing things. They went through a lot of shit, whatever the circumstances were, so you, so I could be in the position I was."[22]

Lee casts Savion Glover as Manray, a choice that highlights the historicity of the film duo's performances while reaffirming the connections to *Invisible Man*. Glover choreographed for and danced within the Broadway show *Bring In Da Noise, Bring In Da Funk*. This musical recounts the history of black people in America through tap, staking a claim to the dance form which has been traditionally used as a means to stereotype black performers and reminding audiences of its critical weight. In the number "Green, Chaney, Buster, Slyde" Glover asserts the influence of tap performers whose goal was to educate, not entertain. In *Bamboozled*, Womack calls Manray's feet educated; a signifyin' categorization that refers back to Bill Robinson's sand dance routine in *Stormy Weather*, as well as marking Manray as a Du Boisian man. In the scene where the duo are offered the show, Delacroix requests Manray change his name to Mantan. Manray says he doesn't care what he's called "as long as I'm hoofin' and gettin' some loot, I'm good, man."[23] When Mantan is asked in a subsequent meeting with Dunwitty whether or not he's willing to wear blackface while he performs, Manray says "As long as the hoofin' is real."[24] This statement reflects a greater complexity than is first apparent. Manray demonstrates that despite Delacroix's power to tag him with a derogatory name, the act of an authentic performance allows Manray agency that Delacroix cannot remove. This attitude echoes within "Green, Chaney, Buster, Slyde."

Glover also tapped in 1989's *Black and Blue* at the young age of 15. This musical revue contained the Louis Armstrong song mentioned within Ellison's novel and was choreographed by Fayard Nicholas, among others. Fayard was the older member of the Nicholas Brothers, the tap performance duo that created the classical tap style in the 1930s. The Nicholas Brothers' parents were both professional musicians who performed in the orchestra pits of black vaudeville in the days leading up to and during the Harlem Renaissance. Like Bert Williams, the Nicholas Brothers would appear in the Ziegfeld Follies, although 20 some years later. They also appeared with Robinson within *Stormy Weather*. Lee chooses Glover because of his connections to tap and history.

Glover's career choices demonstrate his investment in history and education as well. Through these intersections, Lee demonstrates that Manray is a figure to be admired. Manray is not a coon, in the same way that Bert Williams was not. In the context of the film, Manray is less culpable for his actions because he begins with a disadvantage. Delacroix marks him, setting him disingenuously before Dunwitty as a coon, and in the process, both men miss the artistry in his performances. Delacroix's ignorance allows him to misrepresent Manray to Dunwitty. He doesn't understand or honor the trajectory from which Manray arises, therefore he helps maintain an institutionalized attitude about this trajectory. The way Delacroix treats Manray exemplifies the treatment afforded men like Williams and Walker, who were also exploited for their talents, and unacknowledged in their influence on other prominent black personalities. These individuals did them a second injustice by erasing them from history. A wrong that Lee attempts to rectify. For his part, Manray at first demonstrates ignorance of history but chooses to be influenced to act as his knowledge grows. Though he and Delacroix share similar fates, in his final performance before the show's audience, Manray wakes up and makes a stand as himself, sans blackface. And burns his papers.

Manray and Womack demonstrate the greatest growth of all the characters within the film, and next to Sloan, the greatest self-awareness. Both manage to shatter the mask of minstrelsy although not without heavy consequences for Manray. Womack has the clearest understanding of the futility of their work on the show. He says, "I'm not drinking the Kool-Aid"[25] This exchange is crucial to the film's overarching theme of self-determination as the means to achieve autonomy from white formed ideas of blackness. Through the performance of the Uncle Tom stereotype that follows, Womack demonstrates his awareness that he was selected for this role because he fulfilled a stereotype and he cannot continue to play himself. In part, because he understands that he is being limited and used to limit others.

Womack is named after the musical performing family the Womacks, who wrote the song "Woman's Gotta Have It," the title that inspired *She's Gotta Have It*. This naming connects Womack to Lee directly, and although we hear Lee's voice coming from other characters, Womack is perhaps the most similar to Lee's public identity. Cecil and Linda Womack[26] traced their ancestral roots to the Zekkariyas tribe in Nigeria, and thus later adopted the name of the tribe as their surname. This connection demonstrates Womack's desire for knowledge, and pride which enable him to break away from Manray and the show. Womack understands the folly of the undertaking, demonstrating suspicion and offense at Delacroix's suspicious and offensive behaviors from the start. As his immediate needs become less pressing, he finds himself increasingly grieved by his own involvement with the project. Womack's understanding leads him to reject the minstrel show satire as a continuation of the racist past. As Womack says in the film, "It's the same thing, just done over."[27]

Sloan Hopkins

This doing over is reflected in historical echoes Lee encodes through repetition of reference. Minstrelsy, Romanticism, the early race films of Micheaux and others, the Harlem Renaissance, the Black Arts Movement, soul and rap music, and the golden age of black television comedy in the 1980s and 1990s with shows like *The Jeffersons, Good Times, What's Happening!!, Cosby Show, Different World, 227, Amen, Fresh Prince of Bel Air, Family Matters*, and *In Living Color* are signified over and again. Lee casts Damon Wayans because of his association with *In Living Color* and Jada Pinkett-Smith provides connections to Bill Cosby and Will Smith. The film is packed with referents meant to draw attention to patterns and cycles that are being reinforced. Lee lays these out to expose how the space of cultural blackness is maintained and how deep its influence runs. He wants the connections to history to feel permeable.

Through the voice of Sloan Hopkins, Lee introduces the present to its past. The first collectible—the significant Jolly Nigger Bank—is given to Delacroix by Sloan. This gifting marks Sloan as the Mary to Delacroix's *Invisible Man*; and Jean Du Bignon. Through Sloan, we hear Lee's assessment of the objects. "I love these Black collectibles. It reminds me of a time in our history in this country where we were considered inferior ... subhuman, and we should never forget."[28] Lee parades before the viewer a cascade of historic racist imagery—slave ship plans, the n-word and as its physical signifier, blackface—attempting to awaken an abolition of these practices. He takes Micheaux's visual trope of portraits of great black American thinkers like Booker T. Washington and Frederick Douglass off the walls and replaces them with sports figures. Dunwitty uses them to undermine Delacroix's identity as a black man by goading him that he doesn't know who "number 24" is, in order to demonstrate the surface level quality of Dunwitty's perceptions of blackness, but also the loss of priority of and access to knowledge. Lee is mourning forgotten history.

Sloan dedicatedly weaves the threads together and persistently presents the story behind the all the cultural artifacts and practices, functioning as the source of historical fact within the film. Sloan explains the process and the significance of using the traditional method of the burning of the cork to make the blackening paste. She presents the black memorabilia to Manray and Womack that serves as a source of reference for *Mantan* and awakens Womack's conscience. She puts together the montage of racist imagery that Delacroix watches as he dies. Fittingly, her name is taken from William J. Sloan, the author of *The Documentary Film and the Negro: the Evolution of the Integration of Film*. Like Delacroix, Sloan wants to succeed and she is good at her job. But, unlike Delacroix, Sloan desires more to help her people. She calls out her brother's posturing, she tries to clue Manray into what is being done to him, and ultimately she tries to make Delacroix see what he refuses to consider, that his success bears a heavy price tag.

However, like Louise in the race film, *Scar of Shame*, the means for succeeding are closed off to Sloan. Although Sloan strives to be one of Micheaux's race film heroines, she is reduced to the Tragic Mulatto type. Lee enables this reduction by introducing the information that Sloan and Delacroix have slept together. Sloan maintains to Manray that this does not matter in relation to how she got her job—once again Delacroix accuses and degrades. However, in the context of the film, the reveal of this act limits her voice didactically, making her pleas to both Manray and Delacroix less effective than they might be otherwise. Her voice—through the betrayal by Delacroix—becomes filled with the echoes of D. W. Griffiths' mulatto servant in *Birth of a Nation* who used her sexuality to advance her position.

After Delacroix fires Sloan to quiet her influence, Sloan's gift, the Jolly Nigger bank takes up her cries in the wilderness, and Delacroix suffers from a vision that echoes directly a passage from *Invisible Man*,

> Then near the door, I saw something which I'd never noticed there before: the cast-iron figure of a very black, red-lipped, wide mouth Negro, whose white eyes stared up

at me from the floor, his face an enormous grin, his single large black hand held palm up before his chest. It was a bank, a piece of early Americana, the kind of bank which, if a coin is placed in the hand and a lever pressed upon the back, will raise its arm and flip the coin into the grinning mouth. For a second I stopped, feeling hate charging within me then dashed over and grabbed it, suddenly as enraged by the tolerance, or lack of discrimination or whatever, that allowed Mary to keep such a self-mocking image around, as by the knocking. In my hand, its expression seemed more of strangulation than a grin. It was choking filled to the mouth with coins.

How the hell did it get there, I wondered, dashing over and striking the pipe a blow with the kinky iron head. "Shut up!" I screamed....[29]

Through this symbol, Ellison referenced Herman Melville's character Black Guinea from his book *The Confidence Man*. The character Black Guinea performs in blackface and catches pennies in his mouth. In the Melville novel, the crowd watching the performance calls into question the Black Guinea's authenticity. The spectators disbelieve his blackness, suspecting it to be a performance. They view him as a shyster who is swindling them out of their money. Michael Ray Charles has appropriated the Black Guinea as a performative identity statement, inserting the Lincoln penny into each of his paintings as a trademark. in a similar vein to Kara Walker's Negress—a word which Lee uses in *Bamboozled* as a feminine form of the n-word during one build up to the show during which various audience members identify themselves as niggers—[30] In *Bamboozled,* the repetitive clicking of the hand to the bank's mouth operates as Ellison's clanging pipes. The clanging marks a refusal of the past to lie down quietly. For Lee, the Black Guinea forces a question, what work do the images of cultural blackness do?

To answer this question, we should examine what was occurring in television in the late 1990s that may have influenced Lee's decision to undertake this project. According to Mark Anthony Neal, Lee saw television shows being produced during this time for and by black Americans as problematic. *The PJs* was the kind of project that concerned Lee. The series, a foam-a-tion stop-motion animated sitcom, centered on life in the fictional Hilton Jacobs housing projects. It aired on the Fox Network just prior to the production of *Bamboozled*. The title of the show was a slang reference for the projects, which, according to Neal's book *Soul Babies*, were named for the actor who portrayed Freddie Washington on *Welcome Back, Kotter*.[31] The main character, Thurgood Stubbs, is voiced by Eddie Murphy, who also helped produce and create the show, alongside Larry Willmore and Steve Thompkins, both former writers for *In Living Color*.

Bad blood had existed between Murphy and Lee since the release of Lee's critically acclaimed *Do the Right Thing* when Murphy had called Lee a cricket on national television. Lee was also taken to task by Murphy's friend and advocate Arsenio Hall for tearing down the "strong black man," according to Neal.[32] Lee had maintained an adamant and opinionated voice on the subject of black representation or image building for blacks. His statements concerning *The PJs* reflect this. Lee called the show "hateful to Blacks," and maintained that it "showed no love for Blacks."[33]

Sianne Ngai, a professor of film studies in Stanford's English department, drew connections between *The PJs* and the doll made animate by Tod Clifton in *Invisible Man* in her essay "Animatedness." Ngai argues "to be animated in American culture is to be racialized in some way."[34] Ngai asserts that the animation, which brings the doll to life through Clifton's ventriloquism, also animates Clifton, forcing his body to move in a way that is beyond mindful control. *The PJs* characters operate physically and symbolically in the same way for Ngai. Posed by the filmmakers, they become animated and create the same unconscious animation for their puppeteers.[35]

Ngai's connection between animation and racialized portrayals of black Americans can be expanded to include blackface, especially within the context of *Bamboozled*. As a means of creating an animation of an autonomous person, blackface reduces naturally variant skin tones to performative binary design elements, standardizing varying individuality to one true black, and creating a painted animated figure from a human being, indicating through its theatricality a connection to puppetry. Manray then, through the process of blackening up, becomes Mantan, and also, the puppet.

This is evident in specific instances throughout the film. First, Manray dances for Womack, in order to eat, then for Delacroix, ostensibly with the same motivation. The analogy of Manray as puppet is laid bare in a conversation between Manray and Sloan. Sloan asks Manray, "Are you a puppet for Delacroix?"[36] When Manray denies it, Sloan then asks, "Well then, the question is, whose puppet are you?"[37] The implication is that once Manray becomes aware that his actions are being directed, he can exercise the self-determination to stop. For it is Manray who animates Mantan, and therefore, he can make the decision to no longer animate himself as puppet, which is what he ultimately chooses to do.

After refusing to be animated, or to blacken up for the final minstrel show, awakened by first his rejection of Sloan, and then the loss of his partnership with Womack, Manray symbolically performs a revision of his original monologue sans blackface. However, it is too little too late. Like *Invisible Man*'s Tod Clifton—operator of the racist puppet—Manray is kidnapped by the Mau Maus and killed, forced to perform as they shoot at his feet. In the moments before Manray's body is riddled with bullets we are given a glimpse of his genuine genius and talent. The Mau Maus, like the Brotherhood, support a racial murder in order to condemn the racist imagery they see inherent in the *New Millennium Minstrel Show*. In the process, the Mau Maus blacken up hiding their identity within the blackface masks, paraphernalia of the show. Thus, although the Mau Maus disown *Mantan* through the assassination, they also consume the show's images and products. Ultimately, the Mau Maus, in their blackface masks become puppets themselves, as the bullets fired by the policemen enter their bodies and make them dance.

The Mau Maus and Julius Hopkins/Big Blak Afrika

In addition to representing the wrong thinking Brotherhood, the Mau Maus represent the radical black Nationalists of the Black Arts Movement within *Bamboozled* with the members named Blak, Double Blak, Big Blak Afrika and $^1\!/_{16}$ Blak. This final name is a reference to both the amount of lineage needed to legally be termed black under Jim Crow laws, but also refers to a plot device Micheaux frequently used as a vehicle for commenting on both "passing" and, flirting with themes of miscegenation and the constructed nature of blackness. The day would be saved and the couple could be reconciled when it was discovered that the one who was supposedly white was really legally black. One sixteenth Blak demonstrates both the arbitrary nature of the designation of blackness and how related it is to perception. Being $^1\!/_{16}$ black allowed $^1\!/_{16}$ a sense of cultural belonging, and he is wholeheartedly accepted by the Mau Maus. With irony, $^1\!/_{16}$ Blak passes as white during the final shootout with police and is the only member of the Mau Maus who survives.

Big Blak Afrika's name change from Julius references Amiri Baraka's renaming from LeRoi Jones, as well as Malcolm X, but the name he selects calls to mind the racial stereotype Donald Bogle refers to as the black buck.[38] His sister Sloan highlights the disparity between the lineage claimed within the name Big Blak Afrika and the connection the name Julius affirms. "Mama and daddy called you Julius, so that's what I'm gonna call you."[39] Sloan meaningfully points out that he was named by their parents, not the white man. It is worth noting, that Julius is a kingly name of historical distinction, and like Delacroix, Big Blak Afrika disowns his familial heritage in favor of an affectation.

The Mau Maus' name comes from the revolt of Kikuyu ethnic tribe in Kenya against the colonial rule of Britain. The name carries specific connotations, emphasizing the revolutionary mindset of the group, marking them as black Nationalists, and ideologically aligning them with figures like Marcus Garvey. However, there is also a measure of irony to their claim of the name as Mau Mau was not a name that the first revolutionaries took for themselves, it was given to them based on a phonetic misunderstanding. Therefore, the name implies a lack of agency and self-determination. It points to the fact that within *Bamboozled* The Mau Maus react to the ideas of others rather than burning their papers. In addition, while the name Mau Mau raises notions of anti-colonial sentiment, it also references the violent actions the first Mau Maus took against Kenyans who would not take their oath to stamp out the presence of the white man. The Mau Maus within the film—like their historical antecedents—are complicated, not the villains of the piece but not necessarily heroes either.

Historically, the nature of the Mau Mau Rebellion and its influence in establishing independence for Kenya is contested. The conflict arose in response to a variety of issues most of which dealt with access to land and exploitation of labor. In particular, the Kikuyu protested insufficient wages, the need for ID cards called kipande in order to seek and secure employment—British employers would frequently destroy or keep the cards once presented to make it more difficult for the Kikuyu to find other employment—and mass eviction from land. European settlers displaced the Kikuyu from the land they owned and occupied and then permitted them to return to, live on and farm small plots of the land in exchange for their labor, essentially making them into tenant farmers. The land the Kikuyu had occupied was ideal for settling as it was significantly cooler than surrounding areas. Between 1936 and 1946, the colonists' demands for labor increased steadily while the Kikuyu were partitioned into smaller and smaller sections of land. Over this same period of time, the income of the Kikuyu decreased by 30–40 percent. Over 1800 Kikuyu loyalists were killed by the Mau Maus in the rebellion, with the Lari Massacre being the deadliest insurgence with 70 dead from the loyalist village, mostly women and children. Over the course of the entire rebellion, only 32 colonists were killed. However, the counter-insurgency was estimated to be even more deadly, with conservative estimates of 25,000 Kikuyu dead. Until 2003, the Mau Maus were categorized as terrorists in Kenya. Since that time many in Kenya have come to regard them as heroes. Despite the ambiguities, the name has carried strong connotations of ruthless dedication and chaos. It has been used culturally several times in America by groups seeking to assign attitudes of rebellion and danger to themselves.

In the 1950s and early 1960s, during the height of the state of emergency in Kenya, a Puerto Rican street gang from Fort Greene—the same neighborhood from Brooklyn where Lee grew up—operated under the name. One member, Carl Cintron, was arrested for murdering a member of rival gang Sand Street Angels outside the Paramount Theater. Former member Salvador Agron, who later joined the gang The Vampires, mistakenly murdered two youths he believed were from the gang the Norsemen. He had been expecting to encounter this gang. Agron received the nickname The Capeman following the crime because of the red-lined black cape he wore during the attack. He was 16 years old when he was given the death penalty, the youngest person in the State of New York to do so. In 1962, Governor Rockefeller commuted Agron's sentence to life without parole. His story became the basis for the Paul Simon 1998 musical *The Capeman*.

The name makes an appearance elsewhere in music. The L.A. punk group The Mau Maus formed in 1978. The group's founding member Rick Wilder appears within the infamous music documentary film series The Decline of Western Civilization's first punk iteration. The Mau Maus of L. A. were considered to be one of the most underrated groups within the scene. Their lack of recognition was due to the fact that they never secured a recording contract.

The rich historical context of the name and its connections to Lee's stomping grounds demand a respectful consideration for the group despite many of their misguided actions. Lee presents the Mau Maus as a fairly sympathetic didactic tool pointing to a way not to behave, echoing Micheaux's narrative employment of negative stereotypes within his films. Particularly, Micheaux's critique of the black church through Paul Robeson's riveting portrayal of the corrupt the Reverend Jenkins in Body and Soul comes to mind. Sloan even goes so far as to call Big Blak Afrika "ig'n'ant,"[40] referring to a way of speaking that Micheaux uses in the inter-titles of his films to illustrate the difference between the New Negro and the old negro. They are on point within their dislike of *Mantan* and many of its themes, however, this critique is diminished in its efficacy by their unsuccessful attempts to audition for the show and receive help from Sloan to get exposure on television. In addition, the Mau Maus employ the language of rebellion and push back against racial language and images, but reinforce many negative depictions of black people in the mainstream media. Lee's Mau Maus drink malt liquor and do drugs, embracing the gangsta lifestyle as they rigidly perpetuate stereotypes. They are, as the film frequently contends, "keepin' it real."[41]

The Mau Maus work to reaffirm a politically charged understanding of blackness. This relates to a debate in the mid–1960s in response to the possible passage of the Civil Rights legislation regarding imagery. The debate centered on whether or not it was necessary to continue a policy of consensus regarding the portrayal of black Americans by black Americans in response to negative stereotypes perpetuated by white Americans. A platform of uplift had been the policy of previous generations, who had not—to paraphrase Du Bois—cared for any art that was *not* propaganda.

The Spiral Group was formed by Romare Bearden and Hale Woodruff in 1963, to address these issues through debates that were notable for their diversity of response and lack of consensus. The members came to the table without a preordained notion of what that response might be. Ellison's *The Art of Romare Bearden* triumphed Bearden's progressive art techniques that, for Ellison, operated outside traditional culturally black forms.

Amiri Baraka, a founding member of the Black Arts Movement, viewed Ellison's "liberal individualism" as a race betrayal.[42] The Black Arts Movement drew its imagery from a specific vision of black culture, which rejected associations with American/white culture. The writings of Amiri Baraka eloquently express the ideology of this group. As Baraka wrote in the manifesto, black Poem:

> We want a black poem. And a
> Black World.
> Let the world be a Black Poem
> And Let All Black People Speak This Poem
> Silently
> or LOUD[43]

As Darby English wrote, this practice of consensus "discouraged Black artists unrestricted play among the resources available and referred them to a limited range of forms and tropes that could yield an unequivocally ethnic art."[44] Ellison sought to abolish these limitations, to integrate black forms with white forms, in an acknowledgment of the necessity of both in the forging of an American culture. For Ellison, these limitations indicated a "stubborn blindness to the creative possibilities of cultural diversity."[45]

Lee's reliance on the symbolism and narrative structure of Ellison's novel *Invisible Man* highlights Ellison's ideas by invoking history in a similar way. As Ellison's *Invisible Man* alluded to historical figures contemporary to, or just prior to the Harlem Renaissance, WEB Du Bois, Booker T. Washington, Marcus Garvey, etc., Lee engages this debate of the legacy of the Civil Rights era and de-centers the argument to a broader context, indicating Lee's belief that the history beyond the legacy of the 1960s needs to be remembered and learned from. Says Lee;

> I think that there's a lot of young people, both Black and white, that really don't know about the Civil Rights struggle and the Civil Rights movement, and African Americans in particular who today are bearing the fruits of everybody who had to sacrifice and struggle. They have no idea what happened, and they think it was always like this because they were always allowed to vote or go wherever they wanted. That wasn't the case at all. Afro-Americans somehow fear going back and revisiting painful parts of history, nevertheless we need to do it.[46]

This lack of attention can lead to complicity in the reinforcing of stereotypes, of limited representations of blackness. As an artist who makes films about blackness, Lee is concerned about representation and its effect on systems of power. He asserts through this film that makers of images are responsible for what they put out into the world. And so, when the camera pans the crowd, it spies Lee in blackface amongst it, recognizable only by his trademark glasses and hat, placing himself within the debate; asking hard questions about himself, as well as those around him.[47] He shows deference to the history and presents what he sees as its continuity.

9
Signifyin'

> *When I rhyme, something special happen every time. I'm the greatest, somethin' like Ali in his prime.*—50 Cent, "Many Men (Wish Death)"
>
> *It is a peculiar sensation, this double-consciousness, this sense of always looking at one's self through the eyes of others, of measuring one's soul by the tape of a world that looks on in amused contempt and pity.*—W. E. B. Du Bois, *The Souls of Black Folk*, 1903

The language spoken within *Bamboozled* expresses a similar purpose to that of Lee's casting and naming choices. Through Lee's employment of loaded didactic language, the terminology characters use indicates their ideologies and motivations. Linguistics provides the tools for unpacking much of the language of a film, giving us a structure to analyze it more thoroughly, providing a snapshot through which we can unveil the encoded representations present within the dialogue of the film. Three particular linguistic patterns appear in *Bamboozled* under close examination. First, double articulation is present throughout the film. In this process, the repetition of sounds codify layered meaning. Second, Lee uses particular phrases and types of conversation to indicate the genre of the film, and therefore, ratifies the audience. Third, characters employ code-switching to indicate the cultural status of different characters and to differentiate between different subtypes of cultural blackness. In a film about representational space, it is crucial to note how Lee employs all of film's aspects—not just visuality—to highlight the extent to which representational strategies are employed in the culture of images.

Double Articulation, W. E. B. Du Bois, and Double-Consciousness

When examining film, analyses must underscore the importance of language and semiotics. For all films create a symbolic system of dialogue and visual signs through their words and images, which communicate culturally loaded ideas. However, unlike static systems of representation, film is not experienced as an isolated sequence of images. Rather, film occurs across time in a greater complexity than its individual parts. Most events unfold phenomenologically within a film; experienced by the audience members according to a predetermined sequence. The director guides the viewer through the cinematic experience, serving as a curator of its languages. So, the content of the film is located somewhere in the midst of this direction and our reception. Therefore, meaning is created over this experience of the film, not just within its isolated symbols, or frames. It is an unfolding. As a result, things that appear insignificant at first can become pregnant with meaning as the unfolding occurs.

Deleuze wrote about film in relationship to movement-images and time images. He identified four senses of movement that occur within film: first, a physical movement across and within space, the action-movement image; second, the movement of light and matter, the perception-movement image; third, movement in time as unpredictable events unfold and change occurs, unveiling the unseen, the affection-movement image; and fourth, movement that marks remembering and thinking as acts that take place within time, the mental-movement image.[1] The first sense relates to the eye of the camera, panning the space, which influences viewer perception, directing what they see. The second sense is about the movement of things caught within the frame of the film, the natural movement of light and all things that are captured within the camera's framing. Again, this sense also relates to perception. The director and any narrative drive the third sense; the viewer experiences the unfolding of each scene rather than standing as a subject gazing upon an object in opposition as one might experience a painting. The fourth sense occurs when a director forces the viewer out of a mode of perception making them think about what they are seeing. Deleuze's example of this type of movement-image within a film occurs within the work *Frenzy* directed by Alfred Hitchcock.

> The camera follows a man and a woman who climbs a staircase and arrive at a door that the man opens; then the camera leaves them and draws back in a single shot. It runs along the external wall of the apartment, comes back to the staircase that it descends backwards, coming out on to the pavement, and rises up the exterior up to the opaque window of the apartment seen from outside. This movement, which modifies the relative position of immobile sets, is only necessary if it expresses something in the course of happening, a change in the whole which is itself transmitted through these modifications: the woman is being murdered.[2]

According to Deleuze, Hitchcock's introduction of the mental-movement image opened a door to a different way of experiencing time within film. The way a film is shot can allow an experience to either unfold as the audience expects or surprise the viewer within its unfolding and force what Heidegger calls a nooshock. A nooshock is when our mind is forced into a new way of thinking. For Deleuze, the nooshock of film results in a different perception of time. Time within movement-image films is an abstraction. Montage is the vehicle that creates the illusion of the passing of time and the audience perceives the order of events through movements, through the action of the film. Time then is something that counts a beat for the progression of movement. It is subordinated to movement. However, for Deleuze, time isn't experienced as a progression of moments. We don't move from the past to the present to the future, rather "there is no present which is not haunted by a past and a future."[3] Or in the words of Zora Neale Hurston, "The present was an egg laid by the past that had the future inside its shell."[4] These three make up the one whole of time. When we recall the past, we separate from the present and draw up a recollection of a general past which slowly comes into focus as specific memory. When movement image films represent the past, they demonstrate it as a lived present which unfolds no differently than the rest of the narrative. Deleuze asserts that time images—as opposed to movement images—interrupt our experience of time as a measurement of movement. Films which employ the time image decenter the action from the subject and the camera makes its presence known. Within these films, the camera does not serve a narrative progression of time.

In *Bamboozled*, the opening monologue is filmed with a camera and the subject—Delacroix—on a dolly. The audience does not watch Delacroix move, rather we see Delacroix and behind him, we get a view of his apartment-behind-the-clocktower flowing behind him as the camera makes the background a character. We are being shown, in a literal and figurative way, Delacroix is behind the times; stuck in a cycle of regression which appears to him to be progressive. As Delacroix presents the film's genre through his soliloquy, Lee unconceals a connection between the character of Delacroix and Fred Daniels by emphasizing Delacroix's living space. Delacroix views himself as enlightened and yet he wreaks havoc upon those who surround him by his lack of knowledge. This indexical reference is meant to spark a nooshock for the audience, but one whose significance is not clear on first viewing. In moments like these within the film, we see that Lee's greater career project of jump-starting a Wake Up via education motivates the way he directs the audience's experience. This sequence operates as a time image, the first of many.

From the beginning, Lee lets us know what the film is about. He lays it all out on the table for those who will see it. Delacroix is fixed, almost fixated, not hearing the music behind his voice or viewing the apartment as we are. While Delacroix's narration is our guide through this experience, we see more and know more than he does. Through direction and editing, *Bamboozled* provides moments of realization and awakening for various characters to prepare us for our own. In the double articulations within *Bamboozled,* various characters experience an understanding of themselves in a new way. According to Thomas Poell, "One of the great differences between neorealist films, like 'Europa '51,' and the films that fall under the regime of the movement-image, is that the character has become a viewer."[5] When these characters see how they are seen, they break the narrative of progressive time within the film. Through these edits, we enter once again the theoretical realm of Du Bois.

As demonstrated in the previous chapters, *Bamboozled* encounters the work of black artists of the twentieth century through the Du Boisian examination of the color line, art as propaganda, and an investment in righting historical ideas about black Americans through fiction. Lee also references—through visual and linguistic patterns—Du Bois' concept of double-consciousness within these moments of double articulations. Within the context of the film, these articulations tangibly represent Du Bois' application of double-consciousness. In other words, the repetition of the filmic moments reasserts the viewer's experience and emphasizes the phrases through the pattern. The audience member is forced out of experiential viewing into active thinking; creating a nooshock that operates as an enlightenment. Lee employs this technique to add additional layers of meaning. Double-consciousness is, for Du Bois, "The sense of looking at one's self through the eyes of others."[6] It is the moment of realization for all black Americans that how you are perceived is vastly different from your self-perception. Du Bois' reinterpretation of this Hegelian theory marks an awareness of the chasm between one's self-conception and the perception of self by others as understood within the context of the American black/white binary. Lee stands in agreement with the project of Du Bois and uses this framework as a lens through which the film's characters—as well as its viewers—must negotiate a response to the parade of genre and history he has set before them. Lee anticipates the viewer will experience the emphasis contained within the moments of double articulation as their own personal moments of double-consciousness.

In the film, these double articulations are created through moments of dialogue that are repeated exactly by the repetition of a filmed clip. These repetitions occur during moments of a character's awakening or double-consciousness. The following figure demonstrates an example of this within the film.

Double Articulation Example 1:
DELACROIX: Eureka!
SLOAN: Oh my God!
DELACROIX: Eureka!
SLOAN: Oh my God!
DELACROIX and SLOAN: Manray![7]

In this example, Delacroix and Sloan share a realization about the character Manray. As the pair struggles to come up with a television concept in response to their boss Dunwitty's demand for culturally black television shows, Sloan and Delacroix both realize the appropriateness of Manray to fulfill this request. Manray is a self-taught tap dancer, a street performer, and a homeless squatter. Sloan and Delacroix identify Manray as fulfilling the parameters of what Dunwitty desires to see for the network. Manray matches aspects of Dunwitty's preconception of blackness. As a result, a moment of double-consciousness, or a crisis of identity rises inevitably around him. Sloan and Delacroix look at Manray through the lens of the historic racial schema and make a judgment that reflects how they—as black Americans—understand themselves as being seen. Sloan and Delacroix are reading Manray as a stereotype.

This instance is the first double articulation within the film. Lee uses the content of the dialogue to signify how the double clip technique functions. "Eureka!" and "Oh my God!" are both expressions of realization or revelation. Eureka comes from the Greek *heureka* and refers back to the story of Archimedes. According to legend, Hiero of Syracuse asked Archimedes to help him figure out the purity of a gold crown. Hiero believed that the goldsmith who had fashioned the crown had replaced some of the gold with a different metal. Hiero noticed the crown was a different color than the gold he had given to the goldsmith originally. However, the crown still weighed the same amount as the original, so there was no known way to prove that anything untoward had occurred. Archimedes considered the problem as he stepped into a bath, and as he did, the water splashed over the edges of the tub, displaced by his body. Archimedes exclaimed, "Heureka!" He understood that if the gold in the crown was pure it would displace the same amount of water as would another hunk of pure gold that weighed the same because the volume of the two would be equal. A less heavy metal would have a greater volume at the same weight.[8] The word was popularized in America during the mid–1800s in connection with the gold rush. Greatly associated with the discovery of gold, it became the state motto of California. The use of this phrase associates Delacroix's inspired choice of Manray for the lead in his new show with money and financial gain. Also, like many of Delacroix's affectations, this phrasing grounds him as bound by history but not cognizant of it. He uses steeped language, anchored in the past but in a way that indicates he doesn't realize the consequences of the usage. He believes that he is presenting the show in protest but he is fooling himself. Sloan's exclamation—while not tainted by an association with money—indicates she still views Manray as an answer to Delacroix's problem. They both understand that Manray typifies the kind of cultural blackness that Dunwitty seeks. They both also understand how blackness is viewed within his limited lens. But it is Delacroix who sees within Manray the possibility for financial gain and personal advancement. This first occurrence of double articulation, therefore, enframes Manray within a gaze. He is a solution to a money problem Delacroix has been tasked to fix.

Through later instances of double articulation, Delacroix reaches an understanding that he and Sloan are perceived by others with the same gaze he casts upon Manray. The white people working in the office don't communicate important appointments, ideas, and deadlines. Delacroix clearly loses control of *Mantan: The New Millennium Minstrel Show* as soon as he speaks the idea into being. When a very racist claymation opening sequence makes its appearance, offending Womack. Sloan states, "No. This was not supposed to be like this."[9] Because their lack of knowledge and ultimate control has become painfully visible, Womack says to Sloan, "Where do you work? In the basement of the damn place?"[10] Following the precedent, these further instances of double articulation within the film hearken back to the previous audience experience of the same, marking them as revelatory as well. As a result, the audience is allowed a more complex reading of the instances that follow. The next incident of double articulation occurs when Delacroix is meeting with Dunwitty, Sloan, and Myrna Goldfarb.

> Double Articulation Example 2:
> MYRNA GOLDFARB: Finally, our best defense is you.
> DELACROIX: who (…) me?
> DUNWITTY: Yes. You.
> DELACROIX: who (…) me?
> DUNWITTY: Yes. You.[11]

For the first time, Delacroix demonstrates an overt realization that his involvement with the project is seen as an endorsement of its ideology and a defense of its terms; a straightforward presentation of minstrelsy. No irony is apparent, no satirical bent. Beyond Delacroix's initial suggestion, his input is neither heard nor required. Dunwitty considers Delacroix to be the slice of authentic blackness for the show, he is there as the black-face of the show. As Myrna Goldfarb prepares the *Mantan* team for the backlash the show is likely to create, she emphasizes the need for token black players behind the camera as well as in front. Delacroix himself is the justification for moving the idea forward. His culpability for the project is plain, he can't deny his association. Delacroix is being called to defend the show. Instead of refusing to defend the project, he doubles down on his investment. It is at this point in the film that *Mantan* becomes fully earnest rather than partially ironic for Delacroix.

In the third instance of double articulation, Lee frames the shift in consciousness Womack undergoes as a result of his growing knowledge and his growing distaste for putting on the blackening paste.

Double Articulation Example 3:
WOMACK: Show...
MANRAY: [time!]
WOMACK: Show ... time.[12]

This example is broken across time, delayed in it's presencing. We are called as audience members to remember the first instance, as the second instance echoes with the past, a return. First, Womack and Manray say it enthusiastically and within a rhythm, together; in sync and as one mind. As the film's narrative unfolds and the situation behind the show deteriorates, the accolades and the clamor for the offensive imagery rises. Womack grows uncomfortably aware of how his public persona offers up blackness as a joke, or a fad, unattached to history and without respect to the dignity of those that came before him, and without regard for what it is doing to repeat the process into the future. As a result, within the repetition, Womack is disillusioned and saddened that it is once again time to step in front of the camera. This re-articulation marks the origin of the rift between the duo. This rift will only expand as Womack witnesses the callousness Manray exhibits towards his fellow dancers as they rehearse. Manray chastises the dancers, many of whom are young children, treating them poorly for not performing his choreography correctly. For Womack, Manray's behavior constitutes the final straw and demonstrates that Womack has not only turned a corner in his thinking but so has Manray, just in a decidedly more negative way.

The final instance of double articulation happens within the montage Lee sets up that demonstrates the influence of *Mantan* as a phenomenon. The show has taken off and the performers are experiencing their newfound celebrity. Honeycutt does a questionable commercial for the malt liquor beverage Da Bomb. Manray and Womack witness their visages on display as Mantan and Sleep'n'Eat in the bright lights of Time Square. Children appear dressed for Halloween in blackface masks. Delacroix's voice booms:

Double Articulation Example 4:
DELACROIX: Now the latest craze sweeping the nation was blackface!
CHILDREN: Trick or Treat!
DELACROIX: Blackface!
CHILDREN: Trick or Treat![13]

In this example, the double articulation exists solely for the benefit of the audience members. Lee breaks the fifth wall through the double articulation of Delacroix's narration, confronting the viewer with a world permeated by its love of blackface. Because the previous double articulations function as revelation, the same emphasis is ascribed to this instance. Only here, Lee directs the signifying toward the viewer, as the dialogue occurs as an aside to us.

Through the juxtaposition of Delacroix's narration with the chorus of children shouting "Trick or Treat!" Lee designates Delacroix as a trickster type because the reference to trick or treat contains references to masquerade and to the trickster trope. This Halloween tradition's roots are thought to stem from the Scottish practice of guising. In guising, the poor would travel from house to house begging for food or money while dressed in fancy dress or costumes. In exchange, the beggars would stage a play, offer a dance or a song, or recite a poem.

> It seems to be a similar custom, that of the boys of Scotland, who at Hallow tide go about "guising." Three or four of them put on "false-faces," or wizards of pasteboard, and enter a house unceremoniously; [they then stage a sword fight].The wounded combatant is speedily cured, and the "guisers" are ready to depart, enriched with whatever the good people of the house are willing to give.[14]

Guising as trick or treating first shows up in Alberta, Canada, in the town of Blackie, in 1927. However, its current form and level of popularity didn't take hold in until the 1950s in the United States. The idea of playing a trick upon those unwilling to bestow a treat, rather than performing for it, is singularly American in character. According to Steve Matterson, "There is actually a peculiarly American delight in confidence tricksters.... In part, such affection has to do with America's emphasis on and admiration for individual enterprise and ingenuity, which are considered notably 'Yankee' qualities."[15] Henry Louis Gates, Jr., wrote about the trickster in his seminal literary critical analysis, *The Signifying Monkey*. The title comes from a black American folktale in which the Monkey tricks the Lion into fighting with an Elephant. The tale begins with the Monkey confronting the Lion with misinformation about what the Elephant has been saying about the Lion. From the Oscar Brown version,

> Said the signifyin' monkey to the lion one day:
> Hey, there's a great big elephant down the way.
> Goin' 'round talkin', I am sorry to say,
> About your momma in a scandalous way.
> He's talkin' 'bout your momma and your grandma, too.
> And he don't show so much respect for you.
> You want to chat? I sure am glad.
> 'Cause what he said about your momma, it made me mad.[16]

According to Gates, this folktale descends from Yoruba mythology's trickster Esu Elegbara who mediated between men and gods by playing tricks upon them both.[17] Gates used it in critical theory to explore the relationship between the writing exchanges present in the subtext of black writers like Ralph Ellison and Zora Neale Hurston. For Gates, the importance of the tale is that it is a triad between three characters. In other words, the poems serve not as an allegory for a binary between black and white people, as had frequently been assumed prior to Gates writing, but rather it is about those who are capable of maneuvering the space between the literal and the figurative linguistically, and those who are not. According to Gates, "The Lion, realizing his mistake was to take the Monkey literally, returns to trounce the Monkey. It is this relationship between the literal and the figurative and the dire consequences of their confusion, which is the most striking repeated element of these tales."[18]

The trickster Monkey insults the Lion to use him to trounce the Elephant, knowing that whatever the outcome, someone will get trounced, providing entertainment for the mischievous Monkey. Delacroix insults black people through his presentation of minstrelsy; believing that his actions will instill anger amongst black audiences and bring retribution upon the network and upon Dunwitty. However, the audiences do not recognize the insult. Dunwitty's comeuppance does not come. Instead, Delacroix marks himself as the fool that doesn't see the subtext. He has misidentified the Lion and the Elephant because he believes himself to be the Monkey. However, the Monkey is something Delacroix cannot be because he doesn't understand history. His contextual inference range is shallow. Delacroix is still runnin'. Dunwitty is the trickster who has baited Delacroix forcing him to trounce Manray and Womack. Delacroix proves himself to be a literalist. Lee deliberately calls up Gates as another means of identifying Delacroix's folly. Within *The Signifying Monkey*, Gates critiques the work of Richard Wright. According to Hazel Carby's *The Blackness of Theory*,

> Gates peremptorily rejects Richard Wright from his definition of "blackness." Wright's centrality to black modernism is ignored. In terse phrases of condemnation, Wright is accused of creating "a class of ideal individual black selves" that included only himself, and of achieving his humanity "only at the expense of his fellow blacks."[19]

Delacroix believes he is enlightened and lives behind the clocktower, a contemporary for Fred Daniels; laughing at the masses whose faces watch the flickering of their television screens. Like Daniels, he sacrifices those around him for his own ticket to enlightenment. Shoring up treasures he says mean nothing but he still collects. Intent on changing the institutions only to aid his own inclusion.

Delacroix *is* a trickster on a smaller scale. When things don't go his way, he sets Manray against Sloan, removing from his proximity the sole voice of reason. Lee identifies who is the trickster by using minstrelsy's Interlocutor and Mr. Bones. This parody of a Socratic dialogue functions in *Bamboozled* not as a tool for enlightenment, but as a way to reduce an opponent, almost like doing the dozens. The Socratic Dialogue is a genre in which an interrogator who presents himself as knowing nothing, asks questions of a person who has proclaimed himself an expert on the topic in order to demonstrate their wrong thinking and bring about true enlightenment and demonstrate true wisdom. The dozens is an exchange in which insults are traded as a joust between two competitors in a verbal contest. Lee frames these exchanges within the film as a question-and-answer back and forth. The interlocutor is a trickster who is not offering enlightenment but rather insults that degrade Mr. Bones. Lee emphasizes this visually when he places the cutout figures of Mantan and Sleep'n'Eat behind Manray and Delacroix in one such exchange. Thus Lee demonstrates that he too is Signifyin(g). Presenting the tropes of white culture and doubling their meaning. By layering his meaning, despite his public claims to the contrary, he is Signifyin(g) to a ratified black audience.

Genre and Ratified Audience

According to Susan Strauss' and Paratou Feiz's *Discourse Analysis: Putting Our Worlds into Words*, "Genre is a metaphorical frame that provides a structure for discourse."[20] In other words, genre dictates the framework of the languages, shaping the meanings through its limitations and boundaries. Understanding genre requires a foreknowledge of that particular framework. Genre and audience, according to Strauss and Feiz, go hand in hand. Participants within the structure of a genre ratify an audience. Strauss and Feiz write that one text can contain a multiplicity of genres, creating a complex level of discourse.[21] *Bamboozled* operates this way. The primary genre of the film is satire, but because of the sheer volume of genre satirized within the film, the complexity of discourse is heightened. Unpacking the satirical references results in the exposure of a two-fold didactic purpose for Lee's satirical bent. The overt satire of the minstrel show points towards the genre that exists as primarily subtext, the race film, which in turn points to minstrelsy's generational reiterations and differences through its didacticism.

As previously mentioned, one of the conventions of the minstrel show genre involves the exchange between the Interlocutor and Mr. Bones which mocks the Socratic dialogue. After Socrates questioned the assumptive statements of his companion's worldview, the companion would realize—through his own responses to Socrates' questions—the contradictions within his worldview and be brought to enlightenment on the particular subject about which he had demonstrated himself to be a fool. The minstrel show employed this method to comic effect. The interlocutor asked the questions and the respondent, Mr. Bones, served as the comic foil. The characterizations within minstrelsy worked on two levels; the airs put on by the interlocutor rendered him a zip coon, and the foolishness of Mr. Bones demonstrated his quintessential Sambo-like coon-ness. This genre still survives today. In the 1960s and 1970s, the introduction to any number of variety shows used this format, a questioning straight man and a ridiculous fool: *Rowan and Martin's Laugh-In, Sonny and Cher, The Carol Burnett Show,* etc. A more contemporary example would be the interviews conducted by Seth Meyers on SNL News with characters like Stefon, played by Bill Heder. (Seth, you ignorant slut.)

> STEFON: Well, they have a Jewish Dracula.
> SETH MEYERS: Oh. What's his name?
> STEFON: Sidney Appelbaum! [he cracks up and covers his face with his hands]
> SETH MEYERS: Sidney Appelbaum?
> STEFON: [cracking up] Yes! [he continues to crack up, then finally composes himself] For a healthy snack, hit the bar and have some Fraisins—raisins that look like Frasier! Or try your luck with the Human Piñata.
> SETH MEYERS: And what is the Human Piñata?
> STEFON: It's that thing of when a Mexican midget eats a lot of candy, and then he dances until he throws up! [he covers his face with his hands]
> SETH MEYERS: You know, uh, Stefon.... I think "midget" is actually an outdated term.
> STEFON: Sorry. Not "midget"—[making finger quotes] "Fun-sized"! [he covers his face with his hands][22]

Mantan and Sleep'n'Eat's performances on the show within the show are well-crafted presentations of comic forms that are familiar to us and their humor is appealing and historical.

In the minstrel scenes within *Bamboozled,* Lee uses word for word scripts of black minstrel performers from the turn of the twentieth century. And by putting the minstrel show on television, Lee contrasts the racist cultural practices of early twentieth century minstrelsy with the racist cultural practices of 2000. Lee targets television with specificity, much like Michael Ray Charles does with his images in advertising; specifically referencing Williams' and Walker's work and its historical context. Past and present exist within the same conceptual space. This is not about the past.[23] Williams and Walker were talented. Williams and Walker were funny. Williams and Walker performed in blackface because they had no other choice; these were the constraints placed upon black performers at that time. And as is emphasized in previous chapters, this demonstrates a parallel to the situation for Manray and Womack. Financially they are desperate and destitute. They hold very little power both because of their lack of historical knowledge and their lack of wealth. As both of these resources are increased to them as individuals—through their work on the show, their financial situation betters and through Sloan's careful research and presentation of historical materials and objects, Womack first, and then Manray increase in knowledge—their agency increases. Manray and Womack gain the freedom to say no, even though there are consequences for them both.

Lee draws parallels by patterning conversations outside of the show in a question-answer format that mimics the minstrel genre. Below are two examples:

Example 1:

MANRAY: Sloan is the hardest working person I ever met.

DELACROIX: You're a bright young man. How do you think she got the gig in the first place? I hate to burst your bubble, Mantan the Marvelous ... but Sloan is an opportunist.

MANRAY: Naw ... Man. You don't believe that.... I don't believe that.

DELACROIX: Do I have to spell it out for you? In fact ... why don't you go ask her yourself? Ask her. Say, "Sloan, how did you get this gig?"[24]

Example 2:

SLOAN: You want me to hook up you and the Mau Maus? Why would I hook up some ... black, red, green...

BBA: [first of all]

SLOAN: flag-waving pseudo-revolutionaries?

BBA: First, you done messed up the colors first.

SLOAN: What's the colors?

BBA: Damn. Its red, black and green. White folks know its red, black and green.[25]

Damon Wayans (right) as Pierre Delacroix with the Sleep'n'Eat character in Spike Lee's *Bamboozled* (2000).

In both examples, the question-answer format is employed to mark the fool in context of the conversation. They also mark the discourses themselves with folly and detriment. The framework of minstrelsy is used to give indications on how not to behave. These indications, in turn, are markers of the race film genre. This is underscored by one line of dialogue used further into the exchange within Example 2, between Sloan and Big Blak Afrika. Sloan code switches into a racial speech pattern that was used in books like Uncle Remus Stories and in the intertitles of silent films. In saying to Big Blak Afrika, "Y'all ig'n'ant,"[26] the connection is drawn. In the race films of Oscar Micheaux, this affectation of black rural speech was used to draw a line between black Americans who behaved in a way that perpetuated stereotypes, and ones who bettered the race. Notably, although Sloan uses the speech to mark Big Blak Afrika as ignorant, she also makes use of the language to do so, marking herself as she does. By bringing him down, she brings herself down. By creating a film that operates within a race film genre's framework, Lee ratifies the audience as primarily black.

> A number of people would continue to say, "what's the use of having many meanings; why don't we use words and sentences in a clear-cut manner so that nobody is mistaken…" But here multiplicity of meaning, as I have elaborated, is not a question of cultivated ambivalence and ambiguity; it does not derive from a lack of determination or of incisiveness…. Since marginalized people are always socialized to understand things from more than their point of view, to see both sides of the matter, and to say at least two things at the same time, they can never really afford to speak in the singular.[27]

Lee correctly says that his films are not made only for black audiences, but they are specifically ratified towards black audiences. Allan Bell named four types of audience members in his model "Language Style as Audience Design." The types are as follows: addressees, auditors, over-hearers, and eavesdroppers.[28] Black audiences are clearly the addressees for *Bamboozled*, those who are known addressed and ratified. At the opening, Stevie Wonder sings, "We must never be a misrepresented people."[29] The next type, auditors, are audience members who are known and ratified but not addressed. A ratified audience member is one who is the intended audience. A case could be made that Lee intends for the white members of the audience to receive his meaning, even though he does not address them, but the complexity of reference to black culture within the film, much of which is sadly outside of white knowledge base, and the use of Signifyin' forms of speech, lead one to conclude that white audience members are instead over-hearers, audience members of whom the speaker is aware but who are neither addressed nor ratified (intended). Lee is not making *Bamboozled* to find and appeal to white audiences or white sensibilities. Like Ellison and Walker, Lee too is burning the pages from his briefcase.

Blak Is Black: Code Switching

According to a 2004 study by Deric Greene and Felicia Walker, code-switching can involve fluctuation between "two tonal registers, or a dialectical shift within the same language, such as Standard English and Black English."[30] Greene and Walker identify the practice of code-switching as a linguistic tool employed as a satiety for power negotiation by the speaker. Greene and Walker assert this as an awareness of the conventions of multiple registers of speech. This strategy relates to the negotiation of double-consciousness and marks meaning in this context. Gerald Powell, in his analysis of *Bamboozled* and *X*, says African-Americans are "always reminded of their blackness, what that communicates and how it must be negotiated."[31]

Within *Bamboozled,* there are several subtypes of code-switching occurring that have specific functions in context of the script. The first is an employment of the phrase, "I'm keeping it real."[32] Several people repeat this phrase in several contexts. Lee uses the phrase to mark the fluidity and constructedness of cultural blackness. He uses it to emphasize that action needs to be taken to keep it real. Race is something that is done and redone. As Deleuze writes within *The Logic of Sense,* "There is a 'use' of representation, without which representation would remain lifeless and senseless."[33] Dunwitty first uses the phrase over the course of his initial conversation with Delacroix as described earlier in this text. "I'm blacker than you. I'm keepin' it real."[34] As a colloquial phrase, this has one meaning. I'm authentic. I do it old school. But, in context of the greater conversation Lee wants to have, it points toward critical theory and the constructed nature of race. Through the actions Dunwitty is taking he is literally, keeping a certain construction of cultural blackness real. Various characters throughout the film use this phrase to emphasize behavior that reinforces cultural notions of blackness. When Lee employs code-switching in the film, he stakes a claim in the debate over the value of individual manifestations of blackness and how black people are represented in images and chooses to represent their variance.

When Manray prepares to tap in front of Dunwitty, he asks if Dunwitty wants a smooth style or raw flash. Dunwitty replies that he wants raw *dog* flash, and watches Manray tap, repeating several times, "Keep it real, keep it real."[35] Here, several things are happening; first, Dunwitty is exerting power over Manray by code-switching; implying that he has an awareness of black English, even though he is white. Second, he's evaluating Manray's tap routine as doing cultural blackness, which limits the performance, contextually, and codifies it.

The Mau Maus refer to themselves as keeping it real, and Manray as pseudo. If Manray keeps it real according to Dunwitty and is pseudo according to the Mau Maus, the implication is that race integrity is malleable, or contextually based. It also means that Dunwitty doesn't understand cultural blackness as well as he thinks he does, or at least that it is not as limited as he imagines it to be, and in turn, questions his authority to exercise judgment in this regard. However, neither is blackness as limited in the ways the Mau Maus imagine it if blackness can contain both definitions, one which includes Manray within it and one that does not. As Dunwitty, Sloan and Delacroix have done before them, the Mau Maus look at Manray and see a coon. According to their understanding, blackness and coon-ness are not equivalent, so Manray cannot be black. It is within these valuations of Manray's coon-ness that the explicit deliberation inherent to Lee's Williams reference become apparent. Also necessary is Lee's employment of the terminology for blackness from both the Harlem Renaissance and Civil Rights eras. This naming of blackness serves as a second form of code-switching.

Four different terms are used in context of the film: Negro, nigger, black and Blak. Negro is used primarily by Delacroix and demonstrates that he is behind the times. The word also associates him with the Harlem Renaissance, which maintained some of the associations with primitivism and romantic notions of Africa and uplift that later movements would be critical of, citing the movement as an origin point for black respectability politics.[36] Sloan uses it to identify Delacroix, saying, "But that's where you're wrong. He's not black, he's a *Negro*."[37] Her register indicates that this word is intended as an insult; that Negro stands in opposition to black and—as mentioned earlier in the text—that Delacroix ascribes value to one ideology but not the other. Delacroix vocalizes his distaste for a 1960s black Power/black Nationalist definition of black when he says, after hearing the Mau Maus play, "I don't want to be around anything black for a week."[38] While this could be construed as irony, it might also be a straightforward identification of Delacroix as *not* black—in the context of the film. The meanings of the terms as used carry historical weight. They pinpoint the core motivations of the major characters within the film.

The Mau Maus name themselves as Blak, because "it must have been a White boy"[39] who thought of the silent "c." Like the practice of self-determination through renaming, this process re-appropriates racial terminology and imbues new meaning that disassociates itself from what is considered white practices or language. Through the modification of spelling, the Mau Maus criticize the irrationality of English grammar and assign Blak as a self-appointed designation. This process is associated with the ideologies of black Power and black Nationalist movements, as well as the Nation of Islam. Black Nationalists historically rejected terminology that established identities rooted in white or European origins, viewing the terms as connected to oppressors' attempts to exercise control over black personhood. In *Message to the Blackman*, Elijah Mohammed wrote, "You must remember that slave-names will keep you a slave in the eyes of the civilized world today. You have seen, and recently, that Africa and Asia will not honor you or give you any respect as long as you are called by the White man's name."[40] This linguistic practice pushes back against the politics of respectability—associated with ideologies like those of Booker T. Washington—in which pressure is exerted to conform to behavioral norms and expectations of white culture. While Lee holds the Mau Maus responsible for their work in reinforcing negative stereotypes and through their group name demonstrates the folly and divisiveness of their treatment of Manray, he also legitimizes their project of resistance by marking them correct about points of American history, holding them in direct conflict with Delacroix. Big Blak Afrika remarks that slavery lasted for over four hundred years—a correct assessment—while Delacroix says slavery has been over four hundred years, a gross fabrication and denial. This denial originates prior to the creation of the minstrel show. Delacroix's list of shows demonstrate an interest in legitimizing and privileging members of an elite black upper-middle class, of which he sees himself as part. The difficulty with this list under the logic of the film is that Delacroix isolates that experience as ideal but never talks about the difficulties and institutionalized setbacks that stand in the way of true black progress and the ability of most black Americans to achieve the lifestyle he wants to convey. His limited view of blackness turns out to be no more correct then Dunwitty's. As Frederick C. Harris, wrote in Dissent magazine,

> Uplifting stories that leave out structural barriers, let alone the need for political struggle to correct those barriers, can gloss over the enormous challenges the poor face in an era marked by downward mobility. Respectability politics can have the effect of steering "unrespectables" away from making demands on the state to intervene on their behalf and toward self-correction and the false belief that the market economy alone will lift them out of their plight.[41]

Systemic disenfranchisement requires systemic change and is more difficult to overcome without the allegiance of individuals who wield social capital and power. Delacroix is the black man in *Bamboozled* who has both, therefore Lee holds him to a greater degree of culpability. Any reduction of people to one type facilitates prejudice. By identifying a variety within subtypes of cultural blackness, Lee undermines the authority of any monolithic definition of the same. Lee chips away at the construction of race through didacticism and genre and ratified audience.

10
Invoking History

> *It would be a delicate critical practice that struck images with just enough force to make them resonate, but not so much as to smash them.*—W.J.T. Mitchell

Critical theorist and art historian W. J. T. Mitchell penned an insightful analysis of *Bamboozled* in his book *What Do Pictures Want? The Loves and Lives of Images*. Over the greater text, Mitchell considered the question, "What if every theory of images was really grounded in a fear of images that was specific to a historical and cultural situation?"[1] Mitchell divided the text into three subsections: images, objects, and media. He distinguished a difference between the picture—whose defining nature is its ability to be destroyed—and the image, which cannot be destroyed, but instead has its own life and whose power stems from our fears. The image asserts itself into the world as a picture but endures beyond that picture's life. Mitchell said that "images are the thing that allows matter to have memory, as Bergson might have put it, and that the intentional effort to destroy an image always guarantees its survival in some other medium."[2] In *Bamboozled*, Lee invokes the imagery of popular performance at the turn of the century through the use of blackface and black memorabilia in order to draw a line from this racial imagery to media practices contemporary to the film.

Bamboozled's use of blackface and black memorabilia forces a dilemma for the audience. If the images of blackface are part of a long dead past, why do they cause such rancor when they are called up? What fear does the invocation of this history invite? Mitchell argues that *Bamboozled* is important because the film denies the assertion that minstrelsy is in the past. "Just when we thought Black artists were about to disappear into the melting pot or the Rainbow Coalition, just when we had been assured that the moment of Blackness and the 'race problem' in America was well behind us, these two inconvenient figures [Spike Lee and Kara Walker] come along to suggest that there is more to be done."[3] If minstrelsy were dormant, the images representing its ideas would become like Dave Hickey's beauty—senseless form—but instead the images of blackface are vibrantly offensive. They have bite. Lee believes we must examine the fear of this imagery. "Afro-Americans somehow fear going back and revisiting painful parts of history, nevertheless we need to do it."[4] If racist images cannot be destroyed than our only recourse is what Mitchell calls a "'compass' of race, a way of tracking its movements and transmutations in space and time and of tracing the vectors of religion, language, and culture; of biopolitical categories such as species and gender; and of the socioeconomic forces of class."[5] Audience members must critically engage with the media they consume in order to critically examine the culture rather than be swept away by its emotive force. Cultural producers must make use of images in ways that alter perspectives. They must strike the tuning fork with a critical mallet to draw forth a meaning from the image that deeply reverberates into a critical understanding—that awakens within us Deleuze's sublime transcendental problematic Idea—because images once created do not die and cannot be destroyed. Image making is a serious business. A point that Lee would doubtless agree with.

In Mitchell's chapter "Living Color: Race, Stereotype, and Animation in Spike Lee's Bamboozled," he argues that "*Bamboozled* is a metapicture—a picture about pictures, a picture that conducts a self-conscious inquiry into the life of images, especially racial images, and the way they circulate in media and everyday life."[6] Mitchell's identification of a fear of images as occurring within a certain sociocultural context applies directly to the historiographical methodology of Lee's film. The context in which images within the film are made and viewed becomes crucial to our understanding of *Bamboozled*, as does the context for the images and objects of the past, which Lee seeks to make sing a new song. *Bamboozled* critiques the institution, a strategy familiar to Post black artists like Fred Wilson, also mentioned within English's *How to See a Work of Art in Total Darkness,* who used the juxtaposition of objects fetishized by white buyers and viewers—like African masks and black collectibles—to problematize current exhibition practices of institutions like the MoMA. Wilson's exhibition *Hot Mamas (1995)* pointed to the imperialist thinking inherent to exhibitions like MoMA's *Primitivism* of 1984 by posing black collectibles—mammies, coons, and pickaninnies—in groupings that imitated photographs of black families from the same time period in works like *Mine and Yours*. The MoMA had gotten itself into trouble with the *Primitivism* exhibition, which juxtaposed Modernist masterpieces like Pablo Picasso's *Les Demoiselles d'Avignon* against little-researched and decontextualized African artifacts many of which had belonged to the Modernist artists themselves. The comparison the curatorial staff had drawn between these artists and the objects minimized the importance of African artisans, practices, and history in order to maintain the narrative of the invention and supremacy of Modernist avant-garde painters. Additionally, the exhibition as a whole used a logic reminiscent of the Degenerate Art exhibition staged by Adolf Hitler in Nazi Germany, a fact that inconveniently highlighted the link between that regime and the provenance of many of the MoMA's Modernist masterworks.[7] It is precisely the negative reactions and critiques by artists like Wilson that forced institutions like the MoMA to change their habits. Revisiting the imagery of the past draws a fast line between bad faith practices of today with the instances from the past that demonstrate the historic pattern of bad faith and the inherent flaws of the institution. As Nigerian curator, Okwui Enwezor notes, "Any critical interest in the exhibition systems of Modern or contemporary art requires us to refer to the foundational base of modern art history: its roots in imperial discourse, on the one hand, and, on the other, the pressures that postcolonial discourse exerts on its narratives today."[8] Mitchell also points to the colonizing interest of objecthood and the Other within the chapter on objects in his aforementioned text.

Likewise, Lee uses an archival lens, selecting and curating pictures and objects to fill the frames of the film and its invented spaces that service the goals of the film through their specific history. Delacroix, Manray, and Womack encounter the objects that have ascribed white ideas about blackness onto American consciousness and contend with their significance to black identity building. Even when acknowledging the objects' deceitful nature, the black subjects—and *Bamboozled*'s audience—are forced to deal with them. Delacroix's *Invisible Man* moment, where he attempts to silence the Jolly Nigger Bank, expresses a pure frustration of even having to endure the encounter. It is similar to the moment in Boots Riley's *Sorry to Bother You*, in which

Lakeith Stanfield as Cassius "Cash" Green in Boots Riley's *Sorry to Bother You* (2018).

Cassius "Cash" Green—played by Lakeith Stanfield—realizes that he is transforming into an equisapien, against his wishes and as a result of Armie Hammer's deceptions.

The fact that he has not made the choice to become an equisapien does not alter the his reality. However, Green determines his own actions and chooses to fight for the right to self-determination. The injustice has awoken Green's ire, and he sees his position with clarity for the first time. In *Bamboozled*, Delacroix's folly is demonstrated in that he doesn't awaken until it is too late. The objects that overwhelm Delacroix through their colonizing of his space build within the film over time. A few of these objects are given specific emphasis. Through this emphasis, Lee creates a system of objects as signs for a greater bibliographic context. This process—in relation to the notion of Signifyin,' as outlined in the previous chapter—serves two purposes. First, through the objects' inclusion and framing, the film calls up meanings commonly associated with the objects inside American popular culture. The myths that have been built around these objects are complex narratives that support specific ideologies. In *Mythologies*, Roland Barthes uses this example of myth building: the Negro soldier saluting the French flag. The connotations of the image are submission and the supremacy of French Imperialism. Beyond this connotation lies another meaning which can be ferreted out through a critique of the ideology being signified. When the myth of French Imperialism is exposed in its meaning and forms, the distortion contained within the myth becomes clear. So the goal of critique is to make the ideologies visible by revisiting the history and reclaiming all the meanings associated with the objects, thereby enabling a critique of these concepts. When the history of objects or language are forgotten, the critique is not possible, the myth is reinforced. Therefore, secondly, through the reclaiming and remembering of the past, a critique is formed that allows for a subversion of the objects for a new purpose or to expose the work a myth has been doing.[9] As Roland Barthes wrote in *Mythologies*,

> One believes that the meaning is going to die, but it is a death with reprieve; the meaning loses its value but keeps its life, from which the form of myth will draw its nourishment. The meaning will be for the form like an instantaneous reserve of history, a tamed richness, which it is possible to call and dismiss in a sort of rapid alternation: the form must constantly be able to be rooted again in the meaning and to get there what nature needs for its nutriment; above all it must be able to hide there. It is this constant game of hide-and-seek between the meaning and the form which defines myth.[10]

When we forget the connotations of objects, when we are unaware of context, we allow the myth to play the game of hiding itself. Myth, therefore, remains intact, unquestioned. It does not matter if we do not intend to keep the myth real, without the necessary awareness and interrogation, our good intentions cannot prevent the myth from forming. "Even the absence of motivation does not embarrass myth; for this absence will itself be sufficiently objectified to become legible: and finally, the absence of motivation will become a second order motivation, and myth will be reestablished. Motivation is unavoidable."[11] In discussing the work of emphasized objects within *Bamboozled*, the objects' purpose aligns with the goals of the rest of the film, to serve as didactics, pointing towards the illumination of history, the tools for awareness and interrogation.

Renira Rampazzo Gambarato provides a methodology for analyzing objects within film in the essay, "Objects in Films: Analyzing Signs." Gambarato builds upon the work of Roland Barthes' *Introduction to the Structural Analysis of Narratives* which unpacks the metaphorical and indexical function of objects within narrative literature. Gambarato writes that although many early film scholars did work on this topic, this arena of scholarship has lacked a contemporary updating. Gambarato is interested in the idea that objects convince audiences of the material reality of the world the film inhabits and support the narrative.[12] Among the criterion Gambarato employs for the analysis of filmic objects are several of specific interest to this analysis: particularization, surprise, and referential function. Particularization is a strategy through which the importance of an object is emphasized, such as the long shot in which the camera moves very slowly across an object.[13] Surprise occurs when an interaction with an object happens in a way that astonishes the viewer. Gambarato cites the examples of a priest with a gun and a child smoking. Referential-function is when objects are put to use in a way that makes reference to or parodies other artworks or art forms. These methods are useful in unpacking several sets of objects of importance within *Bamboozled*: the photographs on Dunwitty's wall; the black collectibles in Delacroix's office, including the Jolly Nigger Bank and Bill Robinson's tap shoes; the tap dancing puppet; the smiling doorway on the minstrel show; and the Michael Ray Charles' *Bamboozled* painting. In the analyses of these objects' function within the film, we see consistent use of these three methods of emphasis.

Brothas on the Wall

In the case of Dunwitty's photographs, particularization is used when Dunwitty points to them as evidence of his cultural blackness. "Look at all the brothers on the wall."[14]

Several things are significant about this use of particularization. First, Dunwitty has hung portraits of sports figures on his walls. This limited selection of "brothers" points to his investment in racial stereotyping. A varied sampling of black persons of import is not represented. There are no portraits of historians, inventors, critical theorists, writers, Civil Rights leaders, law-

Michael Rapaport as Dunwitty in Spike Lee's *Bamboozled* (New Line Cinema).

yers, pastors, politicians or abolitionists. The portraits reinforce that Dunwitty sees black people as entertainers.

Second, the specific language creates a multi-layered reference. Lee uses the phrase to refer back to Buggin' Out's protest of Sal's restaurant in *Do the Right Thing*. "We want some brothas on the walls!"[15] Lee draws a comparison here between Dunwitty and Sal. There are several points of similarity, but there are also differences. Dunwitty and Sal are both in relative positions of power in the microcosm of their respective films. They are both producers of products that are fed to black consumers. However, though Sal built his restaurant through his own labor, he relies upon the good-willed patronage of the people who live in the neighborhood. Because he interacts with the people he sells to directly, there is a relationship between them. At the end of the film, Sal is still present within the neighborhood, unlike the police who wreak havoc and then run; leaving the neighborhood to burn. Dunwitty, on the other hand, is removed from the black community he claims to participate in. He doesn't see Manray or Womack when he enters or leaves the building each day; as Sloan and Delacroix both do. When Delacroix presents the duo cleaned up within Dunwitty's office, there is no glimmer of recognition, despite the fact that Manray and Womack have clearly positioned themselves outside of this building long enough and often enough to be known

From left: John Tuturro as Pino, Danny Aiello as Sal, three seated actors, Giancarlo Esposito as Buggin Out, and Spike Lee as Mookie in Spike Lee's *Do the Right Thing* (1989).

by name to others. Dunwitty only sees them when they are presented as assets in relation to his business. Dunwitty has risen far enough within the corporate atmosphere at CNS—off the labor of other creative professionals—that his track record of successful shows is the basis for his claim to understanding black culture. Although it is clear that Dunwitty has bosses he reports to and is accountable to—we know this because he has to sell *Mantan: The New Millennium Minstrel Show* upstairs after Delacroix presents the idea—he can make things happen directly in a way that Delacroix cannot. And he is giving audience to Delacroix's scripts. His recitation of their plots is a proof of this. We are never treated to an unbiased assessment of these scripts' quality, Dunwitty is dismissive and later, on the rooftop, Sloan is placating. But nevertheless, he has read them. However, he uses the scripts against Delacroix claiming that they are proof that Delacroix is "fronting, trying to be white."[16]

Dunwitty claims to represent a progress of sorts. He tells Delacroix that he is married to a black woman and that he has two bi-racial kids. He seeks to put shows that depict black people on the air. Dunwitty will put brothas on the wall, and brothas on television. However, he attempts to lay claim to blackness as his own while still maintaining his white male privilege. He has no investment in black uplift and no interest in black history, he wants to be dope and fresh. Dunwitty wants to be in style. He sees blackness as style and surface. There is no progressive platform behind Dunwitty's interest in black culture. He only seeks to add value to his own hipness quotient. Dunwitty wants to live and eat and work and make babies inside the borders of the black community, like Sal. But unlike Sal, there is very little personal knowledge of life in the community demonstrated that reaches beyond a form of self-accessorizing, and no personal growth. This comparison to Sal also points to Dunwitty's business as the catalyst for tragedy.

In a related manner, this conversation about brothas on the wall indicates a correlation between Delacroix and Buggin' Out, another character who misfires in his critique of circumstances and takes a stand in a foolish way that wreaks havoc for those who surround him. Both *Do the Right Thing* and *Bamboozled* are about folly. Both films are also about responsibility. The culminating event of *Do the Right Thing* is not the tragic death of Radio Raheem but Mookie's trashcan thrown through the window at Sal's. All of the events leading up to that moment explain why that moment occurs. In *Bamboozled*, the culminating event is not the death of Manray but rather the probable enlightenment of Delacroix. He finally learns the cost of his actions. By highlighting the correlation between these characters and their story arcs, through the particularization of these objects, Lee reasserts that the moral of these two films is the same; always do the right thing. Doing the right thing frequently does not look the way we imagined and may break down the things we have built rather than keep us comfortable. When we seek to maintain our comfort, we often lose everything. We see that it's Delacroix's folly, vice, and stupidity that are critiqued.

The third bit of work done with this particularization is the reference made to the films of Oscar Micheaux. Micheaux's placement of photographs of great black thinkers on the walls of those dedicated to uplift is inadvertently mocked by Dunwitty through his sports portraits. In this way, Lee demonstrates Dunwitty's ignorance of black history and even black filmic culture, despite his claims to the contrary. Simultaneously, Lee broadens the complexity of reference within his own work and demonstrates himself as operating in a different way then he is depicting. The echoes of meaning pulsate in their inclusion, deliberately didactic, like Micheaux's race films. Lee wants to reference the program of uplift but he has also removed Booker T. Washington's image from the walls, and Lee uses this absence to critique who replaces him. However, Washington was so often the figure in the portraits on the walls of Micheaux's race heroes and heroines that these objects stand in for his presence, absent but looming, like the Founder in Ellison's novel. And because Washington represented the means so many turned to in order to pull themselves up—despite Du Bois critique of the inadequacy of Washington's methods of improvement—the transformation of his portrait into sports figures is all the more poignant, with many black youth viewing sports as their ticket into college and out of poverty.

The portraits also surprise us in Delacroix's inability to identify the person in the portrait when Dunwitty asks him to. His inability to do so upsets stereotypes of black people, demonstrates the constructed nature of race—if black people all know who number 24 is, then Delacroix is not black and blackness is located somewhere outside of skin tone—and undermines Dunwitty's professed authority through contradictory statements. Blackness is either all the qualities of all the people identified as black in skin tone or it is a set of culturally prescribed behaviors that any person can undertake. It cannot be both. So, Dunwitty's expectations that Delacroix can be a source of driving these cultural standards merely because of his skin tone is inaccurate messy thinking grounded in prejudice. Dunwitty, the ostensibly white man, sits in his office knowing the name of the men in his portraits; using the same knowledge as evidence of cultural blackness; ironically, demonstrating the conflict between the definitions.

The Black Collectibles

Delacroix outlines his own confusion over his cultural identity through the black collectibles he amasses within his office. The first collectible is, as previously mentioned, the Jolly Nigger Bank, given to him by Sloan. After the initial introduction of this object, the figures multiply around him, grotesque reminders of history and a link to the past that is an ever-present part of the now. Here, the objects' surprise, function as a referent to Ellison and become more significant through their particularization. Their sheer number is the surprise, they loom in the background quietly overwhelming the space, thrusting Delacroix towards a moment of crisis. When the Jolly Nigger Bank animates under its own volition, it reveals Delacroix's inner conflict, long suppressed. It is the same conflict of Ellison's narrator. When the camera jumps around the room, the eyes of these characters become the focus. They are silent witnesses to the judgment. Delacroix feeds the Jolly Nigger Bank, as assuredly as he feeds the idiot box. The collectibles existence within the film's frame points to an unfolding that occurs off-screen. Delacroix has been locating and purchasing them. They operate like the portrait of Dorian Gray, belying the connection to cultural blackness Delacroix consistently denies. The collectibles represent an image making of the minstrel era and situate themselves within the present, preventing a disconnection from their history. Like Miss Mopsa, they ink the interior of the office.

One of these collectibles—the tap shoes, formerly worn by Bill Robinson—Delacroix gives to Manray. This gift revisits Sloan's gifting but offers a significance through its difference. In the case of the bank, Sloan intends it to be a reminder of the past, and its form—a bank—serves as an admonition. Delacroix should not let money bury his morality. The shoes are not presented to be a reminder of a history, but rather link Manray and Robinson in their talent and their limited ability and opportunity to put that talent to unaffected use. Delacroix again designates Manray as connected to the racist stereotypes of the past. The insidiousness of the parallel Delacroix draws is made clear in his statements about the shoes. Bill Robinson died tapping, within them.[17] This referential function further underscores Manray's diminished agency— as Robinson's roles were primarily limited to Uncle Tom parts, particularly in his Shirley Temple partnerships—and foreshadows Manray's tragic ending, he will go out tapping, just as he hopes he does not. Unlike Sloan's warning, Delacroix's gift seems to be primarily about marking this connection; reaffirming that these things that Delacroix does for Manray are not the pure kindnesses they seem to be. Delacroix's behavior towards Manray is persistently duplicitous. This exchange is something of a Faustian bargain, it both underscores Manray's ignorance and desperation and exposes Delacroix for the devil he is. Surprise is also an element here. Delacroix's gifting is out of character. Consistently, Lee positions Sloan as the source of historical knowledge. If these shoes had come from her, the motivation for the gift would have been markedly different. Because they do not come from her we can be assured that education is not the intent. The only other time where Delacroix extends a gift to Manray is when he first negotiates the deal for the show. When Manray and Womack need to be made over. Delacroix's suggestions are toothpaste and deodorant. He uses the occasion of the gift to insult and ridicule them.

The Tap Dancing Puppet

Through the tap dancing puppet, Sloan provides Manray an illustration of the control she perceives he is under. If he is not Delacroix's puppet, well then, whose puppet is he? As previously noted, this puppet refers back to the one controlled by Tod Clifton in *Invisible Man*. The close-up shot of the puppet animatedly tapping upon Sloan's hand is tied to the paper Sambo dolls Tod Clifton animates with an invisible string. In the book, the language Tod Clifton employs as he animates the puppets points towards images of slavery. "Shake him, stretch him by the neck and set him down."[18] Some in the novel are offended by Clifton's behavior and association with the puppets. However, *Invisible Man*'s narrator views this behavior as potentially ambiguous, because he sees it as inconsistent with Clifton's character as he understands it. The point of final crisis for the narrator turns upon his personal knowledge of

Clifton as an intelligent man of good character. This understanding leaves him unable to draw any conclusion other than that Clifton's actions do not reflect who he is, but rather mark the actions of a good man broken by the circumstances of life, fighting back in the only way left available, to him, by mocking the debased images he peddles, by resisting the police officer and punching him when he is put under arrest. In the same way, Manray's final monologue mocks his initial appearance on the show, he acts—for perhaps the first time—out of his own impetus; eyes opened.

> Cousins…
> I want you all to go to your windows.
> Go to your windows and yell out.
> Scream with all the life that you can muster up.
> Inside your bruised, assaulted and battered bodies.
> I am sick and tired of being a nigger…
> and I am not going to take it anymore![19]

As Manray falls back, hits the ground of the stage beneath him and then springs back to life, beginning his dance, he demonstrates his mastery of the craft and astonishes the audience, including Delacroix and Dunwitty. This performance, while essentially the same in all its elements—the opening monologue, the tapping—is fundamentally changed in relationship to its motivation. Manray dances only for himself, not for Womack, Sloan, Delacroix, Dunwitty or CNS. Delacroix makes clear the stakes that are involved, "Fine, it's your funeral,"[20] and just like Clifton, Manray does not care. He has sacrificed enough of himself for Delacroix's skulking vision. After Dunwitty fires him, turning him away, a willing Honeycutt is ready to take his place. When the Mau Maus pick him up from the alley where Dunwitty leaves him, his fate as a martyr is sealed. However, unlike Spivak's subaltern, his voice occurs within his resistance and final acts of self-determination. Manray can speak. The correct question is do we hear?[21]

Coon Chicken Inn

Although technically not a collectible, the giant smiling faced doorway—through which Manray and Womack enter the stage at the opening of the minstrel show—serves a referential function to a fairly infamous series of black collectibles. This doorway is an imitation of the one that used to be outside the buildings of the restaurant chain Coon Chicken Inn. The roadside restaurant chain opened first in Salt Lake City, Utah in 1925. In 1930, the Seattle location would open on Old Bothell Highway. The grinning image of the winking coon graced not only the entry to the restaurant but every item of service contained within the same. All the plates, cups, menus, even a fan that was a giveaway for children bore the jolly visage. The presence of the doorway within the lore of the show demonstrates how extensive the reach of negative imagery can be, and draws correlations to the advertising imagery employed by Michael Ray Charles. The commercials which appear as a reiteration of this kind of advertising for the show within the film, broadcast contemporary connections proving a return to the past is not necessary for viewing this kind of advertising. The dangers of these *past* representations remain clear to us as their primary connotations have long been exposed. Understanding how their function behaves in relation to contemporary images and advertisements is more difficult, because we believe the myths of our present, and see the folly of the past. Our present understanding allows us perspective on what came before in abundance. However, presentist mindset prevents us from viewing our own time with the same clarity.

The Bamboozled *Painting*

The last significant object is the *Bamboozled* painting by Michael Ray Charles. In the chapter of this book devoted to Charles, an analysis of the content of the painting itself was laid out. For this section, the topic of focus is not the meaning of the painting, necessarily, but the significance of the painting as an object. Its appearance within the film marks a moment of nooshock. The image of the painting flashes across the screen with the speed close to that of a subliminal message. It almost winks across the screen. Like many of the other objects in the film, it is an image of a smiling coon. It is a contemporary image that has been critically contested with a rigor that other contemporary images which share its qualities have not been because it resurrects the past. The painting points to a preference for the past to remain buried.

The style of the appearance mirrors that of the filmed clip. Both are spliced into the action of the film without warning; interrupting the flow of the movement-images. Time is interrupted again. *Bamboozled* the painting breaks into the action like an advertisement, making plain an idea; Deceit and Conquer. Lee places the work in the film in this manner to highlight his alliance with Charles' project and ideas and to refer to the reception of Charles' work and draw a comparison to the reception his own work has received in the past. This conversation—over images and positivity and critique—asks, what is the place of difference between Charles' painting and the images he draws from? It is false to say there is none. What is the difference between blackface minstrelsy at the turn of the century and in *Bamboozled*? When Charles—or Lee—strikes these images to bring forth a new sound, the difference in the repetition sets the images within a new context, reframes them to guide a conversation that remains in progress. The reuse asserts a voice of dissent within a project of positivity that seeks to assert the dormancy of the very images that inspire so great an anger that dialogue shuts down. This reframing inserts a new voice into the narrative, one that intends to pull it all down from the inside.

11
Narrative Structures

I put myself back in the narrative.—Lin Manuel Miranda, *Who Lives, Who Dies, Who Tells Your Story*

I don't think we should ask our artists to worry about the lowest common denominator, or indeed the average common denominator of the response of the American public. I think it's a type of implicit censorship.—Henry Louis Gates, Jr., *Do the Right Thing*

Goodnight, you stupid idiots. Goodnight, you miserable slobs.—Lonesome Rhodes, *A Face in the Crowd*

In 1960's *Anatomy of Satire,* Gilbert Highet wrote that "The final test for satire is the typical emotion which the author feels and wishes to evoke in his readers. It is a blend of amusement and contempt."[1] This quote implies three things about satire. First, the author of the narrative feels amusement and contempt that is specifically directed. Second, that the author intends for the audience—or at least the ratified audience—to share in this amusement and contempt. Third, there is an object of contempt. As many scholars have noted, however, the true nature of that object is often difficult to discern and the audience members may hold biased perceptions that disagree with authorial intent. As a result, satire is one of the most frequently misunderstood forms of narrative. Although the form has a clear structure and markings—pointed and often politically motivated humor and irony, negative characterizations denoting specific types or referring to specific people—its ambiguities allow for incongruous conclusions to be drawn about these authorial intentions and the true meaning of the satire. Such is the case with *Bamboozled*. However, this incongruity can be anticipated and may be used by the author to deepen the critique. Therefore, satire as a form is not limited to a strict simple morality but is rather capable of great complexity. In *Embracing the Ambiguity and Irony of Satire: A Response to Jeff Melton*, Sharon McCoy wrote, "The power of satire lies not in its unambiguous moral target, but in its propensity to force us to make a choice about what that target (or those targets) might be. To both force critical thinking and allow us to laugh it off—if we so choose."[2] These elements—the need for critical thinking and the process of selecting for ourselves the target of the derision—compel our engagement and force us to reveal our own ideologies through our perception of the satire. The elective nature of the reception forces a moral conclusion to be drawn. If that conclusion stands in opposition to the author's ideas, it can very often transform the satire into a critique of its own audience, whose mere variance of viewpoints belie the claim that they are the ones that really get it.[3]

In the case of *Bamboozled*, the film points to the very ambiguity of satire to prove that great caution must be executed when using its forms. Precisely because satire—with its inclusion of negative caricatures—can be misinterpreted in ways that work against authorial intent; especially when that intent is doubly signified—as is the case with a signifier like blackface—because all the connoted meanings are put into play. What or whom is framed as the object of ridicule within *Mantan: The New Millennium Minstrel Show* evolves because Delacroix never really lands his punch. Dunwitty and CNS—whom Delacroix claims to be critiquing—are only derided if they find the show offensive. Once the show airs the objects of ridicule become Mantan and Sleep'n'Eat because the content of the show itself was never a critique of its supposed primary targets. The goal for the show prior to airing was to be so offensive as to command Delacroix's dismissal and to inspire his firing in a way that pointed towards Dunwitty's call for authentic blackness to highlight its racism. However, Delacroix makes an assumption that someone else will say that this line should not be crossed.[4] What Delacroix fails to realize is that he is the person with adequate power and knowledge and *will* to say no. In addition, we see within his previous show suggestions and his affectations that Delacroix has been in such a hurry to break with the past that he hasn't really learned anything from it. Delacroix writes the show in a manner that clearly demonstrates the disdain he feels for the coon character type. But, he also conflates Mantan and Sleep'n'eat with the people, Manray and Womack—as do The Mau Maus. Therefore, the show justifies their denigration through its humor, opening the door to the eventual slaying of Manray.

Delacroix doesn't properly consider the possible end results of his choices. And this ill consideration is magnified by the misinterpretations inherent to satire. Over and again within *Bamboozled*, characters misunderstand and misconstrue other characters' motivations and actions. The bullseye shifts, events unfold as a complex system of blame. The characters' faulty perceptions direct the ridicule towards more innocent targets. Delacroix witnesses the degradation of his critique of the network into a denigration of black people in general because the form's ambiguities allow it and because he never has hold of the reins. The show easily molds to the influence of the network, demonstrating Delacroix has inflated his own importance within the system and yet also missed his chance to be a benefit by crafting a show that subverts the dominant narrative. As a result, Delacroix's culpability for the denigration increases. In this way, Lee illustrates his point that you must be aware of the contexts for the material you put out in the world. You must account for the slippage of meaning, for you will be held accountable for it by your critics.

This point is clear within *Bamboozled*. Although many of the most overtly racist concepts for the show come from white characters, like Dunwitty, the responsibility for them are deflected largely to black characters. Womack holds himself and also Manray culpable. The Mau Maus blame Manray as well as he is the visible face of the renewed blackface phenomenon out in the world and Manray's talent adds weight to the show's concepts. Sloan, of course, attributes the primary responsibility for the show's problems to Delacroix, as do Myrna Goldfarb and Dunwitty. It is important to stress that all of these views have some degree of validity to them. However, the way *Bamboozled* frames the blame overall is to hold Delacroix ultimately most accountable. Authorial intent is key. This space of authorial intent enables the exercise of agency.[5] While the malleability of intertextuality allows for many layers of meaning within a film to be discovered by an audience member, an author forges that content into existence by drawing upon specific signs. Black cultural producers and indeed many black audience members are used to having conversations that are operating on several levels that serve a purpose of subverting the dominant narrative. This process is severely incapacitated when the cultural producer is ignorant of the subtexts. The subversion only works when greater knowledge is on the side of the author. Therefore, in the narratives of the disenfranchised, how the vehicle for that agency is perceived is ultimately less important because audiences can be relied upon to view the content with prejudice, through their own vantage point. Subversion can take place in the space beneath where many audience members cannot see it; even willfully will not see it.

Therefore, within these instances where the author and the audience do not share the same knowledge base or worldview, the object of contempt within a satire can seem unclear and the critique can seem unfocused or misguided or failed and this may be the largest measure of its irony. This point is essential for understanding *Bamboozled*. Lee had to have been aware at least to some degree that the reception of *Bamboozled* would play out exactly as it did. He was, after all, familiar with the reception of Bert Williams, Michael Ray Charles, and even *A Face in the Crowd*. As Roger Ebert pointed out in his review of *Bamboozled*, "That's the danger with satire: To ridicule something, you have to show it, and if what you're attacking is a potent enough image, the image retains its negative power no matter what you want to say about it."[6] Ebert goes on to say that:

> To satirize black shows on TV, Lee should have stayed closer to what really offends him; I think his fundamental miscalculation was to use blackface itself. He overshoots the mark. Blackface is so blatant, so wounding, so highly charged, that it obscures any point being made by the person wearing it. The makeup is the message.[7]

This critique is identical to the one leveled at Michael Ray Charles by Roberta Smith.[8] The argument assumes that for satire to be effective, the audience must receive the intended message of the of the author and respond as expected, but the brilliance of satire is that it levels a critique both when the message is received and when it is not. What if Lee knew that the reception would be exactly what it was? For this point is what separates Lee from Delacroix. Lee is using satire and blackface in order to highlight history and level a critique at black cultural producers who have forgotten that history and are blind to the effects their work has in maintaining these uses for these types of images. Lee uses blackface to underline the gravity of the misrepresentations. Was his use then still a miscalculation, as Ebert later claims within the review? I would argue that it is not. For Lee's use of blackface to be a misfire, Ebert's reaction would necessarily have to be outside Lee's expectations for audience response and this response would not serve the goals of the critique. However, as a result of Lee's work, Ebert is having a discussion with his readers about the ambiguities of satire. And this conversation is precisely the one Lee wants to be having. Lee uses the form to demonstrate the folly of the form's *unwitting* use. The makeup is indeed the message. How does one better say that contemporary portrayals of blackness on television draw parallel to minstrelsy than by linking these two to create one grotesquerie? The problem with *Bamboozled* is not that it misses its mark but that its audience is being told that it has been fooled and—to paraphrase Mark Twain—it is much easier to bamboozle people than it is to convince them they've been bamboozled. The audience is far more offended by Lee's use of minstrelsy than by the masked use of its forms in current culture. It is a difficult prospect to examine why that might be. However, it is unambiguous that Lee is critical of contemporary use of blackface within the film. Lee is very clearly not drawing upon these forms to produce buffoonery; he employs them to blast away at the updated versions of minstrelsy present within many aspects of our culture. Lee is like the Devil in Mark Twain's *The Mysterious Stranger*, chiding us for not seeing the power that lays before us in really putting humor to its best use:

> "There spoke the race!"[9] he said, "always ready to claim what it hasn't got, and mistake its ounce of brass filings for a ton of gold-dust. You have a mongrel perception of humor, nothing more; a multitude of you possess that. This multitude see the comic side of a thousand low-grade and trivial things—broad incongruities, mainly; grotesqueries, absurdities, evokers of the horse-laugh. The ten thousand high-grade comicalities which exist in the world are sealed from their dull vision. Will a day come when the race will

detect the funniness of these juvenilities and laugh at them—and by laughing at them destroy them? For your race, in its poverty, has unquestionably one really effective weapon—laughter. Power, money, persuasion, supplication, persecution—these can lift at a colossal humbug—push it a little—weaken it a little, century by century; but only laughter can blow it to rags and atoms at a blast. Against the assault of laughter, nothing can stand. You are always fussing and fighting with your other weapons. Do you ever use that one? No; you leave it lying rusting. As a race, do you ever use it at all? No; you lack sense and the courage."[10]

This devilish critique of low-grade humor echoes Lee's statements in the press against figures like Tyler Perry, "A lot of stuff that's on today is coonery and buffoonery, and I know it's making a lot of money and breaking records, but we can do better."[11] In addition, Twain's imagery of the brass filings mistaken for gold dust is echoed within Ellison's *Invisible Man* during the battle royal. The competitors put themselves at risk for treasures that masquerade for something of value. The spectators of Ellison's battle royal know that the coins are worthless and laugh and applaud, content to watch the show; content to laugh doubly at the physical spectacle of the competitors and their ignorance and diminished dignity. The coins serve as a means to bring the competitors low, to reduce their humanity, to demonstrate their lack of value. The only protection against this sort of reduction is to have the ability to discern the difference between bronze and gold. Lee asserts within the film that individuals require adequate access to knowledge about the past in order to see the implications of the history within the present. He wants to provoke within *Bamboozled*'s audience a contempt for images that degrade opportunity for nuanced black representations that might rather increase their personal value. As a result, Lee employs heavy-handed didacticism within the film. In order to garner the reaction he strives for, the didacticism is meant to be unmistakable. Lee is using blackface to make these connections unequivocal. The blackest black of Kerry James Marshall's paintings. As *Yo! Is This Racist?*'s Andrew Ti noted within his evaluation of *30 Rock*'s blackface episode, "You need to get more out of blackface if you're going to do it."[12] Lee jam-packs this sign like foie gras.

Didacticism always serves a goal of enlightenment. Satire as a genre is inherently didactic, highlighting folly for the purpose of instruction, to bring the audience to a different level of understanding; to correct misguided behavior. However, even audiences with a clear knowledge of relevant events may misinterpret the object of ridicule within a satire. This point is demonstrated within numerous examples of these so-called failed satires in literature, television, and film. *Bamboozled* is one. So is *A Face in the Crowd*. So is *The Colbert Report*. As Michael Moore says in "Misunderstanding Irony," "These smartly encoded messages have to be decoded, yet not every receiver is able or willing to do so."[13] In 2011, a group of researchers from Ohio State

University—Heather L. LaMarre, Kristen D. Landreville, and Michael A. Beam—published a study entitled "The Irony of Satire: Political Ideology and the Motivation to See What You Want to See in *The Colbert Report*." This study looked at the viewer's political ideology in relation to the message processing of ambiguous political satire within *The Colbert Report* and attempted to determine whether any bias occurred based on this influence. The researchers drew the data from responses by 332 college-aged participants in an online survey and sought to measure the correlation between the viewer's perceptions of Stephen Colbert's political leanings and the participants' individual political leanings. The participants watched a clip from the show, and then answered a series of questions about which elements within the clip were satirical, what they believed to be the true political leanings of Colbert, and what their own political leanings were. Inevitably, the perceptions of Colbert's political leanings corresponded with those of the respondent, while the respondents identified the opposing viewpoint as being the object of the ridicule. According to the report, "Results indicate that political ideology influences biased processing of ambiguous political messages and source in late-night comedy. Using data from an experiment ($N = 332$), we found that individual-level political ideology significantly predicted perceptions of Colbert's political ideology."[14] In other words, we usually allow our preconceptions to dictate how we read satire. Satire is expected to be incongruously received. Therefore, audience reception is not the only measure or even often the most accurate measure of success for a satirical film. Often it takes time to pass for the message of important examples of this genre to become clear. Satire is better appreciated with cognitive distance because hindsight allows for a clearer reception.

The fact that we read satire based on our biases demonstrates how our essential worldview forms our knowledge. It dictates how we as individuals know and perceive truth. Our knowledge about the world is based on what information we are privy to. And this information is formed from facts we encounter within our context. Putting the facts to work to become information and form knowledge is something we all do. This process is critical thinking. However, while facts or data are undeniable in their accuracy—it will always be true that water is required to keep human beings alive, for instance—information is biased; grounded within a worldview, curated. The facts no longer stand alone but are placed alongside other facts in a way that forms patterns. These patterns are interpreted to support claims. In this way, facts are rendered more useful for the purpose of gaining knowledge but are not yet knowledge. The contexts in which the facts are placed can change by the way the facts are perceived. Information can be an instrument of misrepresentation. Therefore, the more facts one has to back up any claims, the more verifiable the information becomes.

When facts are given relevance and directed with purpose—or become information—they always serve the goals of the organizer. If adherence to the truth of facts is less important for the perceiver than maintaining a certain worldview, willful ignorance can result, and informational claims become biased. A biased perceiver can manipulate the facts to aid their perception. In a similar way, if some facts are missing from the perceiver's framework, or unknowable the conclusions that the perceiver arrives at may be proven inaccurate once missing facts are established or become known. In the case of image making or representations, creating accurate ones is reliant upon the cultural producer's broad knowledge of different kinds of people and awareness of a multiplicity of stories. Those who are being represented must be vigilant in safeguarding their representation because they hold the heaviest investment for its depth and those who create representations must create images grounded within genuine understanding or they will visibly mark their ignorance to those who have greater knowledge. Satire serves as a recourse through which a person can critique straightforward forms of limited representation by broadening them through its equivocation. So therefore, by employing satire, Lee not only underscores the very fact that humorous representations can be so persistently malformed because of cultural bias but also provides room for these limited representations to express a double-consciousness through the ambivalence of their construction within this narrative form; just as Bert Williams' and George Walker's performances did. The representations function within a duality which Lee invites us to comprehend but understands that we might not see.

Delacroix's folly is not Lee's. The critical misreadings of *Bamboozled*'s representations arise from a different origin point than the problematics of Delacroix's monstrous vision. *Mantan: The New Millennium Minstrel Show* never critiques CNS directly. Delacroix's exaggerations align with the purposes of the systems they sought to undermine. *Bamboozled* hits its mark, because it secured the aims Lee sought for the film—a dialogue about the folly of ill-considered black representations in media—as demonstrated through the Ebert example. The judgment must be that the *Bamboozled*'s audience has formed inaccurate conclusions about Lee's purposes drawn either from ignorance to its operative function or willful dismissal of Lee's intent. A critique that cites only blackface's apparent singular use isn't sufficient to address why it then operates differently for Lee's film. The opposition to its use becomes a strategy of silence that serves a political purpose. No one argues that Lee advocates for degradation, but rather seek to characterize his choice as either ineffective, misguided, or ill-informed, a notion that doesn't stand up to careful analysis of the film's content.

Lee's emphasis on history and enlightenment within the film affirms that Lee seeks to combat the forgetting of the past that leads to unwitting participation in the perpetuation of demeaning stereotypes. He provides a path to move towards more comprehensive knowledge and understanding. We see multiple characters in the film model this transition. From the film's vantage point, clear perception—true knowledge—equals the awareness of the existence of multiple stories and access to enough facts and assorted experiences that allow an individual to weigh sources of information as to their factual accuracy and to form conclusions about the meaning, thus forging an understanding. To clearly perceive ambiguous forms of narrative, like satire, requires an adequate understanding of the object of the critique. Knowledge then is interdependent with access to adequate information. Knowledge allows for one to interpret facts and create information from them. In turn, perceivers acquire knowledge primarily through accessing the information sources birthed out of previous knowledge, it is therefore a systemic structure. Knowledge, in turn, enables enlightenment to occur. Enlightenment exposes the semantic structures that cause individuals to form beliefs about the information birthed from facts.

This same process of enlightenment is something that is repeatedly emphasized by Lee through his choices of satirical subjects for referents—*Invisible Man, A Face in the Crowd*—which involve a major character's enlightenment, as well as through his greater career project to incite a wake up for his audiences. For Lee, the work is two-fold, to bring adequate information to light sufficient for an awakening and two trigger an awareness of one's own slumber. Before unpacking *Bamboozled*'s references to other satirical narratives, clarification over the usability of the working definition of knowledge identified by this text as occurring within *Bamboozled* is required. It speaks to the success or failure of the project.

Knowledge as a Tool to Expose Semantic Structures

"Knowledge is a true and justified belief." This commonly held definition is more well known as the Tripartite Theory of Knowledge. This theory dates back to Plato. In Plato's *Theaetetus*, Socrates asks Theaetetus "what is knowledge?"[15] First, Theaetetus says that knowledge is perception. Inside Socrates response, Plato outlines a critique of Empiricism, demonstrating that our perceptions alone are inadequate to create an understanding. Theaetetus' second proposed definition is "knowledge is true belief."[16] Socrates dismisses the notion that all true belief is by necessity knowledge. People can believe things that are true without first having the knowledge of these things. Plato also makes plain that just as perception is inadequate for determining knowledge, it is—on its own—incapable of allowing for a distinction between true and false belief. The example of *The Colbert Report* illustrates this point.

Instead, some sort of semantic structure is required which perception fundamentally lacks. Theaetetus then proposes that "knowledge is true belief with an account."[17] Again, nothing is done to justify the distinction between true and false belief, so this definition is not much better than the previous try. Later proponents of this theory necessitate that you can't have knowledge about what is false, it is then not really knowledge, the thing is not known but misunderstood. The accounting aspect requires reasoning for the beliefs or support. This theory of knowledge was generally proved inadequate by Edmond Gettier who demonstrated that all of the conditions for knowledge, according to the Tripartite Theory, can be met—a person holds a true and justified belief—and there can still be no knowledge. Gettier's original example is basically this:

> A man named Smith is up for a promotion, as is a man named Jones. Smith overhears his boss saying that Jones is going to get the job. Later that day, he notices Jones place ten coins in his pocket. Smith muses to himself that the man who will get the job has ten coins in his pocket. This is a belief that is justified by what he has overheard his boss say and what he knows from having seen the ten coins enter Jones' pocket. However, Jones does not get the job. Smith does. It turns out that Smith has ten coins in his pocket as well, so what he has believed is true, however, it doesn't constitute knowledge. (Paraphrased)[18]

Gettier did not offer an assertion of his own conception of knowledge, he merely deconstructed a conception of knowledge as true belief justified. What this passage demonstrates—as does Plato's Theaetetus—is that semantic structures or boundaries need to be in place in order for knowledge to occur. Systems of logic and language provide the limits we apply to data and information to draw conclusions that we claim as knowledge. These systems hold values and operate invisibly and like representations they are being remade and held in force by those individuals—cultural producers among them—who tell the stories. The stories told by Western cultures since the Enlightenment have reflected colonialist values of rationality and power through knowledge and seeing which operated unquestioned until the rise of postcolonial thought in the long 1960s. Knowing therefore involves a colonization, which is combatted only by the awareness of an array of stories and a pushback against the single story. Okwui Enwezor describes what this looks like for contemporary curatorial practices in "The Postcolonial Constellation."

> Foucault's call for the problematization of the concept of thought in relation to critical praxis remains pertinent. The fields of practice in which relations of production, acculturation, assimilation, translation, and interpretation take place confront us immediately with the contingency of the contemporary norm of curatorial procedures that spring from the sovereign world of established categories of art inherited from "the history of art."
>
> The museum of Modern art as an object of historical thought has a social life, as well as a political dimension, and its function cannot be dissociated from the complex arena

of society and culture within which its discourse is imbricated. To that end, then, it is of significant interest to see in the curator a figure who has assumed a position as a producer of certain kinds of thought about art, artists, exhibitions, and ideas and their place amongst a field of other possible forms of thought that govern the transmission and reception of artistic production—someone, that is, who thinks reflexively about museums.[19]

Enwezor's point applies to Lee's desires for films and media. Both museum curators and directors of film are cultural producers. They bare similar responsibilities for determining how stories get told. Enwezor points us towards Michel Foucault's methodology as important for highlighting the problematics of current practices. The other semantic methodology that can be put to use here is Martin Heidegger's conception of truth as Being from *On Being and Time* which links the power of self-determination to knowledge and asserts a form of enlightenment that relates to standing as a fundamental Being inside the world. These concepts function provides a means through which we can establish what is missing from the Tripartite Theory, and how Lee's concept of knowledge parts from it.

Hubert Dreyfus draws a connection between the two philosophers in his article *Being and Power: Heidegger and Foucault*. In it he wrote:

> At the heart of Heidegger's thought is the notion of being, and the same could be said of power in the works of Foucault. The history-of-being gives Heidegger a perspective from which to understand how in our modern world things have been turned into objects. Foucault transforms Heidegger's focus on things to a focus on selves and how they became subjects.[20]

In other words, both men were concerned with the subject-object relationship. The ability to understand any given subject, and attain knowledge in relation to it, has been linked in Western Modernist thought to our ability to look at things objectively. To obtain an understanding of what knowledge is, we must explore how this relationship is constructed.

For Heidegger, Truth is the Greek concept of Aletheia, which he describes as disclosure. Disclosure is "things given." And for Heidegger, what is disclosed is the World. All of our understanding of the World is made possible by the way in which the world is disclosed to us. This assertion means that the facts or data revealed to us and the circumstances under which they are revealed provide the context for how we can perceive what surrounds us and what ways of understanding we can conceive. For Heidegger, while some things are being revealed other things are also being concealed, so even though we have access to ways of conceiving employed by people in say, Colonial times, we cannot experience the World in the way they did. So, how we order information into knowledge is dependent on what aspects of the World are currently in reveal.[21]

For Foucault, as power comes into being, it dictates that the boundaries of knowledge perpetuate its continuity. In this sense, systems of knowledge result from contingencies of history instead of inevitable patterns. Foucault refers to this last concept as Genealogy, which is intended as a reference to Nietzsche's genealogy of morals.[22] Foucault's earlier conception of the archaeology of knowledge conceived of knowledge as an ordering of information, but this model was deemed insufficient for speaking to the way knowledge operated socially and culturally. What knowledge is sought and held onto is determined by who is in power, and therefore different power paradigms employ different systems of knowledge, each putting to use facts which support their understandings.[23] Relating to Heidegger, who is in power dictates which aspects of the World are revealed and which are concealed. This critical space is where agnosis—willful or culturally supported ignorance—comes in. We frequently maintain ignorance of information that opposes our existing viewpoint.

Putting these two ideas together, we can see that at its essence knowledge is information that is selected, curated, and set aside to be consumed in order to reinforce the current mode of understanding. The difficulty with the Tripartite Theory is not within its conception of knowledge as true belief justified, but is rather within our misunderstanding of the significance of Plato's dismissal of the true/false binary. To borrow from Heidegger, let's see the World in its revealing. What if, for Plato, an establishment of knowledge did not require an accuracy of belief, but simply a revealed belief? The concept of truth as accuracy is based on the Roman Veritas, not the Greek Aletheia. If Plato has been misinterpreted through a Roman lens, this implies our conceptions of how truth manifests would produce a skewed model. Western systems of knowledge are instead built upon unlimited facts that may never be disclosed or given to us in their fullness. If this understanding of knowledge is correct then there is no way to establish a system of complete and therefore accurate understanding. Accuracy may not be an impossibility in theory but it is unachievable in practice. The best we can manage is to apply a standard of order that rises out of our current cultural perceptions and that draws upon the widest knowledge base possible. This system of understanding of the world becomes our knowledge regardless of its veracity or lack thereof. The power of more fact-based knowledge then is to challenge the status quo; to provide a means through which to prove the inadequacies of, among other things, limited representations.

Because knowledge is ordered understandings of information we construct from data disclosed by the World all around us, our perception of truth arises out of our knowledge of the World, rather than knowledge arising from Truth. Despite the stability of data as unchanging accurate fact, our inability to access all the data prevents knowledge from being equivalent to a veritas conception of true belief as accurate belief. The implications for *Bamboozled* are that enlightenment is the ability to exercise self-determination and that even when people's beliefs are accurate to the data, when these individuals are willfully disengaged from the facts, a door remains open by which they can lose control over how they are represented and they will not know to challenge the image makers.

Therefore, the objects of contempt within Lee's film are those image makers who willfully disregard the facts in constructing representations—regardless of how those representations end up functioning in relationship to positivity—and those image consumers who can know and do not care that they are being misrepresented because those who are in power—the white men of the West—at best do not see the invisible systems of knowledge that tell their stories and reinforce their power and at worst see them and are actively engaged to keep them in place.

In the case of a controversial film like *Bamboozled*, audiences offended by the vehicle of the message received the vehicle's contempt as equivalent to Lee's message. These audiences remained unmotivated to unpack the context of the imagery Lee used and therefore missed the point of the film, in a final measure of irony: unpacking history and context is necessary to prevent one's own misrepresentation. In other words, while the responsibility for misrepresentation lies first with those who produce the images, it is also born by those who choose to remain ignorant to the misuse. And herein lies the difficulty of the film, that critique is leveled at the audience at all layers. This layering makes audience understanding of the message of the film almost as unpalatable as ignorance and disinterest. On one level, those who misunderstand the film are insulted by its use of blackface, and on the other hand, those who understand the film's intention may be insulted by the vitriol brought against any audience who fails to comprehend its offenses. If not for the pressing theme of enlightenment, a viewer could easily argue that Lee has disdain for those that cannot see things from his viewpoint. The framing of *Mantan's* audience within the film—how Lee presents them—becomes crucial for finding a sympathy for the audience he seeks to enlighten. He makes a point of setting Manray and Womack—arguably the film's most sympathetic characters—in front of a television set when Delacroix speaks of the television as "the idiot box" before the show makes its debut. It's crucial for this moment to occur within the film because the correlations Lee draws are bitter pills to swallow. It is, after all, a turbulent and difficult film.

The difficulty of the message necessitates heavy-handedness on Lee's part in terms of reference, because he doesn't want to leave anybody behind, insulted or brought low. He wants everyone to get the film and to get angry because that anger can be channeled into a platform for action against those who re-make and re-present these types of images. The proof of this assertion can be found in the abundance of references to other satirical sources. From the beginning of the film, Lee strives to be as upfront with his intentions as possible; offering definitions of satire, putting to use several structures of the form within the film. First, the monologue: the opening monologue by Delacroix never actually ends until the film ends. Delacroix's narration serves as one long monologue. Second, the parody—narratively speaking the script parodies not only the PJs, Williams, Micheaux, and Ellison but also *A Face in the Crowd*, *The Producers*, and *Network*. Large chunks of dialogue refer back to these parodied works. Third, the narrative serves as satire by undertaking the form of a cautionary tale and didactic. Ultimately, *Bamboozled* provides the means for the audience to gain the knowledge that would separate them from those who would be ridiculed within its parameters. For the remainder of this chapter, we will unpack these references and talk about the effect of their inclusion.

A Face in the Crowd

In *A Face in the Crowd*, journalist and radio personality Marcia Jeffries discovers Lonesome Rhodes sleeping off a drunk in the local jail. She chooses to highlight his populist antics on her program, "A Face in the Crowd," and delighted by his wit and charm, offers him a job airing his opinions on her station. Lonesome's brand of straight-shooting catches on quickly and soon the local Arkansas radio spot is too small to contain Rhodes' talents and ambitions. He makes his way first to Tennessee and then eventually New York, where he gets a national television show and gains influence in advertising and politics. As his fame grows, so does his ego. Rhodes believes that he is clever, and the more clever he feels, the larger his disdain for his audience grows. Rhodes continues to drink and womanize, leaving Ms. Jeffries to pick up his pieces. Ms. Jeffries believes he will, in the end, reward her loyalty with a marriage proposal. However, instead, Rhodes marries an underage girl, despite the fact that he clearly leads Ms. Jeffries on, flirting heavily with her throughout much of the film, making promises that demonstrate his inherent lack of trustworthiness. Rhodes harshly mistreats his writers and staff. He presumes too much about his power to influence people and cannot view himself as replaceable. His lack of concern for the feelings and loyalties of the people—like Jeffries— who have been with him from the early days of his fame eventually cause them to abandon him. He comes to enjoy being listened to more than audiences even enjoy hearing him. In a fatal error in judgment, Rhodes mocks the audience in front of the camera, believing the sound to be turned off. Ms. Jeffries, in a final act of desperation, broadcasts his insults to his adoring fans. "Goodnight, you stupid idiots. Goodnight, you miserable slobs,"[24] bringing down the monster she helped to create through her blind affection.

Throughout the film, Rhodes self-edits the aspects of his character put on display, presenting a more flattering version of himself. However, importantly, Rhodes is not a good man corrupted by power. He is foul to begin with. The exposure to the spotlight eventually amplifies the character defects already existing within Rhodes and the misplaced adoration of the masses instill him with false confidence; causing him to believe that he can do whatever he wants to do and the audience will still love him. Rhodes presents a false face to the camera, believing he can con audiences the way he has consistently conned people from the opening of the narrative. However, when the audience hears what Rhodes truly says—when they see his genuine feelings about them—they turn on him with lightning speed. He is destroyed before he leaves the building. He arrives at a supper he has thrown in his own honor where no one is in attendance.

A Face in the Crowd does a solid job of critiquing unquestioning positive perceptions of the famous—whom the average person holds little personal knowledge about. While much has changed in this regard since 1957—audiences are more jaded in their perceptions of overall celebrity—too much has not. Audiences are still swayed by the cult of individual personality and convinced by the gleam of branding, frequently accepting images without applying critical judgment towards the same.

The late 1950s marked a growing disillusionment with the rise of consumer culture and beginnings of a postmodern sensibility. Dwight D. Eisenhower became president of the United States and passed the Eisenhower Doctrine, pledging to fight the spread of Communism. This fear of global communism mirrored waning American trust in its own government, which had been shaken by the behavior of HUAC towards U.S. citizens. Accompanying the American public's broadening understanding that governmental power could work against the people—as they had witnessed within Hitler's Nazi party and Stalin's brand of communism—was an understanding that that kind of corruption could exist in any form of government. Oppression could and did surface within a democracy. During this time, advancements were made for social justice. The Rev. Martin Luther King, Jr., helped to form the SCLC and the Civil Rights Movement advanced with greater earnest. However, despite the fact that these ideas were growing among the general public, the film suffered in its reception. While *A Face in the Crowd* served as a warning and an admonition of the very ideas bubbling at the culture's surface—like *Bamboozled*—the film flopped at the box office despite its quality actors, talented director, and scriptwriter. Andy Griffith, Patricia Neal, and Walter Matthau all deliver superb performances. Two time Academy Award winner Elia Kazan directed the powerful script adapted for the screen by poet laureate Budd Schulberg, who also wrote the story the film is based on. The film doesn't miss its mark, its audience of contemporaries simply didn't want to hear it in this form, which perhaps foreshadows the reaction to *Bamboozled*, who follows several of its themes.

First, there is the theme of destitution and elevation. As the savvy Ms. Jeffries finds Lonesome Rhodes and recognizes his appeal, Sloan does for Manray. This match is not an exact mirror, for the Rhodes character most closely resembles Delacroix in the movie, and Sloan's relationship with Delacroix most closely resembles Jeffries and Rhodes. Manray bears similarities to Walter Matthau's Mel Miller, the writer who desires Ms. Jeffries as a romantic partner, but who doesn't stand a chance because Rhodes poisons any possibility of their involvement by stringing Ms. Jeffries along. Delacroix, towards a similar end, poisons any future for Manray and Sloan through his attempts to slut-shame her for her prior involvement with Delacroix. Delacroix also exhibits many of the same character faults as Rhodes does. He looks down on the audience whose attention he seeks. He desires power. He likes money though he does not work very hard. Delacroix is not loyal to those he has used to achieve fame. Most importantly, his initial claims that he wants to get fired are disingenuous. Whenever he envisions a future for the show, it is his own star he sees as rising. Delacroix is accepting an Emmy and offering it to the white presenter. He is performing the coon at his acceptance speech, a la Cuba Gooding, Jr. Delacroix wants to enact the forms he despises and still look down upon those who perform in and watch the show, refusing to see himself as complicit in sustaining the forms' consumption. Success highlights his already generous ego, as much as his lack of success insulted his personal genius.

The Producers

When Mel Brooks released *The Producers* in 1967, it brought shock schtick and low-level humor to new heights. Ebert wrote that "it was one of the funniest movies ever made.... The movie was like a bomb going off inside the audience's sense of propriety. There is such rapacity in its heroes, such gleeful fraud, such greed, such lust, such a willingness to compromise every principle, that we cave in and go along."[25] The main difference between Ebert's description of *The Producers* and the actuality of *Bamboozled* is that *Bamboozled* employs a Juvenalian form of satire rather than a Horatian form—the form employed by Brooks within all of his films including *The Producers*.

These two forms are named after Horatio and Juvenal, the Roman writers who first used them. Horatian satire is gentle and comedic, like The Simpsons. Within this form, the critique is more general, less specific and there is little contempt demonstrated. Juvenalian satire is darker and more biting, like South Park. This form emphasizes contempt over humor. When humor is employed it is through irony. Examples from Modern literature of the two types would be *The Adventures of Huckleberry Finn* and *Lord of the Flies* respectively. So, in this sense, Ebert's comparison of the two films—while Lee is definitely making reference to *The Producers*—is somewhat like comparing apples to oranges.

Juvenalian satire is not necessarily comedic. The BBC series *Black Mirror*—famous for its premiere episode that deals with the kidnapping of a young female member of the British aristocracy who is ransomed in exchange for a public sex act between the British prime minister and a pig—is another example. *Black Mirror* inspires horror rather than guffaws because the point is to be horrified not to laugh. In a similar vein, *Bamboozled* is not funny overall—although there are genuinely funny moments—it is in deadly earnest and the audience should not in good conscience come along. Delacroix, in particular, is also filled with fraud, greed, and lust. He also compromises every principle but we see the consequences as these character flaws play out. The butt of the joke is not an easy, agreeable target like Hitler but Manray and Womack—who Lee calls upon us to empathize with—set up as fools. Delacroix and Sloan stage a failure to save money with the hoped-for result of Delacroix being fired from his contract as quitting would cost him his job, borrowing from *The Producers* its main plot thrust. But in doing so, they wager the reputations and future of others more vulnerable than themselves betting on a bad faith bargain that the show will never make the air. However, as happens within *The Producers,* the show becomes a hit. They are no better judges than Max Bialystock and Leo Bloom are at determining what constitutes a failure or a success. But because *Bamboozled* satirizes *The Producers*, it is pointing the audience to that film's folly. To put on a show that works against ethics for the goal of earning money, when you don't know how it will be received is folly.

The camera pans the audience reaction to *Mantan* just as Brooks does for *Springtime with Hitler* within *The Producers* but shows us a mixture of shock and laughter rather than only shock. White audience members hesitate, unsure if they should laugh or not, looking to the black audience members that surround them for a clue on how to respond and seeing uproarious laughter, they begin to laugh along. The next time we see the audience no one is questioning whether or not it is appropriate to laugh and over time the audience reaction becomes more overtly enthusiastic.

The first inclination of those initial audience members succinctly points to several rules of comedy. First, sometimes what is culturally allowable for one group to laugh at may be inappropriate for another group. Second, sometimes when individuals included within a group laugh at things that are inappropriate for people who are outside the group, the overhearing audience members view this as a form of permission. Third, there is a hierarchy in

Zero Mostel as Max Bialystock (left) and Gene Wilder as Leo Bloom in Mel Brooks' *The Producers* (1967).

comedy. You must always punch *up*. Joseph Amditis wrote in "White Men Can't Joke,"

> First, it must be noted that the success or failure of racial or otherwise controversial humor is largely contingent upon the context in which the material is presented and received. In general, the potential to induce genuine laughter depends on the identity of the person telling the joke. This is especially true of racial, ethnic, and other jokes about marginalized groups in society. These jokes are often considered offensive unless the person who tells them is a member of the marginal group in question.[26]

However, when humor is satirical and the locating the object of the humor becomes murkier, we see slippage in meaning occur. This slippage is the space in which ideologies can shift. Therefore satire requires more work from its audience. A clear example of this point can be seen in the figure of risqué comedian Daniel Tosh. His jokes take advantage of this line to push what people find acceptable to laugh at. Because he is a white male, his jokes often are perceived as mean-spirited and the layers of nuance are often missed or considered insufficient in their critique of the white male troll to make up for the offensive nature of the humor.

A clear example where Tosh pushes this line to make his audience uncomfortable is his joke about what different ethnic groups would taste like if you were a cannibal. The mere use of cannibalism is enough to ride a line of inappropriateness, but when he introduces racial aspects to the humor the line is crossed. Responding fittingly gets stickier in part because the humor is questioning the boundaries of humor and setting whiteness up as the hard punch line of the joke. The largely white audience members laugh at each successive joke because they believe they too will get their turn as the punch line, which eventually they do—"White people taste like macaroni and cheese"[27]—but not before Tosh makes them sweat a little. "You don't eat White people... 'We kind of thought you'd be tossing one in our direction. And now you've pretty much hung us out to dry.'"[28]

Whether Daniel Tosh reads as racist and misogynist relies heavily upon where you believe his satire is directed and what you think he is poking fun at in his humor. Again within audience response to Tosh, we see that political ideology of the viewer heavily influences whether or not the viewer sees Tosh and the white male troll as the ultimate butt of the joke and also dictates whether or not these viewers become offended. In other words, you can have white males who view Tosh's comments as straightforward riffs on the people his jokes appear to be about who hold him up as an icon and fail to see any irony because they stand in agreement with what they believe he represents. But you can also have people of color and women who take his comments as straightforward and find themselves to be the butt of his jokes and therefore find him offensive. Daniel Tosh as a public figure is controversial because much of what he presents breaks the rule that you should always joke upwards, not downwards, unless you see Daniel Tosh as the ultimate butt of his own jokes. In viewing Tosh's humor, an audience member has to make a decision about whether Tosh's standup presence is part and parcel with his personhood, or is an identity statement in order to determine where his humor is directed. In relationship to this point, Amditis reiterates the point of the authors of the *Colbert Report* study—that people process and remember the content that agrees with their established ideas. "That is to say, despite the vast selection of metaphor, meaning, and insight contained within performances from comedians like Dave Chappelle, the majority of audience members will nonetheless subconsciously disregard the overwhelming majority of material—except those narratives that fall in line with their own preconceived notions."[29]

As this point becomes clear to comedians, many choose to draw a line in the sand and forego using tools that are conceptually not necessarily racist or misogynist—fair game according to the above-stated rules—but can be perceived as such in order to prevent the possibility of ambiguous determinations. Mooney operates within the boundaries of this line ever since he butted heads with Michael Richards—of Cosmo Kramer fame—overuse of the N-word. Richards used the word repeatedly to berate a heckler in 2006, causing the Laugh Factory to ban him for life. While Mooney believes—as he has said—that he has earned the right to use the word, as he has too often been the object of its use by others, he does not want his use of the term to justify its abuse by others.

> I have known Michael Richards for something like 20 years. We're friends. But I heard about the tape and I said, "That doesn't sound like a comic routine. That sounds like a breakdown." Then I saw the tape and I had an out of body experience. It was so ugly, so horrible. I hadn't heard (the n-word) like this—from someone I knew. Suddenly, I was directly connected. I was able to look at it not just through my eyes but through the eyes of the world. I had always thought it was endearing. It's NOT. It's not an equal opportunity word. I don't want everyone running around saying it.[30]

In 2012, Tosh was involved in an incident—also at the Laugh Factory—responding again to a heckler. Tosh was doing a bit about how anything can be funny, including rape. The female heckler responded by saying rape is never funny. Differing accounts dispute the circumstances of Tosh's response. In the woman's account on Tumblr, she said she made the statement only after sitting through a litany of offensive, unfunny rape jokes until she couldn't stand to keep silent and that after Tosh's response, she and her friend got up and walked out because she felt so disquieted by the audience laughter in response. The club owner, Jamie Masada, claimed in a Buzzfeed article that an audience member suggested the topic to Tosh; that the woman's comment that rape is never funny followed this audience members' suggestion, not Tosh's jokes and that the woman then sat through the rest of the comedy routine before asking for a refund at the end of the show.[31] Both parties agree that Tosh's comments in response to the woman intimated that she either had been or should be gang-raped by five guys. Many of the articles—like Jeremy Stahl's piece for Slate—and their comment sections about the incident called up the Richards situation.[32] However, saying these two are the same is problematic. They are not. It seems clear that there is a difference in intent—Richards spews a stream of abuse that is not connected to any attempt at humor, while Tosh's comment was an attempt at a joke that miserably failed because of it overstepped the rules of comedy.

In the end, however, this difference doesn't matter because the work that was done in both situations created an atmosphere of fear and intimidation towards the hecklers. The construction of Tosh's joke was aimed directly at the woman. There was nothing that deflected the joke back towards Tosh. Tosh's joke still crossed the line; not punching laterally or upwards; not seeking to create irony. He punched down, and the audience laughed and gave him a standing ovation because they did not see any difference between that failed joke and his more satirical work. For many now the debate over where Tosh's jokes are directed has been answered and closed. Crossing that line closed a door for interpretive possibilities and provided a lens for audience members to view him through. It retrospectively colors everything that went before it. Tosh's own words have given audiences permission to view him as he appeared in that moment. The result is the same within *Bamboozled* for Delacroix. Crossing that line unraveled possibilities for him to protest the racist systems in place at CNS.

Dave Chapelle began to worry he was crossing this same line after a white crew member laughed at the wrong part of a joke, which involved Chapelle dressing up in blackface and appearing over his own shoulder like a devil/angel. This confusion caused him, in part, to abandon his successful Comedy Central show. However, again this situation is not the same as either the Richards or Tosh scenarios. Chapelle was not punching down, nor was he spewing a racist vitriol. While some audience members could choose to mark the three as equivalent—perhaps even find all three funny for similar reasons—this perception doesn't make them the same. But it is still important to be aware of the perceptions and proceed cautiously when riding that line. When you examine the events that unfold after each of these three situations, only in Chapelle's case does the author of the comment become concerned about how the construction of the joke influences the outcome. Only in Chapelle's case does the experience compel the performer to an enlightenment about the complex effects of the joke. The goal of *Bamboozled* seems to be to set up these kinds of awakenings for its audience members, both to see complexity and demand nuance and awareness from the performers. It isn't, necessarily, the goal of the film to hold up only positive images for consumption but to encourage audience members to become more informed image consumers and to patronize television and films that offer this type of complexity. Performers, while not responsible for audience correct response, should nonetheless be cognizant of its effects. While viewers should be responsible for recognizing that they are making choices about their interpretation of humor, and grapple with what that means.

Network

Outside of the influence of *Invisible Man*, no work more clearly asserts its presence within *Bamboozled* than Sidney Lumet's *Network*. The infamous "mad as hell" speech by Howard Beale—played by Peter Finch—makes an appearance twice within the film—first through the voice of Manray as Mantan and then second through Manray as Manray—and echoes the progression of Beale's transition from ratings booster to network critic, in both instances ensuring the tragic fate of Manray and Beale narratively.

Network stands as a prophetic glimpse into the depths television network executives will sink in order to ensure high ratings. At its release, it sparked conversations about the declining morality of television; drawing upon a common idea that these executives were willing to put anything on the air

Peter Finch as Howard Beale in Sidney Lumet's *Network* (1976).

to garner ratings.³³ Looking at today's prevalence of reality television in which unknowns clamor for the spotlight and stand willing to degrade themselves in exchange for their fifteen minutes of fame, its relevance has only increased with time. Shows like Aaron Spelling's HBO offering, *Newsroom* attempt to recreate *Network*'s bite—with *Last Week Tonight* with John Oliver striking this chord more effectively because of its satirical bent. Nevertheless, the authority of Beale's voice within the film is its genuineness. The same holds true within *Mantan: The New Millennium Minstrel Show*, Manray's and Womack's genuine talent and timing produce a show whose performances excel yet whose producers hold the performers up as the butt of the joke. Manray and Womack go through routines that echo the performances they give at the *Bamboozled*'s opening. The main—but not the only—difference is that the producers use blackface to mark these performances as a coon show. Therefore, when Manray speaks and dances with his own voice, and turns the words outward, the change is palpable.

In addition, *Network*'s Ecumenical Liberation Army is fashioned by Lumet and writer Paddy Chayefsky in the image of the Symbionese Liberation Army (SLA) whose most famous action was the kidnapping and possible brainwashing of Patty Hearst. In *Network*, the Patty Hearst character is played by Kathy Cronkite, Walter Cronkite's daughter, in no small measure of irony. The real-life SLA—much like the real-life Mau Maus—often stood in the way of its own stated goals in its actions. On November 6, 1973, the SLA murdered Marcus Foster a superintendent of schools in Oakland, California. The group indicated that Foster was a fascist for instituting ID cards for his schools. In reality, Foster—a politically left-leaning black man—had opposed the cards and had managed to water down earlier renditions of the card policy for the schools. Robert Blackburn, who had been walking with Foster at the time, was also shot by the SLA, suffering 23 entry and exit wounds. As Blackburn stated in an interview in 2002,

> These were not political radicals. They were uniquely mediocre and stunningly off-base. The people in the SLA had no grounding in history. They swung from the world of being thumb-in-the-mouth cheerleaders to self-described revolutionaries with nothing but rhetoric to support them.[34]

Following the death of Foster, recruiting members became increasingly difficult for the group. He had been well-liked and well thought of by the community. In executing him, the SLA eliminated a figure within the system who was working as an advocate for the right to untethered education. Their actions demonstrate their interest in compelling their own propulsion into the spotlight over their political goals. Within the kidnapping of Patty Hearst, the SLA seeks first the release of their own members; only requiring Randolph Hearst to feed San Francisco's poor as an afterthought. Even within this action, their plans created chaos. The media hype that rose in response to the coverage surrounding the kidnapping and ransom drew greater numbers of poor seeking the food to be handed out than anyone anticipated, and those standing in line to be served got pelted with food by the men attempting to distribute it, resulting in riots in many of the locations where the food was distributed. While much of the organizational blame for this situation must fall to Hearst's father, the threat that caused the desperation of the response rose directly from the SLA's actions. Their political aims served as a secondary consideration. The point was always their own publicity and self-aggrandizement. In Lumet's *Network,* this same motivation is made apparent within the contract negotiations with the ELA over the *Mao Tse Tung Hour.* The Angela Davis–esque figure of Laureen Hobbs bemoans the loss of revenue for the Communist cause, claiming that the party will not earn until the series goes into syndication. And slowly the genuine messianic insanity of Howard Beale loses its former appeal as a lead-in as he sinks deeper into madness. Says Hobbs,

> He's plague, he's smallpox, he's typhoid. I don't want to follow his goddamn show. I want out of that 8 o'clock spot. I've got enough troubles without Howard Beale as a lead-in. You guys scheduled me up against "Tony Orlando and Dawn," NBC's got "Little

House on the Prairie," ABC's got "The Bionic Woman." You've gotta do something. You've gotta do something about Howard Beale. Get him off the air. Get him off. Do something. DO ANYTHING.[35]

The Mau Maus in *Bamboozled* are similarly motivated. The film characterizes the group with a mind's eye on *Network*, placing a lust for fame centrally within their actions. He marks them as mediocre and thoughtless through kisses of similarity within the historical referents' backgrounds. The SLA and the Mau Maus both took issue with ID cards, both were economically motivated, both were categorized as terrorist organizations, and both groups used coercion tactics to convert followers. These surface similarities between the two groups allow a connection to be inferred between *Network*'s ELA and *Bamboozled*'s Mau Maus. The Mau Maus' decision to televise their execution of Manray exposes the attention seeking aspect of their actions. The Mau Maus—like Delacroix—feed the idiot-box with the live feed of Manray's execution. All the publicity is good publicity.

In the *New York Times* review of *Network*, Victor Canby questions whether *Network* goes far enough,

> Which leads me to wonder what it will mean when Network becomes—as I'm sure it will—a huge commercial hit with, one assumes, the same audiences whose tastes supposedly dictate the lunacies that Mr. Chayefsky describes in Network. Could it be that Mr. Chayefsky has not carried his outrage far enough or that American audiences are so jaded that they will try anything once, say, Network or Russian roulette? I'm not sure.
>
> I expect that a lot of people will sniff at the film on the ground that a number of the absurdities Mr. Chayefsky and Mr. Lumet chronicle so carefully couldn't happen, which is to miss the point of what they're up to. These wickedly distorted views of the way television looks, sounds, and, indeed, is, are the satirist's cardiogram of the hidden heart, not just of television but also of the society that supports it and is, in turn, supported.[36]

Canby's review gets at the crux of satire in a way that Ebert misses. The goal is to expose the hidden heart of a thing. Lee is angered precisely because he sees minstrelsy's types present within the hidden heart of the entertainment of today. The success of *Network* and the success of *Bamboozled* as satire is not dependent on correct reception, or audience agreement. The cutting nature of Juvenalian satire exposes the gaping rotten heart of the hidden and forgotten things. For an audience member to say, "Tis but a flesh wound,"[37] does not make it so, it merely highlights their inability to acknowledge the possibility.

The Goophered Grapevine

Any analysis of *Bamboozled* requires an awareness of the significance that double-consciousness asserts. This awareness locates the slippage in meaning that is permitted to happen between intention and perception and recognizes what work privileging audience reception over that intent does to the voices of authors of color. The emphasis of its particular importance in reading the work of black authors—or rather authors who are publicly perceived in relation to blackness—is the crux of self-determination. The awareness constitutes a refusal and uses these misperceptions to undermine or critique the wrong-headedness of the perceptions. An example can be found in the work *The Goophered Grapevine* by Charles Chesnutt.

Charles Chesnutt was a major black American novelist writing at the turn of the twentieth century. The Civil War had caused his mother and father, freed slaves, to leave their home in North Carolina and move to Ohio where Chesnutt spent most of his childhood. After the war ended, his family returned to their home in the South, where they struggled to make ends meet in the depressed post-war economy. Chesnutt took advantage of Reconstruction opportunities and became an educator, first a teacher and eventually a principal. He was deeply concerned for the economic disadvantages he witnessed black people endure within the South and was critical of platforms like Booker T. Washington's bootstrap model because he recognized a real barrier existed that prevented hard work from equaling success. Chesnutt began his writing career publishing short stories that were united by their central character Uncle Julius and the narrator John. These tales mimicked the style of Joel Chandler Harris' Uncle Remus stories and gained wide popularity with white audiences. The similarities were mainly superficial, but his largely white audience did not glean the subversions in the text. As Chesnutt expanded his work into novel form, he found his popularity diminished rapidly as readers more widely recognized the motivations. As a result, Chesnutt attributed the meager sales of his novels to the racial content and their clear political voice. In a letter from 1901 he wrote,

> I am beginning to suspect that the public, as a rule, does not care for books in which the principal characters are colored people.... I find a number of my friends advise me to break away from this theme for a while and write something which is entirely disassociated from it.... I am beginning to think somewhat the same way. If a novel which is generally acknowledged to be interesting, dramatic, well constructed, well written ... cannot sell 5,000 copies within three months after its publication, there is something radically wrong somewhere, and I do not know where it is unless it be in the subject.[38]

Although his novels struggled, he never stopped using them as a platform to talk about issues of race. He did, however, express a desire for his work to be taken on its own merit, rather than be marketed as a novelty in terms of subject. Chesnutt believed he was expressing life as he had experienced it. When his publisher Harold Robbins offered up the suggestion that his novel *The House Behind the Cedars* be marketed as a book about passing, he responded by writing, "I rather hope it will sell in spite of its subject, or rather, because of its dramatic value apart from the race problem involved. I was trying to write, primarily, an interesting and artistic story, rather than a contribution to polemical discussion."[39]

The House Behind the Cedars—his most successful novel—told the story of a brother and sister—John and Rena Walden—who were both of mixed-race background. The brother moves South and adopts the surname Warwick; marrying a Southern white woman and assuming a white identity. After his wife passes away—burdened to care for his young son—John returns to his home to ask his sister to live with him and care for the boy. She agrees and assumes the name, Rowena Warwick; effortlessly fitting into white Southern society. Soon Rena/Rowena becomes engaged. This happiness doesn't last long, however. She is found out, her background revealed. Her doting fiancé scorns her, and after this rejection, Rena/Rowena becomes seriously ill. Upon her recovery, she undertakes work to uplift her race, only to suffer an appalling end, fulfilling the trope of the tragic mulatto.

Like the performances of Bert Williams, Chesnutt's stories and novels located cracks in the mortar where the constructed narrative of race appeared less solid and fiddled with them to make them wider. Also like Williams, Chesnutt was professionally active a generation before the Harlem Renaissance and after the rise of that movement, his work fell out of fashion despite the fact that he inspired many of its writers.

Micheaux—who explored similar themes—would adapt *The House Behind the Cedars* twice for film. The 1925 silent version is thought to be lost, but the second version from 1932—entitled *Veiled Aristocrats*—still exists mostly intact. Always the optimist, Micheaux chose to reinvent the ending for the film. In his version, Rena survives by enthusiastically embracing her black heritage and marrying a young black businessman. The difference between Micheaux's and Chesnutt's endings may have reflected each man's level of optimism that arose from their experiences. While not necessarily financially successful, Micheaux mostly directed the events of his life through the force of his personality. Chesnutt on the other hand struggled and saw small reward. Eventually, he was forced to abandon his dream of earning a living as a writer; returning to his daily work teaching. Despite the moral power of works like *The Marrow of Tradition*—a novel that drew its plot from the race riots that occurred in Wilmington, North Carolina in 1898—or perhaps because of it, Chesnutt's most ambitious novel sold miserably and was poorly received by critics. His publishers demanded excessive changes and the end result was marked as a failure. Its reception would effectively end his career as a writer. He wrote his last novel in 1905.

Until recent years, Chesnutt's short stories had been criticized for pandering to racial stereotypes but many scholars have reinvestigated these works finding within them a greater depth than had been traditionally recognized.

Within the text *Race, Rape, and Lynching: The Red Record of American Literature, 1890-1912*, Sandra Gunning notes that "as an ambitious young writer who had begun to attract a national White audience, Chesnutt set himself up as a direct opponent to [Thomas] Dixon in particular."[40] Thomas Dixon's novel *The Clansmen* would become Griffith's *Birth of a Nation*. Both men wrote in response to the problems and racial tensions arising within the Reconstruction and both had enjoyed a great deal of critical success and popularity in the public.[41] However, their intentions could not have been more opposite. Under analysis, Chesnutt's attempts to reclaim and subvert the character forms present within other popular depictions of blackness is clearly demonstrated, while Dixon plays upon the worst fears and prejudices of his audience. The nuances and irony of Chesnutt's stories enable them to reach beyond the types they originate from.

The first story to garner critical attention for Chesnutt was *The Goophered Grapevine*. *Atlantic Monthly* published it in 1885, just four years after Houghton-Mifflin released *Uncle Remus: His Songs and Sayings* by Joel Chandler Harris. *The Goophered Grapevine's* publication marked the first appearance of a black writer in the pages of the magazine, although *Atlantic Monthly* at first did not disclose the author's blackness. Based on the merits of this story, Houghton-Mifflin became interested in Chesnutt's writing, eventually publishing his first collection of short stories entitled *The Conjure Woman* in 1899. The volume was a financial and critical success. The collection's narratives focused on the relationships between slaveholders and slaves, overturning the stereotype of the satisfied and happy go lucky slave so prevalent in popular Southern depictions; conveying instead the humanity, the sharp intellect and quick tongues of the same. In addition, rather than romanticizing the South and the plantation life, Chesnutt's stories depicted the cruelty of the slaveholders, offering a substantially more nuanced vision.

In 2001, Spike Lee would identify characters like Uncle Remus as the Magical Negro trope. Lee made these remarks when speaking out against the character John Coffee within the Green Mile.[42] The Magical Negro was a black man—usually elderly and wise, sometimes mystical—whose sole narrative purpose was to bring about character development within a white character. This character type, although often a positive portrayal, is problematic because the character has no life, meaning or purpose of their own, other than to be in service to the white characters. Black intellect, wisdom, and ability are put to use only in service of whiteness. Chesnutt combatted the Magical Negro trope by infusing the stereotype with a measure of warning aimed at the moral folly of the landowners and allowing the Uncle Julius character agency by leaving room for multiple motivations and subtext to his warnings. Chesnutt also highlighted the landowners' tendency to neglect and dehumanize the men and women who worked the land for them.

Chesnutt accomplished this broadening within *The Conjure Woman* by satirizing Joel Chandler Harris' narrative format—a recounting of folktales told by a black man in a negro dialect—interpreted through a white narrator. Chesnutt's use of this technique bridged a racial and cultural gap that stood as an obstacle to publication and expanded readership to white audiences through the format's familiarity without falling prey to all of its generalizations. Chesnutt's story documents the complexity of race relations in post–Reconstruction America while pointing out the incorrect perceptions and simplistic worldview inherent in Harris' book—both of which were endemic to the time period. Whether or not white audiences perceived these differences was almost beside the point. If they could not see themselves in John the narrator, this lack of perception was only underlined. If they did draw parallels between themselves and the affable but clueless John and alter their perceptions of the simplicity of the race question then so much the better.

Chesnutt understood race relations during this time period as layered interactions that required one to take into account a myriad of circumstances in their analysis. This understanding stemmed from his own personal experience of that complexity. Chesnutt was born to biracial parents, and as a result, had predominately western European facial characteristics and fair skin. This heritage proved an obstacle to integration into either black culture in North Carolina where he grew up or white culture in the South. This alienation led Chesnutt to examine the issues of race in depth. The work that he did in dealing with race within his short stories and novels was quite progressive, broaching themes that investigated the absurdity of the color line and flirted with ideas about passing and miscegenation. He confronted the inability of some people of mixed racial heritage to fit neatly into the categories of black or white; focusing on the special plight of those who defied the binary. As Chesnutt wrote in his journal, "I occupy here a position similar to that of Mahomet's Coffin. I am neither fish, flesh, nor fowl—neither 'nigger,' white, nor 'buckrah.' Too 'stuck-up' for the colored folks, and, of course, not recognized by the whites."[43] The evidence of the influence of Chesnutt's background creeps into *The Goophered Grapevine*. In the story, Chesnutt demonstrates an ease and familiarity with both the Northern and Southern landscapes and ideological narratives. His narrator hails from Ohio, where Chesnutt was born and moved to North Carolina where Chesnutt's parents took up residence during his youth.

> About ten years ago my wife was in poor health, and our family doctor, in whose skill and honesty I had implicit confidence, advised a change of climate. I was engaged in grape-culture in northern Ohio and decided to look for a locality suitable for carrying on the same business in some Southern State. I wrote to a cousin who had gone into the turpentine business in central North Carolina, and he assured me that no better place could be found in the South than the State and neighborhood in which he lived:

climate and soil were all that could be asked for, and land could be bought for a mere song.[44]

In this passage, we learn that the narrator was advised by a family member to buy the piece of property described in the parable that follows. Already, Chesnutt has marked for us the problems that exist with the land. If the climate and soil are excellent, why is the land to be had so cheaply? Upon striking up a conversation with a wary Uncle Julius, the narrator is admonished not to buy the property, that it has been goophered or cursed. Uncle Julius precedes to detail for the narrator the process through which Mars Dugal, the former owner, had his own land bewitched in order to play off what he considered to be the superstitious beliefs of his slaves. Dugal intended to go through the ritual of the bewitching as a visible way to discourage the slaves from eating any of the grapes while they worked; admonishing them that doing so would transfer the curse onto their own bodies.

In the parable, the vineyard stands as a symbol for the South and an allegory for the way in which slavery and the greed for free labor that it stemmed from tainted the South with its rot, ultimately destroying its financial prosperity; damaging its moral compass. As the story unfolds, we learn that one slave, the newly arrived Henry, fails to realize the grapes have been goophered and partakes of the fruit. Henry's body cycles in varying states of well being in unison with the seasons of the vineyard; representing the intertwined relationship of the lives and bodies working the land; existing together in the South. This connection is lost on Dugal.

> "Spec'" I made a bad bahgin when I bought dat nigger. Henry done good wuk all de summer, but sence de fall set in he "pears ter be sorter pinin'" away. Dey ain' nuffin pertickler de matter wid 'im—leastways de doctor say so—"cep'n" a tech er de rheumatiz; but his ha'r is all fell out, en ef he don't pick up his strenk mighty soon, I spec' I'm gwine ter lose 'im.[45]

Henry clearly thrives when the vines do; and then declines over the winter. Here, the relationship between the slaves, the landowners, and the land is made clear. The slaves are physically connected to the land through their work. The landowners attempt to control the land and the people who work it in order to retain the greatest wealth possible, believing that it is their right, denying the investment of the labor of the slaves—in the same way that Sal in *Do the Right Thing* believes there is a line of ownership that justifies which faces go up on his wall, Italian Americans or black Americans. Black patronage's contribution to Sal's success is overlooked because of Sal's simplistic perception of his labor and ownership equaling the pizzeria's viability. Dugal devalues the ideas and beliefs of the workers and uses what he thinks to be *their* ignorance to his own advantage. The narrator John also exercises this same judgment in weighing the truthfulness of Uncle Julius' story and considers his own valuation superior. He believes that Uncle Julius' warnings conceal selfish motivations. Through this disbelief, the John marks Uncle Julius as either a misguided fool or a cunning trickster. He determines to buy the field despite the warnings, dismissing Uncle Julius summarily. The narrator disbelieves the mysticism and determines that Julius wants to work the land to benefit himself, because that is what John himself wants, to put the land to work for his own profit.

It is not clear from the telling what Uncle Julius' motivations might be, however. His morality is ambivalent. Like John, the reader is forced to make a judgment about the character of Uncle Julius, and over what kind of story Chesnutt has written. Is it speculative fiction or realism? Either choice allows for the possibility that the story Uncle Julius tells is an allegory for how to treat those that the narrator hires to work the land. Dugal may have merely cursed himself through his own selfishness, and Uncle Julius may have framed the story so that John can find a truth principle whether the goophering is real or not. John, however, cannot find any benefit for himself in the tale. In the end, it doesn't matter whether the curse is mystical, or a moral parable. Either way, the warning remains unheeded and the cycle repeated. The narrator John has concluded his judgments. The reader must also. And so, while many readers received *The Goophered Grapevine* as a straightforward narrative of a bemused white landowner enthralled by the tale spun by a Magical Negro, a more discerning reader might clearly see the refusal of an ignorant White man to pay attention to the warnings of a black man's experiences. The reception depends on the biases of the reader.

Chesnutt also calls into question Chandler Harris' use of dialect as a means of authenticating the Brer Rabbit stories as folklore. The dialect as written racializes Uncle Remus with a prescribed cultural blackness which is unquestioned by Chandler Harris' choice of third person point of view. This voice claims authenticity and a neutral, anthropological vantage point. Chandler Harris' narrator interrupts Uncle Remus, instructing the audience how to respond to the tales. In addition, the unquestioning and unchanging relationship between Uncle Remus and the little boy who is his audience always retains the same pattern. In Harris' book, the presentation of Uncle Remus' conversation with the child is fixed and overheard. As John Callahan wrote, "In Harris, personality is static."[46]

Chesnutt's narrator and Uncle Julius stand in opposition to each other, presenting differing viewpoints, engaging in a conversation where there is a substantive dialogue. For Chesnutt's narrator, the South is the land of the Other, opposed to the North. The narrator John perceives Difference and marks Julius' speech as such. The frame shifts from being an authentic story about the Southern life recorded by a Southern anthropologist to one that sets up a North which views itself as more rational and with greater knowledge.

The syndicated audience of both men's writing consisted primarily of white Northerners. The approach of the two authors couldn't have been more different. Harris tells this audience what the South is all about, while Chesnutt invites the reader to encounter the South and perhaps disagree with its misguided Northern representative.[47] For while at one level, Chesnutt's narrator affirms these readers self-perceptions, the structure of the story allows for a subtext. Uncle Julius' audience is a white Northerner. He recounts Julius' tale in the first person. The narrator performs his version of the story as surely as Uncle Julius does and this performative quality influences the reader to distrust the narrator and his motivations for telling the story in the first place. The first person point of view also sets up space for the reader to question whether Uncle Julius truly spoke in the exaggerated dialect as portrayed or whether that dialect was part of a racialization process. Chesnutt deliberately sets the narrator up as suspicious. This stands in contrast to Harris, whose *Uncle Remus* writings are told in the third person and are presented as anthropological.

Harris hails from Georgia and took up the project as a means of recording stories he claims to have heard the slaves tell. In the introduction to the collection, Harris acknowledges, in a roundabout way, that the stories he has collected are disavowed in their authenticity by black Americans—"Curiously enough, I have found few negroes who will acknowledge to a stranger that they know anything of these legends"[48]—and that the dialect contained within the stories no longer exists—if in fact it ever was used. "The dialect of the legends has nearly disappeared."[49] He also acknowledges in the preface to the stories that the dialect he writes for the *Uncle Remus* is a characterization of Southern blacks, intended to operate as a type.[50] The subtext of this preface reads that Chandler Harris' *Uncle Remus* draws upon minstrel stereotypes and a romanticized idea of slavery as a happy institution. In the introduction, Chandler Harris goes so far as to ask the reader to imagine a time where a black slave "has nothing but pleasant memories of the discipline of slavery."[51] Chesnutt complicates slavery, however. John's use of the "Uncle Remus" dialect sets up the established characterizations of blackness tropes and connects the narrator to Mars Dugal. His characters interact and are given agency. black and white. Both narrators recount the stories and disagree about the meaning. This negotiation serves as a cue for the reader that the subject is open for discussion.

> I found, when I bought the vineyard, that Uncle Julius had occupied a cabin on the place for many years, and derived a respectable revenue from the neglected grapevines. This, doubtless, accounted for his advice to me not to buy the vineyard, though whether it inspired the goopher story I am unable to state. I believe, however, that the wages I pay him for his services are more than an equivalent for anything he lost by the sale of the vineyard.[52]

Chesnutt has Uncle Julius recount the tale to expose the subtlety of the racist undercurrent in the Northern narrator and to enable us to draw parallels between the first master and the second, one who is in power in the enslaved South and one who is in power following the Reconstruction. Uncle Julius is interpreted by the Northern narrator as a trickster but Chesnutt is telling the reader that John and Uncle Julius are both really tricksters as they are both narrators and as such, completely unreliable. John judges Uncle Julius untrustworthy based on his belief in established stereotypes of blackness. "Black Folks" are magical and superstitious. This transgression mirrors that which caused the issue for the original master, Mars Dugal. It is not the greed of the workers, but the greed of Mars Dugal himself. Just as it is not the greed of Uncle Julius that causes John to not heed Uncle Julius' subtextual warning but his own. Dugal has Aunt Peggy goopher the grapevines because he believes that workers are eating from the vines, even though none have ever been caught doing so.

A belief in the mystical is not necessary to find or heed the warning. Julius is clearly telling John that the fate of the land, the owner and the treatment of the workers are all clearly intertwined. Part of John's inability to see the warning contained in the story is a willful ignorance of the interdependence of these three. The refusal on the part of white Americans like John to recognize the fact that an American South—and therefore, also, America as a whole—did not need to be integrated, but already operated with interactions between black and white Americans on every level of life is represented by the manner in which the Goophering plays out. Mars Dugal does not view himself or his land as connected to the enslaved blacks that work it. And the same is the case with the new owner.

Operating within a time that disavowed black humanity and equality, Chesnutt used the language of the time to access and address these constructed representations and offer alternative imagery, agreeing with Du Bois' notion in *A Criteria for Negro Art* that all art is propaganda and representations in imagery both reflect and reinforce the attitudes of the culture.[53] Therefore, alterations of those representations can alter the culture itself. Through his satire of the dialect and characterizations and the grounding of these within the tragedy of the life and death cycle of the vineyard, and the use of a first-person Northern narrator with suspect motivations, Chesnutt alters the myth established by Harris, challenging its simplicity by deepening the connoted meaning as he exposes John's—and therefore implicitly, Harris'—motives. Chesnutt uses the stereotype of the Magical Negro and offers up his critique perfectly aware of the fact that it may be received in exactly the same manner as John, in fact, receives it. That John doesn't receive the message Julius conveys is inconsequential to its presence within the story. That the reader may not recognize John's ignorance is merely an added irony.

The fact that Julius may have his own motivations for not wanting John to buy the land, doesn't negate the parable of the story and in fact, provides a vehicle for his agency. The same is true for *Bamboozled*. Lee's critique doesn't require correct reception to function or to land its punch. In fact, the blow is all the greater in its impact when all its layers operate as plotted.

12
Keeping It Real: A Conclusion

WAKE UP!—Spike Lee

Bamboozled is a degraded word. Although its origins are unclear, folk etymology suggests a connection between it and drunkenness. Walter Skeat implies that it was the low slang of thieves, a cant before a drink; similar to the word lampoon, which derives its meaning from the French word lampons, meaning "let us drink!"[1] Jonathan Swift objected to its use in his compiled list of words that were corrupting the English language "A Proposal for Correcting, Improving and Ascertaining the English Tongue," from 1710. The vast percentage of entries in this volume come from the mouths of the British lower class, so undoubtedly there is a relationship between the satirical objection to the word by Swift and an objection to those who might use the word and/or do the thing.[2] For to bamboozle is to deceive by tricking the senses, for personal gain.

Through the use of this degraded word as the film's title, Lee points us to many things. Herman Melville uses the word within *Moby Dick*. "'Look here, friend,' said I, 'if you have anything important to tell us, out with it; but if you are only trying to bamboozle us, you are mistaken in your game; that's all I have to say.'"[3] Charles uses it within his painting *Bamboozled* as a reference to Melville's Black Guinea within *The Confidence Man* as well as the board game of the early 1950s. Lee uses it as a reference to himself, and to Malcolm X. The speech that the phrase is framed within—inside the film *X*—is the Harlem Rally in which Malcolm X states that a Negro is the only man who doesn't know his history.[4] Lee wants his audience to snap out of it.

Over and again, throughout a great portion of his films, Lee calls for his audiences to WAKE UP! There can be no doubt that Lee's career project is for people to wake up; to wake up to the futility of bickering between people who should be united; to wake up to the way images and characterizations hold the potential to harm and belittle people; to wake up to the way gun violence is destroying American communities. Recently, at a question and answer session after a screening of Chi-raq at Northwestern University, an audience member asked Lee what the solution to ending gun violence should look like. Lee responded, "Education."[5] Education is not enlightenment, but it sets up the conditions for enlightenment to occur. So, the didacticism of Lee's films point the way to enlightenment, but as this text argues, it is not Plato's enlightenment which seeks to find a Goodness to which these forms represent. The enlightenment within *Bamboozled* opens the audience's eyes to the vestiges of the weighty history to which the images and forms of the film are beholden and marries the film's intent to that of *Invisible Man* and Du Bois' double-consciousness.

In *Bamboozled,* Peerless or Pierre Delacroix is Lee's narrator. The story is Delacroix's, not Sloan's, not Womack's, not Dunwitty's, not Manray's. Like Fred Daniels, he lives behind the scenes. His apartment sits behind the face of a clock tower. Although not a literal cave, Delacroix's apartment exists behind and in relation to invisible systems that exist beyond the conscious mind of most. A clock tower—or a movie theater screen—is not something that most would imagine as an inhabited living space. And Delacroix's ventures into the world and his interactions with others demonstrate that neither he nor they can see him for who he really is. Through these significations, Lee establishes Delacroix as the character who will become importantly enlightened. As in the works by Wright and Ellison, this enlightenment is a journey. Because of his position and education and his understanding of the entertainment industry, Delacroix is the character held most culpable for his actions. Clearly, Lee feels for himself the weight of this responsibility as a black man of relative power and position within the industry and feels justified in calling out others with a similar level of influence to do the same because he has managed it for himself.

Ultimately, the biggest challenge for Lee to overcome is the complexity of his vision. The audience is unlikely to have the full spectrum of information that Lee is privy to and in fact, may be convinced by differing perspectives that are difficult to combat within mission of one film. The intensity of the experience of *Bamboozled* is the inevitable result of this attempt. A fellow art historian once offered up this piece of advice, "You don't have to fit it all within this one paper."[6] The fact that the film manages to be the masterpiece that it truly is despite the weight of its historical burden is an amazing accomplishment. The work manages to convey a strong connection to history and mines a rich tradition of black performative and narrative and visual culture with a measure of success that arguably exceeds any other Spike Lee Joint.

I do not argue that *Bamboozled* is a perfect film. It is uncomfortable to watch in some ways that extend beyond its subject matter, and it is by no means as streamlined or seamless as his masterwork *Do the Right Thing*. However, the common critiques of the film for its use of blackface, that it is denigrating to figures like Bert Williams, that it is a failed satire, that it misuses Savion Glover,[7] these are not validated by an in-depth critique that weaves together all the elements that Lee has carefully threaded. And its message is frequently sorely misinterpreted. The staying power of the film and its cult status despite its near unavailability either through streaming or on video are a testament to its endurability and growing audience. Even if a reader disagrees with the perceptions of the film as outlined in this book, *Bamboozled*'s continuing influence in conversations about representation is undeniable. After the close of the Obama presidency, the rise of Trump and the rise in visibility of movements like #blacklivesmatter, the film only grows in relevance.

Within *Black Skin, White Mask*, Frantz Fanon asserted that all people had one right and one duty. It is the right of human beings to demand humane treatment from others and the duty of human beings to act in ways that don't surrender freedoms, resulting in a loss of agency. Here Fanon says, "I am not a prisoner to history. I should not seek there for the meaning of my destiny. I should constantly remind myself that the real *leap* consists in introducing invention into existence. In the world through which I travel, I am endlessly creating myself"[8] In this passage, Fanon does not intend to discard history, but to assert that the force of history does not compel the future of any people. Agency exists. The choices that are made form what we become and we must be vigilant in the choosing. And so Lee renders a careful line. He does not call for only images of positivity and uplift but for a range of expression that is executed consciously and conscientiously. He employs blackface to subvert the form through the return. The Difference will arise through this Repetition. If *Bamboozled* is to be believed, buffoonery is not merely a style of performance but a yoke that is slipped on when vigilance is relaxed—a lazy comedy. If nothing else is proved within this text, may it be that the meaning found within Lee's films have been considered and executed with weight. *Bamboozled* may be a troubled film but it is not a mess, it is a deliberate calculation. As the man said, "I may have been born yesterday, but I stayed up all night."[9]

Chapter Notes

Preface

1. "bell hooks," Center for Cultural Studies RSS, 2015. Accessed January 8, 2016, http://ccs.ihr.ucsc.edu/inscriptions/volume-5/bell-hooks/.
2. Louis Onuorah Chude-Sokei, *The Last "Darky": Bert Williams, Black-on-black Minstrelsy, and the African Diaspora* (Durham, NC: Duke University Press, 2006), Kindle.
3. Monique Judge, "Green Book Has Great Acting, a Misleading Title and Palatable Racism for White People." *The Grapevine*. November 21, 2018. Accessed March 12, 2019. https://thegrapevine.theroot.com/green-book-has-great-acting-a-misleading-title-and-pa-18305 72839.
4. James Baldwin as he spoke in the film about his life, *The Price of the Ticket*. See also Baldwin, "Dark Days," in *The Price of the Ticke*t (New York 1985), 666.
5. David Rodeiger, *The Wages of Whiteness: Race and the Making of the American Working Class* (London: Verso, 1991), 6.

Introduction

1. W. E. B. Du Bois, *The Souls of Black Folk*, Third Edition (Chicago, IL: A.C. McClurg & Co., 1903).
2. W. E. B. Du Bois, "Postscript," *The Ordeal of Mansart* (Oxford, UK: Oxford University Press, 1957).
3. Cornel West, "The New Cultural Politics of Difference," October 53 (1990): doi:10.2307/778917.
4. Many scholars have varied in the spelling of the term Post Black. The fallback position has been post-black. I disagree with this spelling for two reasons. First, I capitalize Black here because Du Bois requested the capitalization of Negro in one of his published papers and J. Franklin Jameson refused to capitalize the word. Second, because it is not my intention to indicate an era or an art that is occurring "after" Blackness, I find this to be an inaccurate spelling of this descriptor. Post Black refers to a manifestation of art that attempts to deal with the metanarrative of Blackness after the rise of Postmodernity. Although these influence each other they are more separate than a hyphen would allow them to be. So this is how I will spell the term throughout, unless I am quoting the work of another.

Historiography

1. Jason Vest, *Spike Lee: Finding the Story and Forcing the Issue* (Oxford, UK: Praeger), 185.
2. W.J.T. Mitchell, *What Do Pictures Want?* (Chicago: University of Chicago Press), 340.

3. Mitchell, 14.
4. Gilles Deleuze, *Difference and Repetition* (New York: Columbia University Press, 1994), 147.
5. Stuart Hall, *Representation: Cultural Representations and Signifying Practices* (London: Sage, in Association with the Open University, 1997).
6. Deleuze.
7. *Ibid.*
8. Thelma Golden, et al., *Freestyle* (New York: Studio Museum in Harlem, 2001).
9. Michael Germana, *Standards of Value: Money, Race, and Literature in America* (Iowa City: University of Iowa Press, 2009).
10. Chude-Sokei.
11. *Ibid.*
12. Jacqueline Najuma Stewart, *Migrating to the Movies: Cinema and Black Urban Modernity* (Berkeley: University of California Press, 2005).
13. Cedric Robinson.
14. Donald Bogle, *Toms, Coons, Mulattoes, Mammies, and Bucks; an Interpretive History of Blacks in American Films* (New York: Viking Press, 1973).
15. Thomas Cripps, *Slow Fade to Black: The Negro in American Film, 1900–1942* (New York: Oxford University Press, 1977).
16. "Birth of a Quotation: Woodrow Wilson"; and "The Journal of the Gilded Age and Progressive Era," accessed August 8, 2016, http://journals.cambridge.org/action/displayAbstract?aid=7951339.
17. "Progressive Era to New Era, 1900–1929," Browse by Topic (Library of Congress). Accessed August 8, 2016, http://loc.gov/topics/content.php?subcat=10.
18. Corey Capers, Lectures, UIC, History 496, 2013.
19. David Waldstreicher, *Slavery's Constitution: From Revolution to Ratification* (New York: Hill & Wang, 2009), 19.
20. *Ibid.*
21. Capers.
22. Capers.
23. David R. Roediger, *The Wages of Whiteness: Race and the Making of the American Working Class* (London: Verso, 1991).
24. Hall, 1.
25. Capers.
26. This moral standard would give birth to politics of Black Respectability.
27. Roediger.
28. W. E. B. Du Bois, *The Souls of Black Folk: Essays and Sketches* (Greenwich, CT: Fawcett Publications, 1961).
29. Frantz Fanon, *Black Skin, White Masks*.
30. The practice of socially limiting the access of active forms of resistance to Black people continues even today. The recent backlash against #blacklivesmatter for the possible interruption of the 2015 Twin Cities Marathon is an example. The conversation within social media was framed around an interest in protestors respecting the rights of the runners to complete the race. The protest was acceptable as long as it didn't interrupt the experience of the runners.
31. Hosea Easton, *A Treatise on the Intellectual Character, and Civil and Political Condition of the Colored People of the United States and the Prejudice Exercised Toward Them*.
32. Mark Twain would translate this work as *Slovenly Peter*, arguably the most popular work in the 1891.
33. In 1875, they published *Ten Little Niggers*, a counting book that would later give its title to the Agatha Christie novel—ultimately retitled *And Then There Were None*, the last line of the verse—whose text provides the form for the murders.
34. Vincent Dill, and Thomas A. Cuzner, *Little Miss Consequence* (New York: McLoughlin Bros Publishers, 24 Beekman St., N.Y., 1859).

35. Michele Gillespie, Randal L. Hall, and Cherlene Regester, Thomas Dixon, Jr., and the Birth of Modern America (Baton Rouge: Louisiana State University Press, 2006), 170.
36. Eric Lott, Love and Theft: Blackface Minstrelsy and the American Working Class Kindle Edition (New York: Oxford University Press, 1993), loc. 87.
37. David Krasner, Resistance, Parody, and Double Consciousness in African American Theatre, 1895-1910 (New York: St. Martin's Press, 1997).
38. Krasner, 160-161.
39. Chude-Sokei, 42.
40. *Ibid.*
41. *Ibid.*
42. Spike Lee, *Bamboozled*, 40 Acres and a Mule Productions, 2001.
43. *Ibid.*
44. In 2000, the year of Bamboozled's release, Savion Glover would win the Flo-Bert award for advancing the field of tap.
45. *Ibid.*
46. *Ibid.*
47. W. E. B. Du Bois, "Criteria of Negro Art (1926)," *An Anthology of African American Literary Criticism from the Harlem Renaissance to the Present Within the Circle*, 2012, 60-68, doi:10.1215/9780822399889-007.
48. *Ibid.*
49. *Ibid.*
50. Roger Ebert.

Chapter 1

1. This violent reaction to the duo's performances sans blackface is echoed in Manray's final performance for the minstrel show. When Dunwitty sees Manray appearing onstage without makeup, he becomes irate—even before his speech—and removes him from the building, making him vulnerable to kidnapping.
2. In the film, the Mau Maus exercise control over Manray's bodily autonomy forcing him to perform. Despite the pressure of the bullets flying towards his feet, Manray performs with a brilliance that demonstrates the freedom that his ability affords him. The dance is his, not theirs. Just as Williams performance belongs to him.
3. Ann Charters, *Nobody: The Story of Bert Williams* (New York: Macmillan, 1970).
4. George Walker, "A Real 'Coon' on the American Stage," *Theatre Magazine* 6, August 1906, 224-6.
5. This flattening is also performed upon the use of blackface in *Bamboozled*. Attempting to determine the meaning of the film—without allowing for the possibility that the sign operates in multiple ways—closes the door to any subversive purposes of the text.
6. Robinson distinguishes within his text between "minstrelsy," the overall genre, "blackface minstrelsy," performance by white men in blackface, and "Black minstrelsy," blackface performance by black performers.
7. Cedric J. Robinson, *Forgeries of Memory and Meaning: Blacks and the Regimes of Race in American Theater and Film Before World War II* (Chapel Hill: University of North Carolina Press, 2007).
8. Chude-Sokei, 25.
9. *Ibid.*
10. *Ibid.*
11. It is important here to note that just because things are constructed does not mean that they are not real, only that they are made and therefore someone is doing the work to make them. Like buildings, without upkeep, constructed representations and identities change over time.
12. Bogle, xxi.

13. *Ibid.*

14. Spike Lee's *Bamboozled* (2000) makes a similar claim, expanding the praxis to include black performing history in general and the history of the representations of black bodies in blackface minstrelsy specifically.

15. Deleuze.

16. English, 36.

17. Bert Williams.

18. Chude-Sokei, 247.

19. In the film, Lee categorizes—through Sloan Hopkins' voice—Williams as "brilliant."

20. Lee, *Bamboozled*.

21. In this section, a reminder that Black is used as a social-cultural designator while black refers to a color or an equivalent to an American idea of white as a racial concept.

22. These same community members later profit by turning in the gamblers, after the judge gives them the kitty as a reward.

23. Lee includes the clip of this performance within *Bamboozled* with Sloan marking it as one of the moments of performative history necessary for Manray and Womack to learn about.

24. Metropolitan Museum of Art, *Lime Kiln Field Day Didactics*, 2013.

25. Indianapolis Freeman, March 7, 1908:5.

26. David Krasner, *Resistance, Parody, and Double Consciousness in African American Theater, 1895–1910* (New York: St. Martin's Press, 1997), 159.

27. One wonders if this is not the true intention of Damon Wayans improbable portrayal of Delacroix. He is the zip coon to Manray's sambo. A point Lee emphasizes when he places Manray and Delacroix in front of the two cardboard figures of Mantan and Sleep'n'Eat in Manray's apartment within the film.

28. MoMA Didactics.

29. "Bert Williams Discovery at MoMA | UCLA Film & Television Archive," Bert Williams Discovery at MoMA | UCLA Film & Television Archive. Accessed August 15, 2015, https://www.cinema.ucla.edu/blogs/archival-spaces/2014/12/05/bert-williams-discovery-moma.

30. David Ragan. *Who's Who in Hollywood*, 1918.

31. Aida Overton Walker, interviewed by Constance Beerbohm, "The Cake-Walk and How to Dance It: A Chat with the Prima Donna of 'In Dahomey.'" *Tattler*, No. 5 (July 1, 1903):13.

Chapter 2

1. "Spike Lee's *Bamboozled*—15 Years Later." *BAM Blog*. October 26, 2015. Accessed March 16, 2019, http://blog.bam.org/2015/10/spike-lees-bamboozled-15-years-later.html.

2. Race films were pictures produced in the early twentieth century directed toward specific audiences—Black or Jewish audiences, for example—outside the mainstream of the Hollywood Studios. Oscar Micheaux was arguably the most memorable director of this genre.

3. Joan Scott, 383.

4. The bitterness of the split, and the contentiousness of his relationship with his father-in-law, a respected reverend, would feed Micheaux's critique of the Black church in his novels and films.

5. Oscar Micheaux, Open Letter, *Chicago Defender*, 1910.

6. John R. Howard, *Faces in the Mirror: Oscar Micheaux and Spike Lee*, Kindle, Ch. 2, para. 41.

7. W. E. B. Du Bois. *The Negro Problem: A Series of Articles by Representative American Negroes of Today* (New York: James Pott & Co., 1903), 33.

8. W. E. B. Du Bois, *The Souls of Black Folk*.

9. Jacqueline Stewart, *Migrating to the Movies: Cinema and Black Urban Modernity* (Berkley: University of California Press, 2005), Kindle, Ch. 7, para. 2.

10. Lee would revisit the theme of miscegenation in *Jungle Fever*, complicating the story

by de-romanticizing the lens. Whereas the differences between Micheaux's characters would disappear upon a discovery of similarity, Flipper and Angie are isolated from their communities and have little in common. The space they share at the film's end is not what they had imagined it might be.

11. Griddlestone would turn out to be Sylvia Landry's biological father within the film.

12. Pearl Bowser, and Louise Spence, *Writing Himself into History: Oscar Micheaux, His Silent Films, and His Audiences* (New Brunswick, NJ: Rutgers University Press, 2001), 181.

13. This subject of positive portrayal would be revisited by both Ralph Ellison within *Invisible Man* and the essay "The Art of Romare Bearden," and Spike Lee within *Bamboozled*. This trajectory stands in contrast to the arc of Black Nationalism presented by figures like Marcus Garvey, Amiri Baraka, and complicatedly within many of the other films of Spike Lee, including *Do the Right Thing*. The influence of artist Michael Ray Charles upon Lee's work in *Bamboozled* is significant. In *Bamboozled*, Lee is employing history within a specific mode of working that mirrors the intent of artists like Charles, and also Kara Walker and Glenn Ligon who employ history as a lens for both showcasing the accomplishments of the past and questioning its hold on identity. For these artists, and for Micheaux, negative portrayals paint a picture of blackness that is varied and complicated, not monolithic and pristine.

14. Willis Huggins, Open Letter, *Chicago Defender*, 1921.

15. Carl Sandburg, *The Chicago Race Riots*, 1.

16. William Henry, Open Letter, *Chicago Defender*, 1925.

17. In the same way, Delacroix brings down Manray as a result of his own desire for fame and recognition and his own ignorance.

18. Note the connection to Lee's brothas on the walls in *Bamboozled* and Buggin' Out's desire for brothers on the walls of Sal's Pizzeria in *Do the Right Thing*.

19. Micheaux, *Body and Soul*.

Chapter 3

1. John Sanford, "Scholars Examine the Enduring Legacy of Invisible Man," Stanford University, April 24, 2002. Accessed June 29, 2018. Retrieved from: https://news.stanford.edu/news/2002/april24/ellisonsymposium-424.html.

2. Orville Prescott, "Book of the Times," *New York Times*, April 16, 1952. Accessed June 29, 2018. Retrieved from: https://archive.nytimes.com/www.nytimes.com/books/99/06/20/specials/ellison-invisible2.html?scp=16&sq=invisiblemanellison&st=cse.

3. Ellison, 577.

4. Ralph Ellison, "Change the Joke and Slip the Yoke," *Shadow and Act* (New York: Vintage International, 1995), 57.

5. *Ibid*.

6. *Ibid*.

7. Ellison's notation that he places the narrator in a coal cellar instead of a sewer separates his intention from that of Richard Wright's *The Man Who Lived Underground*.

8. *Ibid*.

9. Arnold Rampersad, *Ralph Ellison: A Biography* (New York: Knopf, 2007), Kindle, Ch. 1, para. 19.

10. Douglas Brinkley, "Unmasking Writers of the W. A. Published: August 2, 2003. Retrieved from: www.nytimes.com/2003/08/02/books/unm.

11. Ellison.

12. Rampersand, Ch. 4, para. 81.

13. Carol Palsgrove. *Divided Minds: Intellectuals and the Civil Rights Movement* (New York: William Norton & Co. 2001).

14. Richard Wright, "Richard Wright," *The God That Failed* (New York: Harper & Row, 1944), 168.

15. Du Bois.
16. Alfred Chester and Vilma Howard, "Interviews: Ralph Ellison, The Art of Fiction, No. 8," *The Paris Review*, August 1954.
17. Richard Wright, "The Man who Lived Underground," *Cross Section: A Collection of New American Writing*, ed. Edwin Seaver (New York: Fisher, 1944), 58–102.
18. Richard Wright, "The Man who Lived Underground," *Cross Section: A Collection of New American Writing*. Ed. Edwin Seaver. New York: Fisher. 1944. 58–102.
19. Ellison, 573.
20. Jean Paul Sartre (tr. Philip Mairet.), *Existensialism Is Humanism* (London: Methuen, 1948).
21. Robin McNalllie, "Richard Wright's Allegory of the Cave: 'The Man Who Lived Underground,'" *South Atlantic Bulletin* 42.2 (1977): 80.
22. Ralph Ellison, "The Art of Romare Bearden," *The Collected Essays of Ralph Ellison* (New York: Modern Library, Random House, 2003).
23. W. E. B. Du Bois.
24. Harry Brooks, Andy Razaf, and Fats Waller "(What Did I Do to Be So) Black and Blue?" *Hot Chocolate*, 1929.
25. *Ibid.*
26. *Ibid.*
27. *Ibid.*
28. The concept of a Battle Royal is a popular one of late as a theme for dystopian novels. The Hunger Games are a battle royal, which is meant to be a battle to the death with the last member standing named the winner. Takami's 1999 novel about a dystopian version of Japanese culture entitled *Battle Royale* is another example of this in popular culture.
29. W. E. B. Du Bois.
30. Ellison, 143.
31. Zora Neale Hurston, "How It Feels to Be Colored Me," *The World Tomorrow*, May, 1928.
32. William Shakespeare, *Macbeth*, Act V, Scene 5.
33. Ellison, 680.

Chapter 4

1. W. E. B. Du Bois., January 1946, quoted by Horne, Malika, "Art and Artists" in Young, 13–15.
2. A Gathering of the Tribes, "David Hammons: Concerto in Black and Blue," Publsihed: July 2, 2001. Retrieved from: www.tribes.org/web/2001/07/02/david-hammons-concerto-in-blacl-and-blue/.
3. English, 3.
4. Patricia Sipion, *AIDS and the Policy Struggle in the United States*. Washington D.C.: Georgetown Univeristy Press, 2002.
5. *New York Times*. Roberta Smith, "At the Whitney, a Biennial with a Social Conscience," Published: March 5, 1993. Accessed from http://www.nytimes.com/1993/03/05/arts/at-the-whitney-a-biennial-with-a-social-conscience.html.
6. Smith.
7. David Hickey, "Enter the Dragon: On the Vernacular of Beauty," *The Invisible Dragon: Four Essays on Beauty* (Los Angeles: Art Issues Press, 1993), 15–24.
8. W. E. B. Du Bois, 26.
9. W. E. B. Du Bois, 115.
10. English.
11. Roberta Smith.
12. Maurice Berger.
13. Tina Dunkley.

14. English.
15. Interestingly, the work of artist Michael Ray Charles drew criticism for his reinterpretation of racist imagery from poster art in this same article for the IRAA. However, in the discussions of Charles work, the subject of his character or his personal being is never brought up. This leads one to wonder if the disparaging remarks are connected with Walker's gender and the frank sexual content of her work.
16. Darby English, "This Is Not About the Past," *Narratives of a Negress* (Cambridge, MA: MIT Press. 2007).
17. Venise Wagner.
18. Frantz Fanon, *Black Skins, White Masks*.
19. Kara Walker, *Narratives of a Negress* (Cambridge, MA: MIT Press, 2007).
20. Alfred Chester, and Vilma Howard.
21. Gwendolyn Du Bois Shaw, *Kara Walker: Seeing the Unspeakable* (Cambridge, MA: MIT Press, 2004).
22. English.
23. English.
24. In discussing issues of race, in the context of the South, Faulkner is definitely at least as problematic as Walker herself, due to his racist tendencies. The recent use of this particular quote by President Obama as a means of addressing his associations with the Rev. Jeremiah Wright, bracket the particular span of history which Walker operates inside, perhaps serving to contextualize her work. It is with this mindset and a cautious pen that this quote is used. For further reading on Faulkner and issues of race: Arthur F. Kinney, "Faulkner and Racism," *Connotations* 3.3 (1993–94): 265–278.
25. James Hannaham.
26. Hannaham.
27. Hannaham.
28. Griffin.
29. Webster's Dictionary (black n.d.).
30. Stuart Hall, "Old and New Identities."
31. Page.
32. Walker.
33. Walker.
34. Walker.
35. Talty, "Spooked," *The Atlantic Monthly*, 2008.
36. Shaila Dewan, "The Art of Darkness," *Houston Press*, June 12, 1997.
37. Dewan.
38. Heller Books, Michael Ray Charles, "On Racial Stereotypes," Retrieved from: www.hellerbooks.com>dialogues_charles. Accessed December 13, 2015 (n.d.).
39. Glenn Ligon. Tate Museum, "Glenn Ligon," 2009.
40. *Ibid*.
41. Richard Meyer, "Light It Up, or How Glenn Ligon Got Over," ArtForum, FindArticles.com, October 5, 2011.
42. Ligon.
43. Recently, in an Artforum article about his work, Ligon was quoted about why he had returned to this work after having stopped making Pryor paintings, specifically due to this incident at the Whitney, he said: "So why have I returned to Pryor after all these years? Perhaps it is that Pryor is funny again. Not that he wasn't funny back in the seventies, it's just that all his militancy, his rage at social and economic injustice, his breaking down of sexual taboos seems amusing now, almost quaint. The jokes don't scare me anymore because the world they promised to bring seems even farther away than it did then. As Pryor says, 'Remember the Revolution brother? It's over. Lasted six months.' When I listen to Pryor records now, I laugh and am a little sad—nostalgic for my fear, I guess."
44. Golden, Tate.
45. Dewan.

Chapter 5

1. Paul Willistein, "Controversy at School Leaves Spike Lee Dazed, "*The Morning Call.* Retrieved from: articles.mcall.com/1988-02-12/entertainment/2617404_1_school-daze-morehouse-college-benefit-screening. February 12, 1988.
2. Willistein.
3. Willistein.
4. Sarah Larson, "Do the Right Thing at Twenty-five," *The New Yorker*, July 4, 2014. Retrieved from: www.newyorker.com/culture/sarah-larson/do-the-right-thing-at-twenty-five.
5. Spike Lee, *Do the Right Thing*, A Spike Lee Joint, Forty Acres and a Mule Productions, 1989.
6. Virginia Slave Code, 1705.
7. W. E. B. Du Bois, "Let Us Reason Together," *The Crisis*18 (September 1919): 231.
8. Bosley Crowther, "The Screen: 'Bye Bye Birdie' Arrives at Radio City Music...." Accessed June 9, 2015, http://www.nytimes.com/movie/review?res=980CE2D7103CE63ABC4D53DFB2668388679EDE.
9. Spike Lee, *Jungle Fever*, A Spike Lee Joint, Forty Acres and a Mule Productions, 1991.
10. Lee, *Jungle Fever*.
11. *25th Hour*, dir. Spike Lee, perf. Edward Norton, Philip Seymour Hoffman (United States: 40 Acres and a Mule Productions, 2002), transcript.
12. Lee, *Northwestern University Speech*.

Chapter 6

1. "The Independent—1908—Eastern Illinois University." Accessed June 19, 2015, http://www.eiu.edu/past_tracker/AfricanAmerican_Independent65_3Sept1908_RaceWarInTheNorth.pdf.
2. William Edward Burghardt, Du Bois, 1868–1963, Back to Africa in Century Magazine 150 no. 4:539–548 (February 1923) (New York: Century Co., 1923), 539–548.
3. "Economics of Negro Emancipation: WEBDuBois.Org," Economics of Negro Emancipation: WEBDuBois.org. Accessed August 19, 2016, http://www.webDuBois.org/dbEcNeEmUS.html.
4. "W. E. B. Du Bois: The Fight for Equality and the American Century, 1919–1963," Nashville Public Library VuFind, 536. Accessed December 19, 2015, https://catalog.library.nashville.org/GroupedWork/ef07dc5a-b1ed-178b-460d-d5b29105bc46.
5. W. E. B. Du Bois, Black Reconstruction in America; an Essay toward a History of the Part Which Black Folk Played in the Attempt to Reconstruct Democracy in America, 1860–1880 (New York: Russell & Russell, 1966), 726.
6. Du Bois, *The Ordeal of Mansart*, Postscript.
7. Du Bois, *The Ordeal of Mansart*.

Chapter 7

1. Armond White, "More Trash by Spike Lee," Manhattan, New York, NY | News. Accessed August 14, 2018, http://www.nypress.com/more-trash-by-spike-lee/.
2. *Ibid.*
3. *Ibid.*
4. *Ibid.*
5. "The Little Known Story Behind Do the Right Thing," Mental Floss, June 28, 2015. Accessed August 14, 2018, http://mentalfloss.com/article/57249/little-known-story-behind-do-right-thing.
6. Lena Williams, "Spike Lee Says Money from Blacks Saved X," *New York Times*.

Retrieved from: https://www.nytimes.com/1992/05/20/movies/spike-lee-says-money-from-blacks-saved-x.html.

7. Manufacturing Intellect, "Spike Lee Interview on "Bamboozled" (2000)," YouTube, August 31, 2016. Accessed November 4, 2018, https://www.youtube.com/watch?v=9_7NF_KS7tM.

8. Peter Travers, "Movie Reviews: Bamboozled," *Rolling Stone* Movie Reviews Category. Accessed November 4, 2018, https://www.rollingstone.com/movies/movie-reviews/.

9. This number does not include the documentaries.

10. Thomas Chatterton Williams, "The Culture Caught Up with Spike Lee," *New York Times*. Accessed from https://www.nytimes.com/2017/11/21/magazine/the-culture-caught-up-with-spike-lee-now-what.html.

11. Christopher Orr, "The Remarkably Lazy Woody Allen," *The Atlantic*, October 2017. Accessed March 20, 2018, https://www.theatlantic.com/magazine/archive/2017/10/woody-allen-wonder-wheel/537876/.

12. Jerome Christensen, "Spike Lee, Corporate Populist," *Critical Inquiry* 17(3), 1991, 582–595.

13. Andrew Dewaard, "Joints and Jams: Spike Lee as Sellibrity," *Fight the Power! The Spike Lee Reader* (New York: Peter Lang, 2009), 347.

14. "The Angriest Auteur," *New York Magazine*, NYMag.com. Accessed March 16, 2019. http://nymag.com/movies/profiles/19144/.

15. Sherry B. Ortner, "Against Hollywood: American Independent film as a critical cultural movement," 2012 HAU: *Journal of Ethnographic Theory* 2 (2): 1–21.

16. White.

17. Ibid.

18. Ibid.

19. Venise Wagner, "CROSSOVER," *SFGate*, April 19, 2012. Accessed November 4, 2018, https://www.sfgate.com/magazine/article/CROSSOVER-3495140.php.

20. Venise Wagner—who wrote the passage about Crouch—is the same critic who wrote the scathing review of Kara Walker's work.

21. Alissa Wilkinson, "Spike Lee's BlacKkKlansman Draws a Ham-Fisted Line from White Supremacy's Past to Its Present," *Vox*, May 15, 2018.

Chapter 8

1. Stuart Hall, "Learning Resources," Stuart Hall: Representation and the Media. April 22, 2015, http://lr.library.uq.edu.au/items/26473A49-5ED3-31E0-D7BC-AF331A68E4A1.html.

2. Spike Lee, *Bamboozled*, 40 Acres and a Mule Productions, 2000.

3. Lee, *X*.

4. W. E. B. Du Bois, "Postscript," *The Ordeal of Mansart*, Oxford University Press: Oxford, UK. 2007.

5. Lee, *Bamboozled*.

6. Ibid.

7. Stevie Wonder, "Misrepresented People," film performance by Stevie Wonder, 2000.

8. John Shepard, and David Horn, *Continuum Encyclopedia of Popular Music of the World*, Vol. 8 (Edinburgh, UK: A&C Black: 2012), 97.

9. Eric Lott, *Love and Theft: Blackface Minstrelsy and the American Working Class* (New York: Oxford University Press, 1993), 39.

10. Lee, *Bamboozled*.

11. Ibid.

12. Ibid.

13. Ibid.

14. Ibid.

15. *A Prisoner's Dictionary*. Accessed April 22, 2015, http://aren.org/prison/documents/dictionary/words.htm.

16. We see the evidence of this through Delacroix's interactions with his coworkers before and after the advent of the show.
17. Lee, *Bamboozled*.
18. Malcolm X, *By Any Means Necessary: Speeches, Interviews and a Letter by Malcolm X* (New York: Pathfinder Press, 1970), 35–61.
19. Lee, *Bamboozled*.
20. Deborah Root, *Cannibal Culture: Art, Appropriation, and the Commodification of Difference* (Colorado: West View Press, 1996), 21.
21. Lee, *Bamboozled*.
22. Fuchs, 162.
23. Lee, *Bamboozled*.
24. Lee, *Bamboozled*.
25. Lee, *Bamboozled*.
26. Linda Womack's maiden name is Linda Cooke. She is the daughter of Sam Cooke.
27. Lee, *Bamboozled*.
28. *Ibid.*
29. Ralph Ellison, *Invisible Man* (New York: Vintage Books, 1998), 250.
30. PBS.
31. Mark Anthony Neal, *Soul Babies* (Routledge, NY: Routledge, 2002), 124.
32. Neal, 124–125.
33. *Ibid.*
34. Sianne Ngai, "Animatedness," *Ugly Feelings* (Cambridge, MA: Harvard University Press, 2005), 95.
35. Ngai, Pg. 111.
36. Lee, *Bamboozled*.
37. *Ibid.*
38. This is a probable reference Amiri Baraka, and also Ras the destroyer, given the context of the debate.
39. Lee, *Bamboozled*.
40. *Ibid.*
41. *Ibid.*
42. Michael Germana, *Standards of Value: Money, Race, and Literature in America* (Iowa City: University of Iowa Press, 2009), 121.
43. Amiri Baraka, "Black Art," *Selected Poems of Amiri Baraka/LeRoi Jones* (Baltimore, MD: Black Classic Books, 1979).
44. Darby English, *How to See a Work of Art in Total Darkness* (Cambridge, MA: MIT Press, 2007), 65.
45. Ralph Ellison, "The Art of Romare Bearden," *The Collected Essays of Ralph Ellison* (New York: Modern Library, Random House, 2003), 115.
46. Cynthia Fuchs, *Spike Lee: Interviews* (Jackson: University Press of Mississippi, 2002), 140.
47. While the figure in the audience doesn't necessarily need to be Spike Lee, I contend that it is. The presence of an audience member who resembles Lee, knowing that Lee frequently appears in his own films, seems too coincidental to not be purposeful.

Chapter 9

1. Gilles Deleuze, *Cinema 2: The Time-Image* (London: Continuum, 2005).
2. *Ibid.*
3. *Ibid.*
4. Zora Neale Hurston, *Moses, Man of the Mountain* (New York: HarperPerennial, 1991), 240.
5. Thomas Poell, "Movement and Time in Cinema." Accessed October 1, 2015, http://papers.ssrn.com/sol3/papers.cfm?abstract_id=2154302.

6. Du Bois, *The Souls of Black Folk*, 351.
7. Spike Lee, *Bamboozled*, 40 Acres and a Mule Productions, 2000.
8. Susan Zannos, *The Life and Times of Archimedes* (Hockessin, DE: Mitchell Lane Publishers, 2005).
9. Lee, *Bamboozled*.
10. This quote also makes reference to "The Man Who Lived Underground" by Richard Wright, the story that in part inspired Ellison to write *Invisible Man*.
11. Lee, *Bamboozled*.
12. *Ibid*.
13. *Ibid*.
14. "British and American Halloween Words | OxfordWords Blog," OxfordWords Blog, 2012. Accessed May 23, 2015, http://blog.oxforddictionaries.com/2012/10/history-of-halloween-words/.
15. Stephen Matterson, "Indian-Hater, Wild Man: Melville's Confidence-Man," *Arizona Quarterly: A Journal of American Literature, Culture, and Theory Arizona Quarterly* 52, no. 2 (1996):, doi:10.1353/arq.1996.0019.
16. Oscar Brown, "Signifyin' Monkey," *Spotify*. Accessed August 8, 2015, https://open.spotify.com/track/03rt5RZu0zkWFrzl4VEVx9.
17. Henry Louis Gates, *The Signifying Monkey: A Theory of Afro-American Literary Criticism* (New York: Oxford University Press, 1988). 60–61.
18. *Ibid*.
19. Hazel Carby, "The Blackness of Theory," in *Cultures in Babylon: Black Britain and African America* (London: Verso, 1989), 235.
20. Susan G. Strauss and Parastou Feiz, *Discourse Analysis: Putting Our Worlds into Words*.
21. *Ibid*.
22. Seth Meyers, "SNL Transcripts: Katy Perry: 12/10/11: Weekend Update with Seth Meyers," SNL Transcripts: Katy Perry: 12/10/11: Weekend Update with Seth Meyers. Accessed June 8, 2015, http://snltranscripts.jt.org/11/11iupdate.phtml.
23. English, *Narratives of a Negress*.
24. Lee, *Bamboozled*.
25. *Ibid*.
26. *Ibid*.
27. Trinh Thi Minh-Hain conversation with Annamaria Morelli. 1996, "The Undone Interval," in Iain Chambers and Lidia Curti (ed). *The Post Colonial Question: Common Skies, Divided Horizons*, London: Routledge, 8.
28. Allan Bell, "Language Style as Audience Design" (1984).
29. Wonder.
30. Deric M. Greene and Felicia R. Walker, "Recommendations to Public Speaking Instructors for the Negotiation of Code-Switching Practices Among Black English-Speaking African American Students," *The Journal of Negro Education* 73, no. 4 (2004): 435, doi:10.2307/4129627.
31. Gerald A. Powell, *A Rhetoric of Symbolic Identity: An Analysis of Spike Lee's X and Bamboozled* (Dallas: University Press of America, 2004).
32. Lee, *Bamboozled*.
33. Gilles Deleuze, Mark Lester, and Charles Stivale, *The Logic of Sense* (New York: Columbia University Press, 1990), 146.
34. Lee, *Bamboozled*.
35. *Ibid*.
36. E. Patrick Johnson, "Going Home Ain't Always Easy: Ethnography and the Politics of Black Respectability," Out in Public: doi:10.1002/9781444310689.ch3. 54–70.
37. Lee, *Bamboozled*.
38. *Ibid*.
39. *Ibid*.

40. Elijah Muhammad, *Message to the Blackman in America* (Phoenix, AZ: Secretarius MEMPS Ministries, 2009).
41. Frederick Harris, "The Rise of Respectability Politics | Dissent Magazine," *Dissent Magazine*. Accessed November 18, 2015, https://www.dissentmagazine.org/article/the-rise-of-respectability-politics.

Chapter 10

1. Orrin Nan Chung Wang, W.J.T. Mitchell, and William John Thomas. "The Last Formalist, or W.J.T. Mitchell as Romantic Dinosaur." *Romantic Circles*, August 1, 1997. Accessed March 16, 2019, http://www.rc.umd.edu/praxis/mitchell/interview/mitch-interview.html.
2. W.J.T. Mitchell, *What Do Pictures Want? The Love and Lives of Images* (University of Chicago Press, 2005), 301.
3. W.J.T. Mitchell, *Seeing Through Race (The W. E. B. Du Bois Lectures)* (Harvard University Press, Kindle Edition, 2014), 60.
4. Fuchs, 140.
5. Mitchell, *Seeing Through Race*, 61.
6. Mitchell, *What Do Pictures Want*, 295.
7. "Provenance Research Project | MoMA," Lee Bontecou, Untitled, 1959 | MoMA. Accessed November 26, 2018, https://www.moma.org/collection/provenance.
8. Okwui Enwezor, *Contemporary African Art* (New York: Thames & Hudson, 1999), 31.
9. Roland Barthes and Annette Lavers, Mythologies (New York: Hill and Wang, 1972), 119.
10. Barthes, 118.
11. Barthes, 126.
12. Renoira Rampazzo Gambarato, "Methodology for Film Analysis—The Role of Objects in Films," Academia.edu. Accessed August 17, 2015, http://www.academia.edu/5218752/Methodology_for_Film_Analysis_The_Role_of_Objects_in_Films. 1.
13. *Ibid.*
14. Spike Lee, *Bamboozled*, 40 Acres and a Mule Productions, 2000.
15. Spike Lee, *Do the Right Thing*, A Spike Lee Joint, Forty Acres and a Mule Productions, 1989.
16. Lee, *Bamboozled*.
17. Although it is stated in the film, I cannot find any evidence verifying that Robinson passed away while dancing. He died of cardiovascular disease, however, and a strong physical exertion under these conditions may have been capable of killing him.
18. Ellison, 259.
19. Lee, *Bamboozled*.
20. *Ibid.*
21. Gayatri Chakravorty Spivak, "Can the Subaltern Speak?," *Marxism and the Interpretation of Culture*, 1988, 313, doi:10.1007/978-1-349-19059-1_20.

Chapter 11

1. Gilbert Highet, *The Anatomy of Satire* (Princeton, NJ: Princeton University Press, 1962), 21.
2. Sharon McCoy, "Embracing the Ambiguity and Irony of Satire: A Response to Jeff Melton," *Humor in America*, 2012. Accessed June 11, 2015, https://humorinamerica.wordpress.com/2012/10/30/embracing-the-ambiguity-of-satire/.
3. I realize in stating this that I am revealing through the writing of this book my own ideologies and likely prejudices. This understanding is why the book is formed as it is, to demonstrate a reliance on history for the forming of my arguments.

4. This argument does not ignore the voiced objections of Sloan Hopkins over the course of the film, just acknowledges that she has limited authority in determining what gets put on the air, and Delacroix refuses to hear her objections anyway.

5. Jameson.

6. Roger Ebert, "Bamboozled Movie Review & Film Summary (2000) | Roger Ebert," All Content. Accessed June 11, 2015, http://www.rogerebert.com/reviews/bamboozled-2000.

7. *Ibid.*

8. Ebert also draws parallels between Bamboozled's use of blackface and The Producers' satirical portrayal of Hitler, noting that The Producers would be less effective if the satire within the film depicted prisoners of the Holocaust, a critique remarkably similar to the one leveled at Kara Walker by the IRAA.

9. It should be pointed out here that Twain is using the word race to refer to the human race.

10. Mark Twain, and William M. Gibson, *The Mysterious Stranger* (Berkeley: University of California Press, 1970), 131.

11. "War of Words: Tyler Perry Vs. Spike Lee," *NPR*, "All Things Considered." Accessed September 15, 2015, http://www.npr.org/2011/04/21/135610190/war-of-words-tyler-perry-vs-spike-lee.

12. Andrew Ti, "Yo! Is This Racist?" Accessed June 11, 2015, http://yoisthisracist.com/.

13. Micheal Moore, X.J. Kennedy, and Dana Gioia, *Literature: An Introduction to Fiction, Poetry, Drama, and Writing* (Boston: Pearson, 2013), 243.

14. Heather L. LaMarre, Kristen D. Landreville, Michael A. Beam, "The Irony of Satire: Political Ideology and the Motivation to See What You Want to See in The Colbert Report," *International Journal of Press/Politics*, April 2009, Vol. 14, No. 2 212–231. doi: 10.1177/194016 1208330904.

15. Plato, and Francis Macdonald Cornford, *Plato's Theory of Knowledge: The Theaetetus and the Sophist of Plato* (New York: Liberal Arts Press, 1957). 186a.

16. Plato, 187b4–8.

17. Plato, 201d–210a.

18. Edmund L. Gettier, "Is Justified True Belief Knowledge?" *Analysis* 23, no. 6 (1963): 121, doi:10.2307/3326922.

19. Okwui Enwezor, "Postcolonial Constellation," *Antimonies of Art and Culture* (Durham: Duke University Press, 2008), 231–232.

20. Hubert L. Dreyfus, "Being and Power: Heidegger and Foucault," *International Journal of Philosophical Studies* 4, no. 1 (1996):, doi:10.1080/09672559608570822.

21. Martin Heidegger, *On Time and Being* (New York: Harper & Row, 1972), 69, translation amended. Cited in Nikolas Kompridis, *Critique and Disclosure: Critical Theory Between Past and Future* (Boston: MIT Press, 2006), 189.

22. Michel Foucault, *Discipline and Punish: The Birth of the Prison* (New York: Vintage Books, 1995).

23. Foucault.

24. *A Face in the Crowd*, dir. Ela Kazan, screenplay by Budd Schulberg, perf. Andy Griffith, Patricia Neal, Walter Matthau (Lucerne Films, 1957), streaming on iTunes.

25. Roger Ebert, "The Producers Movie Review & Film Summary (1968) | Roger Ebert," All Content. Accessed September 12, 2015, http://www.rogerebert.com/reviews/great-movie-the-producers-1968.

26. Joseph Amditis, "White Men Can't Joke: Racial Hierarchy and Traditional Race Narratives in Humor and Comedy," Academia.edu. Accessed September 9, 2015, http://www.academia.edu/3539690/White_Men_Cant_Joke_Racial_Hierarchy_and_Traditional_Race_Narratives_in_Humor_and_Comedy.

27. "True Stories I Made Up," by Daniel Tosh, September 9, 2015. Comedy Central Records, CCR0036, track 9.

28. *Ibid.*

29. Amditis.

30. Erin Texeira, "Kramer Aftermath: Paul Mooney Renounces N-word after Michael Richards Rant," Recordonline.com. Accessed September 9, 2015, http://www.recordonline.com/article/20061129/ENTERTAIN/61129019.

31. Amy Odell, "Comedy Club Owner Says Daniel Tosh Incident Has Been Misunderstood," *BuzzFeed*. Accessed August 17, 2015, http://www.buzzfeed.com/amyodell/comedy-club-owner-says-daniel-tosh-incident-has-be.

32. Jeremy Stahl, "Daniel Tosh Is Like Michael Richards—But Not for the Reasons You Think," *Slate* Magazine, 2012. Accessed July 1, 2015, http://www.slate.com/blogs/browbeat/2012/07/13/daniel_tosh_is_like_michael_richards_but_not_for_the_reasons_you_think_.html.

33. Robert L. Hilliard, *Hollywood Speaks Out: Pictures That Dared to Protest Real World Issues* (Oxford: Wiley-Blackwell, 2009), 243.

34. "FORGOTTEN FOOTNOTE/Before Hearst, SLA Killed Educator," *SFGate*. Accessed October 17, 2015, http://www.sfgate.com/bayarea/article/FORGOTTEN-FOOTNOTE-Before-Hearst-SLA-killed-2754621.php.

35. *Network*, dir. Sidney Lumet, prod. Howard Gottfried, by Paddy Chayefsky, perf. Faye Dunaway, William Holden, Peter Finch, Robert Duvall, and Lee Richardson (United States: United Artists, 1976).

36. "Movie Review—NETWORK—NYTimes.com," *New York Times*, Victor Canby. Accessed October 4, 2015, http://www.nytimes.com/movie/review?res=EE05E7DF173CB82CA6494CC1B7799A8C6896.

37. *Monty Python and the Holy Grail*, by Terry Gilliam, Terry Gilliam, Graham Chapman, John Cleese, and Eric Idle, perf. Graham Chapman, John Cleese, and Eric Idle (Londres: Columbia Tristar Home Entertainment, 2002), streaming on Netflix.

38. Charles Waddell Chesnutt, Letter to Houghton, Mifflin & Co., December 30, 1901.

39. Charles Waddell Chesnutt, Letter to Harry D. Robins, September 27, 1900.

40. Sandra Gunning, *Race, Rape, and Lynching: The Red Record of American Literature, 1890–1912* (New York: Oxford University Press, 1996), 53.

41. *Ibid*.

42. "Stephen King's Super-Duper Magical Negroes," Strange Horizons Articles: by Nnedi Okorafor-Mbachu. Accessed February 1, 2016, http://www.strangehorizons.com/2004/20041025/kinga.shtml.

43. Charles Waddell Chesnutt, Journal, "Charles Waddell Chesnutt (1858–1932)," Regionalism and Local Color. Accessed December 7, 2015, http://blogs.cofc.edu/english-362-01-spring-2012/2013/02/18/charles-waddell-chesnutt-1858-1932/.

44. Charles Waddell Chesnutt, *The Goophered Grapevine* (Boston: Houghton, Mifflin, 1887).

45. Chesnutt.

46. John F. Callahan, *In the African-American Grain: The Pursuit of Voice in Twentieth-century Black Fiction* (Urbana: University of Illinois Press, 1988).

47. "2002 Conference: Historical Reconstructions Atlanta, Georgia, May 16–18," Historically Speaking 3, no. 2 (2001):, doi:10.1353/hsp.2001.0073.

48. Joel Chandler Harris, and A.B. Frost, *Uncle Remus, His Songs and Sayings* (New York: D. Appleton & Co., 1909), 7.

49. *Ibid*.

50. *Ibid*.

51. *Ibid*.

52. Chesnutt.

53. Du Bois.

Chapter 12

1. Walter W. Skeat, *An Etymological Dictionary of the English Language* (Oxford, Clarendon Press, 1909).

2. Swift, "A Proposal for Correcting, Improving and Ascertaining the English Tongue." Accessed January 16, 2016, https://andromeda.rutgers.edu/~jlynch/Texts/proposal.html.
3. Herman Melville, *Moby Dick*, adapted by Shirley Bogart (New York: Baronet Books, 1990), Kindle.
4. Malcolm X, and George Breitman, *By Any Means Necessary: Speeches, Interviews, and a Letter* (New York: Pathfinder Press, 1970).
5. Spike Lee, *Chiraq*, screening, Northwestern University, 2015.
6. Hannah Higgins, UIC. 2012.
7. "More Trash by Spike Lee," *NY Press*. Accessed April 16, 2015, http://www.nypress.com/more-trash-by-spike-lee/.
8. Fanon, *Black Skin, White Masks*. 228.
9. Spike Lee, *Mo' Better Blues*, A Spike Lee Joint, Forty Acres and a Mule Productions, 1990.

Bibliography

Amditis, Joseph. "White Men Can't Joke: Racial Hierarchy and Traditional Race Narratives in Humor and Comedy." Academia.edu. Accessed September 9, 2015. http://www.academia.edu/3539690/White_Men_Cant_Joke_Racial_Hierarchy_and_Traditional_Race_Narratives_in_Humor_and_Comedy.

Andrews, William L. *The Literary Career of Charles W. Chesnutt.* Baton Rouge: Louisiana State University Press, 1980.

Atlantic Monthly. "Spooked." December 2008: 24–25.

Baraka, Amiri. "Black Art," *Selected Poems of Amiri Baraka/Le Roi Jones.* Black Classic Books: Baltimore, MD. 1979.

Barthes, Roland, and Annette Lavers. *Mythologies.* New York: Hill & Wang, 1972.

"bell hooks." Center for Cultural Studies RSS. N.p., 2015.

Bell, Allan. *Language Style as Audience Design.* 1984.

Berger, Maurice. "Kara Walker." *New York Magazine,* 2007.

"Bert Williams Discovery at MoMA | UCLA Film & Television Archive." Bert Williams Discovery at MoMA | UCLA Film & Television Archive. Accessed August 15, 2016. https://www.cinema.ucla.edu/blogs/archival-spaces/2014/12/05/bert-williams-discovery-moma. Web. 8 Jan. 2016.

Biber, D. Johansen, G.S. Leech, S. Gonard, and E. Finnegan. *The Longman Grammar of Spoken and Written English.* London: Longman, 1999.

Branson, Johanna. *The Feminist eZine.* Lillith Gallery. http://www.feministzine.com/feminist/books/Kara-Walker.html (accessed 10/30/2010).

"British and American Halloween Words | OxfordWords Blog." OxfordWords Blog. 2012. Accessed May 23, 2015, http://blog.oxforddictionaries.com/2012/10/history-of-halloween-words/.

Brown, Oscar. "Signifyin' Monkey." *Spotify.* Accessed August 8, 2015, https://open.spotify.com/track/03rt5RZu0zkWFrzl4VEVx9.

Callahan, John F. *In the African-American Grain: The Pursuit of Voice in Twentieth-century Black Fiction.* Urbana: University of Illinois Press. 1988.

Carby, Hazel. "The Blackness of Theory." In Dispatches from the Multicultural Wars, 232–36.

"Charles Waddell Chesnutt (1858–1932)." Regionalism and Local Color. Accessed August 16, 2016. http://blogs.cofc.edu/english-362-01-spring-2012/2013/02/18/charles-waddell-chesnutt-1858-1932/.

Charters, Ann. *Nobody: The Story of Bert Williams.* New York: Macmillan, 1970.

Chesnutt, Charles Waddell. "The Goophered Grapevine." Boston: Houghton, Mifflin, 1887.

Chesnutt, Helen M. *Charles Waddell Chesnutt, Pioneer of the Color Line.* Chapel Hill: University of North Carolina Press, 1952.

Chude-Sokei, Louis Onuorah. The Last "Darky": Bert Williams, Black-on-Black Minstrelsy, and the African Diaspora. Durham: Duke University Press, 2006. Kindle.

Clarke, Terence. *Red Room*. October 21, 2008. http://redroom.com/author/terence-clarke (accessed 11 7, 2010).
Cooper, Andrew M. "Blake and Madness: The World Turned Inside Out." *ELH* 57 Autumn, no. no. 3 (1990): 585–642.
Creative Tools 4 Critical Times. November 4, 2009. Accessed November 7, 2010, http://ct4ct.com/Kara_Walker.
Cripps, Thomas. *Slow Fade to Black: The Negro in American Film, 1900–1942*. New York: Oxford University Press. 1977.
Crowther, Bosley. "The Screen: 'Bye Bye Birdie' Arrives at Radio City Music Hall." Accessed June 9, 2015. http://www.nytimes.com/movie/review?res=980CE2D7103CE63ABC4D53DFB2668388679EDE.
Cutler, Jody. *Americana: Journal of American Pop Culture 1900 to Present*. 2009. Accessed November 12, 2010, http://www.americanapopularculture.com/journal/articles/fall_2009/cutler.htm.
Deleuze, Gilles, Mark Lester, and Charles Stivale. *The Logic of Sense*. New York: Columbia University Press. 1990.
Deleuze, Gilles. *Cinema 2: The Time Image*. London: Continuum, 2005.
Deleuze, Gilles. *Difference and Repetition*. New York: Columbia University Press. 1994.
Dreyfus, Hubert L. "Being and Power: Heidegger and Foucault." *International Journal of Philosophical Studies* 4, no. 1 (1996): 1–16. doi:10.1080/09672559608570822.
Dreyfus, Hubert L. *Lecture Notes*. Aarhus: Aarhus Universitet, 1998.
Du Bois, W. E. B. "Back to Africa." *The Century Magazine* 150, no. 4:539–548, February 1923. New York: Century Co., 1923. 539–548.
Du Bois W. E. B. *Black Reconstruction in America: An Essay Toward a History of the Part Which Black Folk Played in the Attempt to Reconstruct Democracy in America, 1860–1880*. New York: Russell & Russell. 1966.
Du Bois, W. E. B. "Criteria of Negro Art (1926)." *An Anthology of African American Literary Criticism from the Harlem Renaissance to the Present Within the Circle*. 2012. 60–68. doi: 10.1215/9780822399889-007.
Du Bois, W. E. B. "Economics of Negro Emancipation." WEBDuBois.Org. Accessed December 18, 2015. http://www.webdubois.org/dbEcNeEmUS.html.
Du Bois, W. E. B. "Postscript" *The Ordeal of Mansart*. Oxford University Press. 2007.
Du Bois, W. E. B. *The Souls of Black Folk*. Third Edition. Chicago: A. C. McClurg & Co. 1903.
Ebert, Roger. "The Producers Movie Review & Film Summary (1968) | Roger Ebert." All Content. Accessed September 12, 2015, http://www.rogerebert.com/reviews/great-movie-the-producers-1968.
Ebert, Roger. "Bamboozled Movie Review & Film Summary (2000) | Roger Ebert." All Content. Accessed June 11, 2015, http://www.rogerebert.com/reviews/bamboozled-2000.
Ellison, Ralph. "The Art of Romare Bearden *"The Collected Essays of Ralph Ellison*. New York: Modern Library, Random House. 2003.
Ellison, Ralph. *Invisible Man*. New York: Vintage Books. 1998.
English, Darby. *How to See a Work of Art in Total Darkness*. University of Chicago Press. 2007.
A Face in the Crowd. Directed by Ela Kazan. Screenplay by Budd Schulberg. Performed by Andy Griffith, Patricia Neal, Walter Matthean. Lucerne Films, 1957. Streaming on ITunes.
Fanon, Frantz. *Black Skin, White Masks*. Translated by Charles L. Markham. New York: Grove Press. 1967.
Faulkner, William. *Requiem for a Nun*. New York: Random House. 1951.
"FORGOTTEN FOOTNOTE / Before Hearst, SLA Killed Educator." *SFGate*. Accessed October 17, 2015, http://www.sfgate.com/bayarea/article/FORGOTTEN-FOOTNOTE-Before-Hearst-SLA-killed-2754621.php.
Foucault, Michel. *Discipline and Punish: The Birth of the Prison*. New York: Vintage Books. 1995.
Fuchs, Cynthia. *Spike Lee: Interviews*. Jackson: University Press of Mississippi. 2002.
Gambarato, Renoira Rampazzo. "Methodology for Film Analysis—The Role of Objects in

Films." Academia.edu. Accessed August 17, 2015, http://www.academia.edu/5218752/Methodology_for_Film_Analysis_The_Role_of_Objects_in_Films.

Gates, Henry Louis. *The Signifying Monkey: A Theory of Afro-American Literary Criticism.* New York: Oxford University Press. 1988.

Germana, Michael. *Standards of Value: Money, Race, and Literature in America.* Iowa City: University of Iowa Press, 2009.

Gettier, Edmund L. "Is Justified True Belief Knowledge?" *Analysis* 23, no. 6 (1963): 121. doi:10.2307/3326922.

Greene, Deric M., and Felicia R. Walker. "Recommendations to Public Speaking Instructors for the Negotiation of Code-Switching Practices Among Black English-Speaking African American Students." *The Journal of Negro Education* 73, no. 4 (2004): 435. doi:10.2307/4129627.

Griffin, Kevin. "Kerry James Marshall Makes Black Visible." *Vancouver Sun*, May 13, 2010. Accessed November 13, 2010, https://vancouversun.com/news/staff-blogs/kerry-james-marshall-makes-black-visible.

Gunning, Sandra. *Race, Rape, and Lynching: The Red Record of American Literature, 1890–1912.* New York: Oxford University Press. 1996.

Hall, Stuart. "Learning Resources." *Representation and the Media.* Accessed April 22, 2015, http://lr.library.uq.edu.au/items/26473A49-5ED3-31E0-D7BC-AF331A68E4A1.html.

Hall, Stuart. "Old and New identities; Old and New Ethnicities." In *Culture, Globalisation, and the World System: Contemporary Conditions for the Representation of Identity.* ed. Anthony King. Minneapolis: University of Minnesota Press. 1997. 31–68.

Hannaham, James. "Pea, Ball, Bounce." *Interview*, November 1998.

Harris, Frederick. "The Rise of Respectability Politics." *Dissent Magazine.* Accessed November 18, 2015, https://www.dissentmagazine.org/article/the-rise-of-respectability-politics.

Harris, Joel Chandler, and A. B. Frost. *Uncle Remus, His Songs and Sayings.* New York: D. Appleton & Co. 1909.

Heermance, J. Noel. *Charles W. Chesnutt; America's First Great Black Novelist.* Hamden, Conn: Archon Books, 1974.

Highet, Gilbert. *The Anatomy of Satire.* Princeton, NJ: Princeton University Press. 1962.

Hilliard, Robert L. *Hollywood Speaks Out: Pictures That Dared to Protest Real World Issues.* Oxford: Wiley-Blackwell. 2009.

Horn, David, and John Shephard. *Continuum Encyclopedia of Popular Music of the World*, Vol. 8. Edinburgh, UK: A&C Black. 2012.

Hurston, Zora Neale. *Moses, Man of the Mountain.* New York: HarperPerennial. 1991.

"The Independent—1908—Eastern Illinois University." Accessed June 19, 2015, http://www.eiu.edu/past_tracker/AfricanAmerican_Independent65_3Sept1908_RaceWarInTheNorth.pdf.

Johnson, E. Patrick. "Going Home Ain't Always Easy: Ethnography and the Politics of Black Respectability." *Out in Public*: 54–70. doi:10.1002/9781444310689.ch3.

Keller, Frances Richardson. *An American Crusade: The Life of Charles Waddell Chesnutt.* Provo, UT: Brigham Young University Press. 1978.

Kennedy, X. J., and Dana Gioia. *Literature: An Introduction to Fiction, Poetry, Drama, and Writing.* Boston: Pearson. 2013.

Kredel, Karsten. *d-b art info.* Accessed November 7, 2010, http://www.db-artmag.com/archive/01/e/magazin-karawalker02.html.

Krasner, David. *Resistance, Parody, and Double Consciousness in African American Theatre, 1895–1910.* New York: St. Martin's Press. 1997.

LaMarre, Heather L.; Landreville, Kristen D.; Beam, Michael A. "The Irony of Satire: Political Ideology and the Motivation to See What You Want to See in The Colbert Report," International Journal of Press/Politics, April 2009, Vol. 14, No. 2 212–231. doi: 10.1177/1940161208330904.

Lee, Spike. dir. *Bamboozled.* 40 Acres and a Mule, Productions. 2000.

"The Little Known Story Behind Do the Right Thing." *Mental Floss.* June 28, 2015. Accessed

August 14, 2018. http://mentalfloss.com/article/57249/little-known-story-behind-do-right-thing.

Lott, Eric. *Love and Theft: Blackface Minstrelsy and the American Working Class.* New York: Oxford University Press. 1993.

Lobel, Michael. *Robert Colescott Press.* Edited by Art Forum. October 2004. http://arthurrogergallery.com/press.

Matterson, Stephen. "Indian-Hater, Wild Man: Melville's Confidence-Man." *Arizona Quarterly* 52, no. 2 (1996): 21–35. doi:10.1353/arq.1996.0019.

McCoy, Sharon. "Embracing the Ambiguity and Irony of Satire: A Response to Jeff Melton." *Humor in America.* 2012. Accessed June 11, 2015, https://humorinamerica.wordpress.com/2012/10/30/embracing-the-ambiguity-of-satire/.

"Manufacturing Intellect." "Spike Lee Interview on 'Bamboozled' (2000)." *YouTube.* August 31, 2016. Accessed November 4, 2018, https://www.youtube.com/watch?v=9_7NF_KS7tM.

Melville, Herman, adapted by Shirley Bogart, *Moby Dick.* New York: Baronet Books, 1990. Kindle.

Merriam Webster Dictionary Online. http://www.merriam-webster,com/dictionary/black (accessed 11 12, 2010).

Meyers, Seth. "SNL Transcripts: Katy Perry: 12/10/11: Weekend Update with Seth Meyers." SNL Transcripts: Katy Perry: 12/10/11: Weekend Update with Seth Meyers. Accessed June 8, 2015. http://snltranscripts.jt.org/11/11iupdate.phtml.

Minh-Ha, Trinh Thi in conversation with Annamaria Morelli. 1996. "The Undone Interval." in Iain Chambers and Lidia Curti (ed). The Post Colonial Question: Common Skies, Divided Horizons, London: Routledge, 3–17.

Mitchell, W.J.T. Seeing Through Race (The W. E. B. Du Bois Lectures) (p. 61). Harvard University Press. Kindle Edition.

Mitchell, W.J.T. *What Do Pictures Want? The Lives and Loves of Images.* University of Chicago Press, 2005.

Mo' Better Blues. Directed by Spike Lee. Produced by Spike Lee. By Spike Lee. Performed by Spike Lee, Denzel Washington, Wesley Snipes, and Giancarlo Esposito.

Monty Python and the Holy Grail. By Terry Gilliam, Terry Gilliam, Graham Chapman, John Cleese, and Eric Idle. Performed by Graham Chapman, John Cleese, and Eric Idle. Londres: Columbia Tristar Home Entertainment, 2002. Streaming on Netflix.

"More Trash by Spike Lee." *NY Press.* Accessed April 16, 2015, http://www.nypress.com/more-trash-by-spike-lee/.

"Movie Review—NETWORK—NYTimes.com." *New York Times.* Accessed October 4, 2015. http://www.nytimes.com/movie/review?res=EE05E7DF173CB82CA6494CC1B7799A8C6896.

Muhammad, Elijah. *Message to the Blackman in America.* Phoenix, AZ: Secretarius MEMPS Ministries. 2009.

Neal, Mark Anthony. *Soul Babies.* Routledge, NY: Routledge. 2002.

Network. Directed by Sidney Lumet. Produced by Howard Gottfried. By Paddy Chayefsky. Performed by Faye Dunaway, William Holden, Peter Finch, Robert Duvall, and Lee Richardson. United States: United Artists, 1976.

Ngai, Sianne. "Animatedness." *Ugly Feelings.* Cambridge, MA: Harvard University Press. 2005.

Okorafor-Mbachu, Nnedi. "Stephen King's Super-Duper Magical Negroes." Accessed February 1, 2016. http://www.strangehorizons.com/2004/20041025/kinga.shtml.

Page, Thomas W. "The Real Judge Lynch." *Atlantic Monthly,* 1901.

Pierce, Charles. *Collected Writings* (8 vols.). 1931–58. Ed. Charles Hartshorne, Paul Weiss and Arthur W. Burks. Cambridge, MA: Harvard University Press.

Plato, and Francis Macdonald Cornford. *Plato's Theory of Knowledge; the Theaetetus and the Sophist of Plato.* New York: Liberal Arts Press. 1957.

Poell, Thomas. "Movement and Time in Cinema." Accessed October 1, 2015, http://papers.ssrn.com/sol3/papers.cfm?abstract_id=2154302.

Powell, Gerald A. A Rhetoric of Symbolic Identity: An Analysis of Spike Lee's X and Bamboozled. Dallas: University Press of America, 2004.

A Prisoner's Dictionary. Accessed April 22, 2015, http://aren.org/prison/documents/dictionary/words.htm.

"Progressive Era to New Era, 1900–1929." Browse by Topic (Library of Congress). N.p., n.d. Web. 8 Aug. 2016.

"Provenance Research Project | MoMA," Lee Bontecou. Untitled. 1959 | MoMA, accessed November 26, 2018, https://www.moma.org/collection/provenance.

Reid, Calvin. *Bomb Magazine 62: Kerry James Marshall.* Winter 1998. Accessed November 12, 2010, http://bombsite.com/archive/Kerryjamesmarshall.

Render, Sylvia Lyons. *Charles W. Chesnutt.* Boston: Twayne Publishers. 1980.

Robinson, Cedric J. *Forgeries of Memory and Meaning: Blacks and the Regimes of Race in American Theater and Film Before World War II.* Chapel Hill: University of North Carolina Press, 2007.

Roediger, David R. *The Wages of Whiteness: Race and the Making of the American Working Class.* London: Verso. 1991.

Root, Deborah. *Cannibal Culture: Art, Appropriation, and the Commodification of Difference.* Colorado: West View Press, 1996.

Roundthwaite, Adair. *Making Mourning from Melancholia: The Art of Kara Walker.* November 2007. Accessed November 7, 2010, http://www.imageandnarrative.be/inarchive/autofiction/autofiction.htm.

Saltz, Jerry. *The Art Review.* November 1, 2007. Accessed November 7, 2010, nymag.com/nymag/critics/art/archive.

Shaw, Gwendolyn Du Bois. *Seeing the Unspeakable: The Art of Kara Walker.* Duke University Press, 2004.

Skeat, Walter W. *An Etymological Dictionary of English Language.* by Walter W. Skeat, New Ed. Oxford: Clarendon Press. 1909.

Smith, Roberta. *Art & Design: Robert Colescott, Artist Who Toyed with Art and Sex, Dies at 83.* June 9, 2009. (accessed November 17, 2010).

Spivak, Gayatri Chakravorty. "Can the Subaltern Speak?" *Marxism and the Interpretation of Culture*, 1988, 271–313. doi:10.1007/978-1-349-19059-1_20.

Stahl, Jeremy. "Daniel Tosh Is Like Michael Richards—But Not for the Reasons You Think." *Slate* Magazine. 2012. Accessed July 1, 2015. http://www.slate.com/blogs/browbeat/2012/07/13/daniel_tosh_is_like_michael_richards_but_not_for_the_reasons_you_think_.html.

Stewart, Jacqueline Najuma. *Migrating to the Movies: Cinema and Black Urban Modernity.* Berkeley: University of California Press, 2005. Print.

Strauss, Susan, and Parastou Feiz. *Discourse Analysis: Putting Our Worlds into Words.* New York: Routledge. 2014.

Swift, Jonathan, "A Proposal for Correcting, Improving and Ascertaining the English Tongue." Accessed January 16, 2016. https://andromeda.rutgers.edu/~jlynch/Texts/proposal.html.

Texeira, Erin. "Kramer Aftermath: Paul Mooney Renounces N-word after Michael Richards Rant." Recordonline.com. Accessed September 9, 2015. http://www.recordonline.com/article/20061129/ENTERTAIN/61129019.

Ti, Andrew. "Yo! Is This Racist?" Accessed June 11, 2015. http://yoisthisracist.com/.

Tosh, Daniel. *True Stories I Made Up.* September 9, 2015.

Travers, Peter. "Movie Reviews: Bamboozled." *Rolling Stone* Movie Reviews Category. Accessed November 4, 2018. https://www.rollingstone.com/movies/movie-reviews/.

Twain, Mark, and William M. Gibson. *The Mysterious Stranger.* Berkeley: University of California Press, 1970.

25th Hour, A Spike Lee Joint. Directed by Spike Lee. Performed by Edward Norton, Philip Seymour Hoffman. United States: 40 Acres and a Mule Productions, 2002. Transcript.

"2002 Conference: Historical Reconstructions Atlanta, Georgia, May 16–18." *Historically Speaking* 3, no. 2 (2001): 30–33. doi:10.1353/hsp.2001.0073.

Wang, Orrin Nan Chung, W.J.T. Mitchell, and William John Thomas. "The Last Formalist, or W.J.T. Mitchell as Romantic Dinosaur." *Romantic Circles.* August 1, 1997. Accessed March 16, 2019. http://www.rc.umd.edu/praxis/mitchell/interview/mitch-interview.html.

Wagner, Venise. "CROSSOVER." *SFGate*. April 19, 2012. Accessed November 4, 2018. https://www.sfgate.com/magazine/article/CROSSOVER-3495140.php.

Wagner, Venise. "For this Artist the Joke's on Us." *The San Francisco Examiner*. February 16, 1997.

Waldstreicher, David. *Slavery's Constitution: From Revolution to Ratification*. New York: Hill & Wang, 2009. Print.

Walker Art Center. *Learn*. 2005. http:/learn.walker.org/karawalker/Main/Biography (accessed 11 8, 2010).

Walker, Kara. *Narratives of a Negress*. Edited by Ian Berry, Darby English, Vivian Patterson and Mark Reinhardt. Cambridge, MA: MIT Press. 2007.

"War of Words: Tyler Perry Vs. Spike Lee." *NPR*. Accessed September 15, 2015. http://www.npr.org/2011/04/21/135610190/war-of-words-tyler-perry-vs-spike-lee.

"W. E. B. Du Bois: The Fight for Equality and the American Century, 1919–1963." Nashville Public Library VuFind. Accessed December 19, 2015. https://catalog.library.nashville.org/GroupedWork/ef07dc5a-b1ed-178b-460d-d5b29105bc46.

West, Cornel. "The New Cultural Politics of Difference." October 53 (1990): 93. Web.

White, Armond "More Trash by Spike Lee," Manhattan, New York, NY | News. Accessed August 14, 2018, http://www.nypress.com/more-trash-by-spike-lee/.

Wonder, Stevie. "Misrepresented People." Film performance. 2000.

X, Malcolm, and George Breitman. *By Any Means Necessary: Speeches, Interviews, and a Letter*. New York: Pathfinder Press. 1970.

Zannos, Susan. *The Life and Times of Archimedes*. Hockessin, DE: Mitchell Lane Publishers. 2005.

Index

Page numbers in **_bold italics_** indicate photographs

Ain't Misbehavin' 55
American Revolution 17, 84
Americanness 17–18, 53
The Answer 32, 107
Armstrong, Louis 55, 60, 115; *see also* "(What Did I Do to Be So) Black and Blue?"
Artaud, Antonin 13; *see also* nooshock

Baldwin, James 4, 76, 103
Baraka, Amiri 44, 54–55, 102, 120, 122–123; *see also* Jones, LeRoi
Barthes, Roland 116, 143–144
Basinger, Kim 3
battle royal 52, 56, 157; *see also* Invisible Man
Bearden, Romare 47, 54, 122
Berger, Maurice 65
Best, Willie 113–114; *see also* Sleep'n'Eat
Big Blak Afrika 109, 120, 122, 136, 139; *see also* Hopkins, Julius
Birth of a Nation (1915 film) 16, 27, 30, 32, 37–39, 42, 88, 103, 118, 178; *see also* Griffith, D. W.
Black and Blue (musical) 115
The Black Flame Trilogy 95; *see also* Du Bois, W. E. B.
Black Male (exhibition) 13, 30, 40, 63, 77, 87; *see also* Colescott, Robert; Golden, Thelma; Ligon, Glenn
Black Nationalism 55, 57, 94, 120, 138; *see also* Garvey, Marcus
Black Panther 4
Black Reconstruction in America 94
The BlacKkKlansman 3, 103–**_104_**, 105
blackness 2, 4, 10, 14, 16–18, 21, 27–29, 38–40, 44, 53, 55–59, 64–65, 69–71, 73–74, 77, 95, 98, 102, 108–113, 116, 118, 120, 122–123, 124–125, 128–130, 137–139, 142, 146–148, 154, 156, 176, 178, 181–183, 188

Bledsoe, Dr. A. Herbert 52, 57; *see also* Invisible Man
Body and Soul 36, 40–**_41_**, 42, 122; *see also* Micheaux, Oscar; Robeson, Paul
Bogle, Donald 15, 27, 120
Bowser, Pearl 14–15, 35, 38–39, 43
briefcase, emptying the 60, 72, 136; *see also* Invisible Man
Bring Da Noise, Bring Da Funk 21, 31, 114; *see also* Glover, Savion
Brother Jack 48, 58; *see also* Invisible Man
The Brotherhood 52, 57–58, 119–120; *see also* Invisible Man
Bunker, Archie 105
Bye Bye Birdie **_86_**

The Capeman (musical) 121
Capers, Corey 13
The Carol Burnett Show 134
cave allegories: in Ellison 45, 54, 58, 60; in Lee 186; in Plato 54; in Wright 50–54
Charles, Michael Ray 7–8, 10–11, 14, 44, 61, 65, 98, 118, 134, 144, 151, 155–156
Chayefsky, Paddy 173; *see also* Network
Chesnutt, Charles 176–183; *see also* The Goophered Grapevine
Chicago Defender 33, 40, 42
The Chicago Race Riots (poem) 40
Chi-raq 99, 186
Chude-Sokei, Louis 2, 13, 20, 23, 26
Civil Rights 4, 16, 34, 48, 56, 85, 92–94, 107, 122–123, 138, 144, 166; *see also* Jim Crow
Clark, Ashley 10, 32, 66
Clifton, Tod 45, 53, 58, 119, 149–150
Colescott, Robert 70, 75, 77; *see also* Black Male (exhibition)
"The Comet" 39; *see also* Du Bois, W. E. B.
Communism 47–48, 166, 175

Concerto in Black and Blue (installation) 10, 59; *see also* Hammons, David
The Confidence Man 75, 118, 185; *see also* Melville, Herman
The Conquest (book) 39; *see also* Micheaux, Oscar
Crawford, Romi 2, 13
Cripps, Thomas 15
Criteria of Negro Art 22, 39, 61, 64; *see also* Du Bois, W. E. B.
Cronkite, Kathy 174
Cronkite, Walter 174

Daniels, Fred 50–54, 126, 132, 186; *see also* "The Man Who Lived Underground"; Wright, Richard
Delacroix, Eugene 113
Delacroix, Pierre 11, 21, 23, 28, 32, 80, 107–120, 126–133, **135**–139, 142–150, 154–156, 159, 164–165, 167–168, 172, 175, 186; *see also* Dothan, Peerless
Deleuze, Gilles 9, 12–13, 53, 125–126, 137, 141; *see also* difference
difference 2, 9, 13, 18, 27, 52–53, 55, 59, 63, 73, 90, 106, 133, 149, 152, 181, 187; *see also* Deleuze, Gilles
Dixon, George 28; *see also* Jim Crow
Do the Right Thing 2–3, 80–82, 86, 88, 98, 100, 108, 118, 145–**146**, 147, 153, 180, 186
Dostoyevsky, Fyodor 53
Dothan, Peerless 111; *see also* Delacroix, Pierre
double-consciousness 18, 21, 30, 53, 96, 124, 127–128, 137, 159, 175, 186; *see also* Du Bois, W. E. B.; Hegel, Georg
Douglass, Frederick 93, 117
Driving Miss Daisy 3
Du Bois, W. E. B. 7–8, 11, 13–14, 16, 18, 20–22, 23, 32, 34, 38–39, 43, 44, 49, 55–56, 60–61, 64–65, 68, 79, 85, 91, 92–96, 102–103, 107–108, 111, 122–123, 124
Dunwitty, Thomas 11, 23, 28, 109–111, 113–115, 117, 128–129, 132, 137–139, 144–148, 150, 154–155, 186; *see also* Rapaport, Michael

Ebert, Roger 22, 98, 102, 155–156, 159, 167–168, 175
Ellison, Ralph 7–8, 10–11, 13–14, 44–58, 60–61, 68, 75, 93, 96, 102–103, 108, 118, 123, 132, 136, 147–148, 157, 165, 186; *see also Invisible Man*
English, Darby 4, 10, 27, 59, 123–124, 127, 147, 183, 186
enlightenment 49–54, 60–61, 127, 132–134, 147, 157, 160, 162, 164, 172, 186; *see also* cave allegories
The Enlightenment 17
Existentialism 51–53

A Face in the Crowd 153, 155, 157, 160, 165–166

Fanon, Frantz 10, 18, 67, 187
Faulkner, William 68
40 Acres and a Mule Productions 11
The Founder 56, 147; *see also Invisible Man*

Garvey, Marcus 14, 49, 57–58, 93, 121, 123; *see also* Ras the Destroyer/Exhorter
Gates, Henry Louis, Jr. 131, 153; *see also* signifyin'
Germana, Michael 13, 75
Get Out 103–**104**
Glover, Savion 21, **24**, 31, 98, 112–115, 187; *see also Bring Da Noise, Bring Da Funk*; Manray; *see also* Mantan
Golden, Thelma 13, 62, 73, 77, 116; *see also Black Male* (exhibition); *1993 Whitney Biennial*
Gooding, Cuba, Jr. 107, 167; *see also Jerry Maguire*
The Goophered Grapevine 175–176, 178, 181; *see also* Chesnutt, Charles
The Great Migration 33, 36, 46–47, 49
Green Book 3–4
Griffith, Andy 166; *see also Network*
Griffith, D.W. 16, 19, 27, 32, 37, 118, 178; *see also Birth of a Nation* (1915 film)

Hall, Stuart 13, 18, 71, 106
Hammons, David 10, 59; *see also Concerto in Black and Blue*
Harlem Renaissance 14, 20, 26–27, 47, 49, 113, 115–116, 123, 138
Harris, Joel Chandler 38, 49, 176, 178–182; *see also* Uncle Remus
Hearst, Patty 174; *see also* Symbionese Liberation Army (SLA)
Heder, Bill 134
Hegel, Georg 127; *see also* double-consciousness
Hickey, Dave 63–64, 141
Highet, Gilbert 153
The Homesteader (book) 35; *see also* Micheaux, Oscar
The Homesteader (film) **35**–36; *see also* Micheaux, Oscar
hooks, bell 1, 80
Hopkins, Julius 120; *see also* Big Blak Afrika
Hopkins, Sloan 28, 80, 96, 109, 111, 113–122, 127–129, 132, 135–136, 138, 145–150, 155, 167–168, 186
Horak, Jan Christopher 30
Hot Chocolates 55
Hurston, Zora Neale 47, 57, 76, 126, 132

"I Don't Know, You're Not So Warm" 26
In Living Color 112, 116, 119
Invisible Man (book) 7, 10–11, 44–49, 52, 54–56, 58, 60–61, 68, 93, 96, 102–103, 111–112, 114, 118–119, 123, 142, 149, 157, 160, 172, 186; *see also* Ellison, Ralph

Jerry Maguire 107; *see also* Gooding, Cuba, Jr.
Jim Crow 28, 34, 75, 85, 120
Jolly Nigger Bank 11, 13, 44, 50, 53, 75, 117–118, 142, 144, 148; *see also Invisible Man*
Jones, LeRoi 54, 120; *see also* Baraka, Amiri
Judge, Monique 3
Julien, Isaac 10, 60
Junebug 44, 111–112; *see also* Mooney, Paul
Jungle Fever 86, 88

"Keepin' it real" 8, 110, 122, 137
Ku Klux Klan 58, 69, 72

Last Week Tonight 173
Ligon, Glenn 10, 60, 63, 73, 76–77; *see also Black Male* (exhibition)
Lime Kiln Field Day 29–31
Lumet, Sidney 172, **173**; *see also Network*

Malcolm X 62, 88–**89**, 106–107, 113, 120, 185
Malcolm X (film) 88–**89**, 98–99
"The Man Who Lived Underground" 49, 50, 52; *see also* Daniels, Fred; Wright, Richard
Manray 21, 23–**24**, 28, 31, 45, 80, 96, 98, 109, 111–120, 128–130, 132–135, 137–139, 142, 146–150, 154–155, 164, 167–168, 172–**173**, 179, 186; *see also* Mantan
Mantan (character) 27, 113–115, 119, 130, 133–**135**, 154; *see also* Manray
Mantan: The New Millennium Minstrel Show **24**, 65, 106, 111, 113, 117, 119, 122, 129–130, 146, 154, 159, 164, 168, **173**
Marxism 5, 15, 94
Mastadon Minstrels 24
Matthau, Walter 165; *see also A Face in the Crowd*
The Mau Maus (fictional rap group) 109, 113, 119–122; *see also* Big Blak Afrika; 1/16 Blak
The Mau Maus (Kenyan political group) 121
The Mau Maus (L.A. punk band) 122
The Mau Maus (Puerto Rican gang in Brooklyn) 121
McCoy, Sharon 153–154
McKay, Claude 14
Melville, Herman 13, 49, 75, 112, 118, 185; *see also The Confidence Man*
Meyers, Seth 134
Micheaux, Oscar 7–8, 11, 13–15, 32–43, 117, 120, 122, 136, 147, 165, 177
Mitchell, W.J.T. 11–13, 140–142
MoMA 30–31, 141–142
Mooney, Paul 112, 170; *see also* Junebug; Pryor, Richard
Mooreland, Mantan 21, 113–114
Murphy, Eddie 118

NAACP 15, 93, 94; *see also* Du Bois, W. E. B.
Narratives of a Negress 67; *see also* The Negress; *see also* Walker, Kara

Natural Born Gambler 28–**29**; *see also* Williams, Bert
Neal, Mark Anthony 118
Neal, Patricia 165
The Negress 66–70, 72, 118; *see also* Walker, Kara
Network 7, 165, 172–175
The New Negro 36, 38, 111–112, 122
Ngai, Sianne 119
The Nicholas Brothers 115
1993 Whitney Biennial 13, 62, 77; *see also* Golden, Thelma
nooshock 12, 126–127, 151; *see also* Artaud, Antonin
The North 37, 42, 93, 181
Norton, Edward **90**

Octoroons 25–26
Oliver, John 173
1/16 Blak 120; *see also* The Mau Maus (fictional rap group)
optic white 57, 70; *see also Invisible Man*
The Ordeal of Mansart 7, 65, 107; *see also* Du Bois, W. E. B.
Oscars (Academy Awards) 3

Peele, Jordan 103–**104**
The Philadelphia Negro 95; *see also* Du Bois, W. E. B.
Pinkett-Smith, Jada 96, 116; *see also* Hopkins, Sloan
The PJs 118–119, 165
Plato 13, 54, 160–161, 163, 186
Pope.L, William 10, 60
portraits on the wall 11, 101, 117, 144–**145**, 147
Post black 7, 13, 44–45, 61, 73, 98, 102, 141, 189
Powell, Gerald 15, 137
Preer, Evelyn **33**, **35**, **37**, 39; *see also Within Our Gates*
The Producers (1967 film) 7, 165, 167–**169**, 174
The Progressive Era 16, 20, 122, 126–127, 147
Pryor, Richard 76–77, 112; *see also* Ligon, Glenn

Raengo, Alessandro 10
Rampersad, Arnold 44, 46, 48
Rapaport, Michael 109–**110**, **145**; *see also* Dunwitty, Thomas
Ras the Destroyer/Exhorter 57–58; *see also* Garvey, Marcus; *Invisible Man*
Ray, Charles 9
Reconstruction 16, 20, 37, 94–96, 178–179, 183
Robeson, Paul 40–**41**, 42, 122; *see also Body and Soul*
Robinson, Bill 114–115, 144, 149
Robinson, Cedric 15, 26

Roediger, David 4, 17
Roma 4
The Root 3
Rowan and Martin's Laugh-In 134
Russian Revolution 94

Saar, Betye 66–67
Salley, Rael 2, 13
Sambo 28, 44–45, 53, 74–75, 134, 149
Sartre, Jean Paul 53
Saturday Night Live 78, 112, 134
Shaw, Gwedolyn Du Bois 68
She Hate Me 22
She's Gotta Have It (film) 79–80, 116
signifyin' 114, 131, 133, 136, 143
simulacra 13
slavery 11, 16–18, 22, 65–66, 73, 111, 139, 150, 180, 182
Sleep'n'Eat 28, 113–114, 130, 133–134, 154; see also Best, Willie; Womack
Sloan, William J. 117
Sonny and Cher 134
Sorry to Bother You 4, **142**
The Souls of Black Folk 34, 56–57, 61, 92, 124; see also Du Bois, W. E. B.
The South 25, 30, 36–37, 40, 42, 46–47, 57, 68–70, 72, 74, 111–112, 176, 178–182
Spelling, Aaron 173
Spence, Louise 14–15, 35, 38–39, 43
Stanfield, Lakeith **142**–143
Stewart, Jacqueline 14, 35–36
Summer of Sam 2, 90, 97
Symbionese Liberation Army (SLA) 173–175

Tarantino, Quentin 109; see also Rapaport, Michael
Thomas, W.I. 95
Tosh, Daniel 169–170
trickster 14, 28, 131–133, 181, 183
Tuskegee Institute 47, 56
Twain, Mark 49, 156–157
25th Hour **90, 108**–109

Uncle Julius 176, 178, 180–184
Uncle Remus 38, 136, 176, 178, 181–182; see also Harris, Joel Chandler

Vest, Jason 9

Wagner, Venise 67
"Wake Up" 1, 22, 108, 126, 160, 185
Waldstreicher, David 17
Walker, Aida Overton 26, 31; see also Walker, George
Walker, George 23–24, 26, 28, 30–31, 114, 159; see also Walker, Aida Overton; Williams, Bert
Walker, Kara 10–11, 43, 60, 65–68, 97–98, 118, 141
Walker Art Center 66
Washington, Booker T. 11, 14, 16, 21, 34, 42, 49, 56, 92, 102, 117, 123, 139, 176
Washington, Freddie 118
Wayans, Damon 111, 113, 115, **135**; see also Delacroix, Pierre; Dothan, Peerless
(What Did I Do to Be So) Black and Blue 55, 60
whiteness 1–5, 17–18, 53, 57, 87, 90, 95, 170, 179
Wilkinson, Alissa 103, 105
Williams, Bert 7–8, 11, 13–15, 20–22, 23–31, 42–43, 45, 65, 73, 98–99, 108, 114–115, 134, 138, 156, 159, 165, 177, 187
Wilson, Edith 55
Wilson, Fred 10, 60, 141–142
Wilson, Woodrow 16
Within Our Gates 32–**33**, 36–**37**, 38–40, 42
Womack 27–28, 31, 98, 109, 112–117, 119, 129–130, 132, 134–135, 146, 149–150, 154–155, 164, 168, 173, 186; see also Sleep'n'Eat
WPA (Works Progress Administration) 47
Wright, the Rev. Jeremiah 90
Wright, Richard 45–54, 132, 186

Ziegfeld Follies 26, 30
Znaniecki, Florian 95